THE COMPLETE GUIDE TO

Calligraphy

THE COMPLETE GUIDE TO

Calligraphy

Oceana

AN OCEANA BOOK

This book is produced by
Quantum Publishing Ltd
6 Blundell Street
London N7 9BH

ISBN 0-681-28864-7

QUMCGT4

Manufactured in Singapore by
Pica Digital Pte. Ltd

Printed in Singapore by
Star Standard Industries Pte. Ltd

CONTENTS

BASIC CALLIGRAPHY   6

Chapter 1   Introduction   8
Chapter 2   Materials and Equipment   26
Chapter 3   Layout & Design   48
Chapter 4   Mastering Letterforms   90
Chapter 5   The Alphabets   136

ADVANCED CALLIGRAPHY   224

Chapter 6   Advanced Techniques   226
Chapter 7   Illuminated Letters   316
Chapter 8   Advanced Projects   380

Glossary   442
Index   445

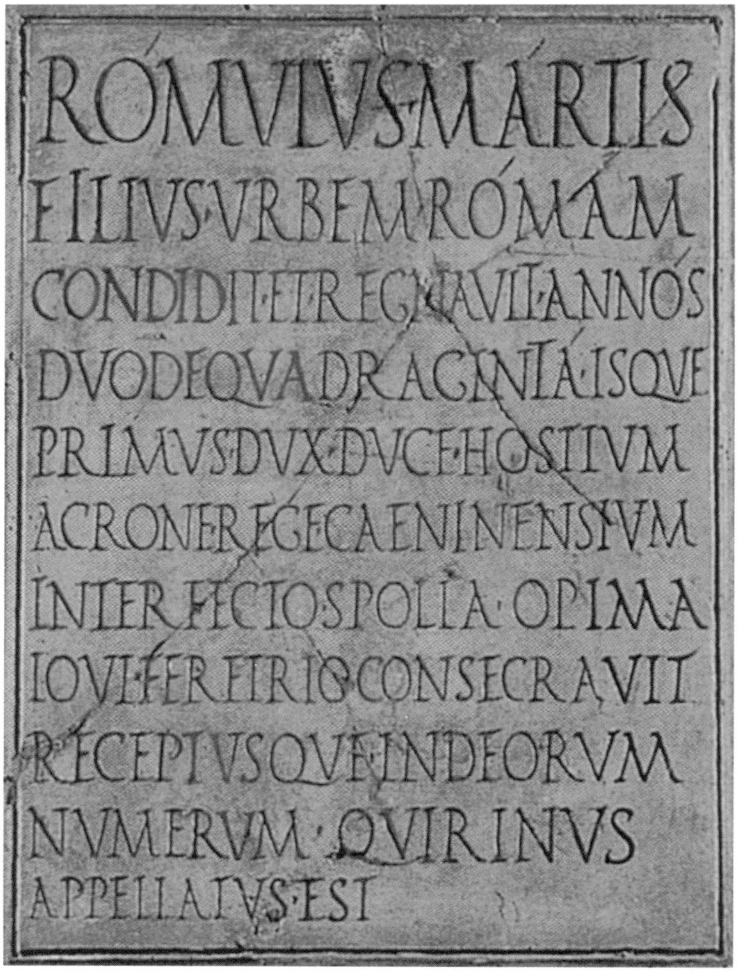

ROMVIVS MARTIS
FILIVS VRBEM ROMAM
CONDIDIT ET REGNAVIT ANNOS
DVODEQVADRAGINTA ISQVE
PRIMVS DVX DVCE HOSTIVM
ACRONE REGE CAENINENSIVM
INTERFECTO SPOLIA OPIMA
IOVI FERETRIO CONSECRAVIT
RECEPTVSQVE IN DEORVM
NVMERVM QVIRINVS
APPELLATVS EST

BASIC
CALLIGRAPHY

INTRODUCTION

Writing is an essential part of our culture. We need to be able to communicate with others by writing, to keep records of our own thoughts and to preserve calculations and information of all kinds. Perhaps more importantly, we need to be able to read what others have written, so that we can absorb their wisdom and knowledge, profit from their experiences and learn from their discoveries. We can take a book on any subject and glean information from it. We can take a work of fiction and be transported by the skill of the author into realms beyond our own imagining. We can read of thoughts and deeds committed to writing thousands of years ago.

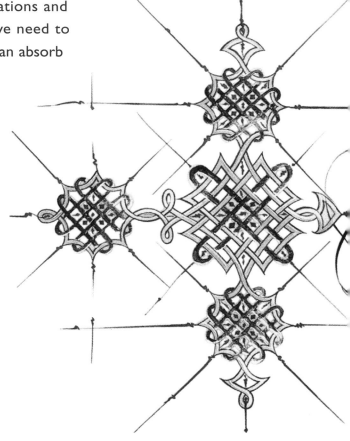

All this is available to us because humans both learned language and devised ways in which to set this language down in a form that could be understood by others. It is true that there are many different languages spoken in the world and, that there is a variety of ways in which to set them down, but scholars can learn these different scripts and languages and then translate them so that ordinary people, who only need to know a language for everyday use, can read translations of anything that has ever been written, anywhere in the world.

No doubt, computers will soon be readily available that will not only be able to transcribe spoken words, but will also simultaneously translate these words into any number of languages, so that all human knowledge and information will become universal. Humans alone, of all creatures, starting from the first primitive beings, had the intelligence to develop the most amazing ability to speak to each other, not only of the basic necessities of life, but also to express feelings and emotions and construct beautiful poetry. Not only did humans learn to vocalise these things, but they furthermore learned to write them down so that others could share their innermost thoughts and ideals. What is also astonishing is that people in various parts of the world independently but simultaneously developed their own different systems of speaking and writing.

The Power of Language

We probably all have an image in our minds of our early ancestors, their daily rounds of work done, seated around the fire in the dark of night, listening to tales of brave deeds, fierce battles, or of ancient myths and legends. Although listening, they had probably heard it all before. However, the words would be reinforced in their memories and, when they became too old to follow an active life they in turn would tell the stories to their families, thus playing their part in confirming the verbal traditions.

It would be nice to think that, as humans learned to write, these ancient tales and legends were written down, but this does not seem to have been the case, for it appears that the first efforts at writing were made to record transactions, and that writing was thus first used for the mundane ends of trade.

The First Types of Writing

Picturegrams: these were the earliest symbols used as a form of writing to convey a meaning, and each stylised symbol represented a meaning by its image. By combining several together, it became possible to express an idea.

i) A bird and an egg may have meant 'fertility'.

ii) Strokes descending from heaven may have meant 'rain'.

Ideograms: these evolved from picturegrams, and their symbols were used to represent idea.

     i) Crossed lines may have meant 'enemy'.

     ii) Parallel lines may have meant 'friend'.

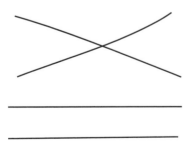

Rebus; this further development came about when one or more symbols were employed to represent something with a similar sound. (This device later became popular in the Middle Ages for use as personal badges or emblems. Abbot Ramrydge at St Albans, for example, used a ram's head with 'rydge' written on its collar; Ashton had an ash tree growing from a ton, and Sir John Peché adopted a peach with an 'é' written on it).

Phonograms: once it was accepted that symbols could represent sounds, they became more stylised and their numbers were reduced. An alphabet began to emerge.

HISTORY OF CALLIGRAPHY

One of the oldest civilisations of which we have evidence was that of the Sumerians, who inhabited the fertile region of Mesopotamia around the rivers Tigris and Euphrates, an area which now falls within the boundaries of modern Iraq. Their agricultural society was highly organised, using irrigation from the rivers and making use of domesticated animals in farming. From the fourth century BC until they were overrun by the Babylonians in 1720BC, the Sumerians established towns and cities, set up a basic system of regional government and were sufficiently prosperous for citizens to perform services beyond the basic requirements of agriculture and trade, such as skilled craft and medicine.

The earliest evidence of a writing system in Sumer is a limestone tablet from the city of Kish, dating to about 3500BC. This shows several pictograms, including a head, foot and hand. Pictograms are pictorial symbols that directly represent a particular object. Gradually, by associating, the symbol could represent a less concrete image - the sun, for example, could also stand for 'day'. A symbol extended in this way is also known as an ideogram. The Sumerians at one time had about 2,000 such symbols forming the elements of their written language.

A further development occurred when it was realised that a symbol representing one word could also be used for a similar sounding word, and that such symbols could be put together to form composite words, by reference to syllabic sounds. These phonograms, or symbols representing sounds, were freed from the original, illustrative conventions of pictograms. This meant that the number of symbols could be reduced and their forms stylised. The essence of an alphabet system had come into being.

The impression of the stylus left wedge-shaped marks

the majority of people have been right-handed.)

The development of Egyptian civilisation was concurrent with that of Sumerians; Egypt upheld its cultural traditions through centuries

The Sumerians mainly used soft clay as a writing surface, inscribed with a stick or reed stylus. Drawing on clay is difficult because ridges of clay build up in front of the tool; the symbols tend to be more angular because curved shapes are so difficult to form. The Sumerians gradually evolved the method of pressing the stylus into the clay in a series of small marks. The impression of the stylus left wedge-shaped marks; Sumerian writing is known as *cuneiform*, from the Latin word cuneus meaning 'wedge'. Speed in writing also reduced the complexity of individual symbols and increased the intention to abstraction.

To prevent the clay from hardening before the writing was finished, small tablets were used for note-taking in business and administrative affairs; important data were then transferred to a more permanent record. The small note-tablets could be held in one hand while written in the other. This gave a slanted direction to the symbols, towards the left-hand edge of the tablet. This was later incorporated into the formal, conventionalised cuneiform signs, giving them a definite horizontal emphasis. (Most of the evidence of early writing styles also suggests that throughout history

The earliest writing was in pictograms, the best-known example of which is Egyptian hieroglyphics. This example (left) is from a relief found in a tomb at Sakkara, probably dating from the 5th Dynasty (2560-2420BC). The Hittites, who founded a powerful ancient civilisation in Asia Minor between three and four thousand years ago, also used a form of hieroglyphics (centre). This /Assyrian script, typical of the period between the eighth and ninth centuries BC, was used in many copies of earlier texts made in the seventh century BC for Assurbanipal's Royal Library in Nineveh (far left). By the time of the Greeks, a recognisable alphabet had been developed. This writing, relating omens derived from the flight of birds, is from Ephesus and dates from the sixth century BC (bottom left).

of peace, war and invasion before collapsing under external influences. Egypt was, like Sumer, a well-organised agricultural society with a system of central government, land ownership and taxation that generated much administrative work. From about 3000BC the Egyptians used a form of picture writing known as hieroglyphics, meaning 'sacred, carved writing'. Within 200 years a script, had been developed, known as hieratic script. A thousand years later a less formal script, known as demotic, was also in use. Hieratic evolved as a simplified version of hieroglyphics, whereas demotic was a cursive, practical hand.

The Egyptians, like the Sumerians, had developed their writing through pictograms to ideograms and then phonograms. By 1500BC they had established an alphabet of 24 consonantal symbols, although this was never fully detached from the hieroglyphs and ideograms; the various forms were written together or side by side, as if to ensure that the text could be understood one way or another.

A major influence on the development of forms in Egyptian writing was their use of reed brushes with liquid ink to paint the pictograms and signs, instead of relying on inscribed symbols.

Top: Ideograms/Pictograms

Middle: Cuneiform 3500-2000BC

Bottom: Hieroglyph 3000BC

Furthermore, they wrote on papyrus, a thin, flexible, fabric, rather than stone, clay or wood, although these materials were cheaper, everyday alternatives. Prepared animal skins were even more expensive than papyrus and were reserved for documents of outstanding importance. The written papyri were rolled for storage and reading convenience. Until the 12th Dynasty (1991-1786BC) the writing was arranged in vertical lines and the sequence ran from right to left. After this period lines were arranged horizontally in narrow, vertical columns, but still read from right to left.

The Egyptians were the first civilisation to have official scribes and a system of education that required a tedious copying of sample writing and admired pieces of literature. Trainee scribes and the sons of noblemen had to spend days memorising the innumerable signs and the sequences of the writing. Nevertheless, this is indicative of the value Egyptians placed on their literacy and the dissemination of knowledge; although many of the scribes were slaves, they were rigorously trained to carry out their particular duties.

The Egyptians were the first civilisation to have official scribes

In the time of Ptolemy 1 (323-285BC) the official court language was Greek, and Alexandria became a centre of learning based on Greek scholarship. The Egyptian 24-letter alphabet is thought to have had some bearing on the rather different and certainly more advanced alphabet of the Semitic tribes of eastern mediterranean lands. These tribes then passed their own alphabet to the Greeks, where it was gradually adapted to form the basis of the alphabet used today in the western world.

The most influential people among the Semitic tribes were the Phoenicians, who lived on the Levantine coast of the Mediterranean (now Lebanon and Syria). Their civilisation was contemporary with the rise of the Egyptian Old Kingdom from 2700BC. The Phoenicians were a skilled and intelligent people, energetic traders, with a merchant fleet that sailed as far as the shores of Britain in the interests of business and commerce.

The oldest known alphabetic inscription of the Phoenicians dates from 1000BC. It is not known precisely how their symbols were evolved, but there are ancestral links with Sumerian pictography and the cuneiform symbols taken over by the Babylonians. There were a number of different Phoenician settlements and local variations of written forms. However, by 1000BC there was at least one alphabet system in existence with only 30 symbols, each sign representing a single consonantal sound. These symbols were entirely abstract, not suggestive of pictures or associative

Fragments of Greek (above) and Roman (below) lettering in stone show the similarity of certain letterforms and the way in which the Romans developed a more formal stately interpretation as the full alphabet sequence evolved. The slight roughness of the Greek letters indicates the difficulty of carving the linear forms into stone, a skill which the Romans brought to a high art.

ideograms. Phoenician culture survived a period under the Assyrians, who conquered and took control of their land from 850 to 722BC. The Phoenician alphabet emerged intact from this experience and was passed on to the Greeks in th form of 24 consonantal signs. It was also influential as the basis of Persian and Arabic scripts.

The Beginning of Calligraphy

The earliest examples of the Roman alphabet we use today date from the third century B.C.

These early Roman capitals were mostly found incised into stone. Although later there were pen-written Roman capitals, the inscriptional forms – in particular those on Trajan's Column (c.A.D.114) in Rome – remain unsurpassed as a historical reference.

Other pen-made scripts in use in Roman times include Roman square capitals (quadrata), Rustica (there are also brush-made forms of this script in existence), and Roman cursive – a flowing, everyday script, which was inscribed into clay and lead tablets and also

The prevalence of Roman lettering on a wide range of artifacts testifies to a relatively organised society:

Right: Informal street notices, such as this first century graffiti from Pompeii, were painted on walls with brushes.

Below: The clean proportions of Roman squared capitals are preserved in stone-carved monumental inscriptions, such as this senatorial address in honour of the Emperor Augustus, found damaged but still legible in the forum at Rome. The weight of the lettering and subtle thick/thin variation in the strokes is perfectly maintained through both the large and smaller-scale letters.

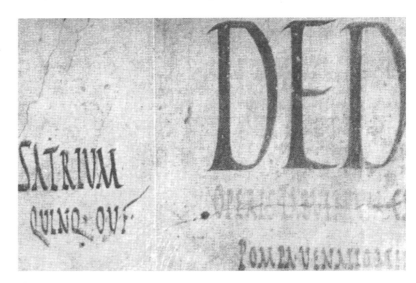

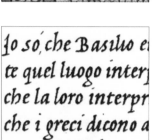

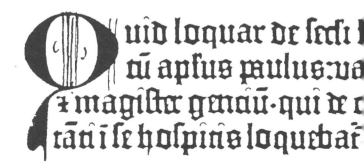

written on papyrus. This last script was the first in which we see ascenders and descenders.

After the decline of the Roman Empire, the main scripts to be developed were uncials, and half uncials, both influenced by Roman precedents. The half uncials found in the English Lindisfarne Gospels, and the Irish Book of Kells mark the highpoint of fine writing during the Dark Ages in Europe.

The court of the Emperor Charlemagne was the source of the next major development in scripts. In 789 Charlemagne, seeking to standardize the great variety of scripts in use throughout his domains, decreed that the round bookhand that we now know as Carolingian minuscule be used. The capitals most often used with this script were pen-made, built-up versions of Roman capitals—versals. They were often highly decorated.

The later medieval period saw the evolution of a variety of forms of Gothic (or Black-letter) scripts, many of which are extremely complex and difficult to read.

Top Left: Book of Kells
This supreme example of half uncials, with its delicate ornamentation, was written by Irish scribes in the eighth century.

Right: 15th C printed book

Top Middle:
Humanistic Minuscule 15th C

Middle: Humanistic Italic 16th C

Top Right: Script 17th C

Middle Right: Copper Plate 18th C

The Introduction of Italic

The re-kindling of interest in classical learning during the Italian Renaissance, and the discovery of ancient texts, led to a revival of Roman capitals and Carolingian minuscules as a basis for formal writing. The Humanist minuscule was an evolution of the latter. The greatest writing landmark of the Renaissance was, however, the development of one of our most beautiful and useful scripts—italic. With its slanting, compressed and flowing letters, it was the joy of the writing masters and appeared in its myriad variations in the great writing manuals, including those of Arrighi, Palatino and Tagliente. Its long ascenders and descenders lent themselves to decorative flourishing, while its speed made it practical as a chancery script too.

SAMPLE SHEET
Edward Johnston
Working in the early part of the 20th century, Edward Johnston produced this roundhand script based on the letterforms of the 10th century Ramsey Psalter.

The Late 19th Century Revival

In the period following the Renaissance, edged-pen writing fell into decline, with the growing ascendancy of pointed-pen copper-plate writing. It was not until the late 19th

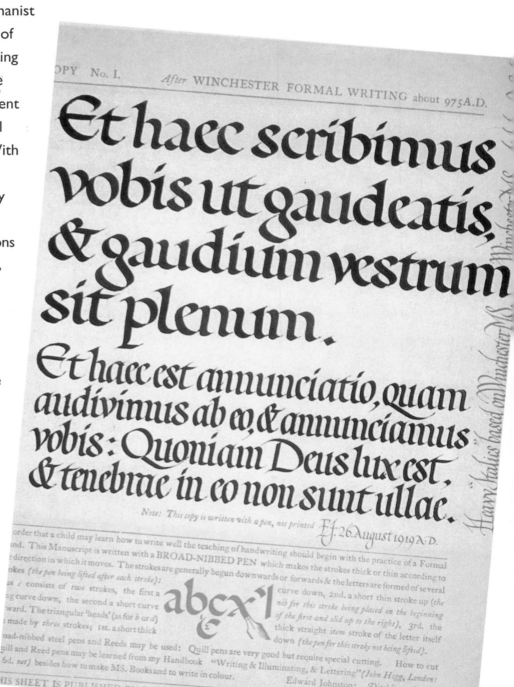

18

I WENT TO THE WOODS BECAUSE
I WISHED TO LIVE DELIBERATELY
TO FRONT ONLY THE ESSENTIAL FACTS OF LIFE
& SEE IF I COULD NOT LEARN
WHAT IT HAD TO TEACH   Thoreau
AND NOT, WHEN I CAME TO DIE
DISCOVER THAT I HAD NOT LIVED

century that the practice of edged-pen callig-raphy was revived by William Morris, the key figure in the Arts and Crafts Movement. He owned, and was influenced by Renaissance manuscripts, and, through his own manuscript books, he engendered an appreciation of the potential of calligraphy in a contemporary setting.

The calligraphic revival was taken further by Edward Johnston, whose pioneering work in the early part of this century involving the study of historical manuscripts resulted in a formal analysis of the letterforms and the principles of edged-pen calligraphy.

In the United States, the revival of edged-pen skills was led in the early part of this century by Ernst Detterer, who had studied with Johnston and, independently, John Howard Benson, a Rhode Island stone cutter,

I WENT TO THE WOOD
John Nash
This elegant panel of poetry by Henry David Thoreau, written in built-up versal-type capitals, shows the timeless craftsmanship of fine calligraphy. Dimensions: 22in x 9in (56 cm x 23 cm).

ALPHABET DESIGN
Donald Jackson
This eye-catching alphabet design shows a delicate tension between elegant gilded classical Roman capitals and the freely written uncial-influenced capitals. Dimensions: 10in x 8in (25.5 cm x 20.5 cm).

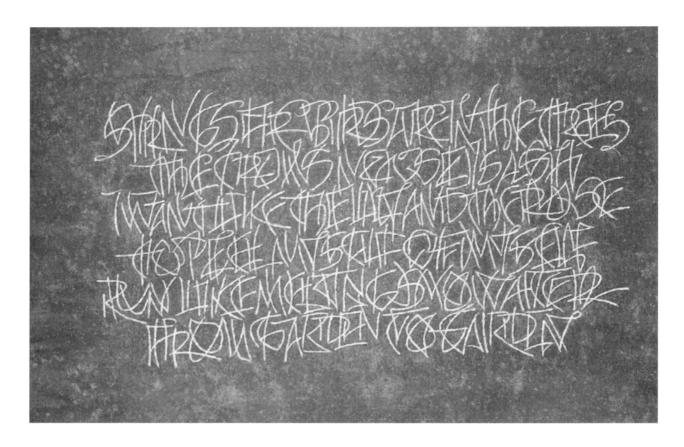

and Graham Casey, who, inspired by Johnston's manual, wrote Elements of Lettering.

Calligraphy in the Modern World

From the middle of this century onwards, many fine calligraphers have emerged on both sides of the Atlantic. The increasing use of calligraphy in graphic design has provided an additional impetus. The craft is now witnessing a popularity unprecedented in terms of the number of practitioners, not only in Britain and the United States, but also in Australia and throughout Europe. The great variety of cultural traditions in which today's calligraphers work has given contemporary calligraphic work a wonderful breadth and vigour.

Calligraphy is now viewed as a tradition with contemporary relevance, rather than an outmoded and archaic practice.

Today's calligraphers have a superb heritage of over 2,000 years of development of the Roman alphabet on which they can draw for their scripts. However experimental you may wish your calligraphy to be, the use of these historical scripts as a basis for your work is vitally important. Such precedents are the roots of modern calligraphy, and have a vast wealth of inspiration to offer to every contemporary calligrapher.

Not only does calligraphy have commercial potential, particularly in graphic design, but it is also growing in popularity as an expressive art form, and continuing to hold an ever-increasing following as a fine craft. Calligraphy is a skill that is open to all. Whether you have had formal art training or not, there are unlimited possibilities for development along individual paths. Calligraphy brings much creative satisfaction, whatever your level of interest and expertise.

Right: THE SHIELD OF ACHILLES
Florian Kynman
An unusual and exciting rendering
of a poem by W.H. Auden.
Dimensions: 17¹/₂in x 24in (61 cm x 95 cm).

Left: SPRING'S FIREBIRD
Ewan Clayton
In this panel the Roman capitals
illustrate how a traditional letterform can be
taken in a contemporary direction.
Dimensions: 20in x 30in (51 cm x 76 cm).

TEXT BY APOLLINAIRE
Julia Vance
The delicate and striking texture of these capitals
(left), punctuated by subtle use of color, has a
powerful presence. Dimensions: 18in x 22in (46
cm x 56 cm).

The classical art of lettering is recovered in this modern reworking of Roman capitals (left) in this instance carved in the more yielding material of plaster rather than stone, but still finely calculated in the proportions and relationships of the letters. A free and vigorous interpretation of letters decorates a geometric motif accompanied by a printed text (right), making use of the contrasts of white, black and a mid-tone blue. Lombardic lettering (far right) is treated to an experimental process. The original pen lettering was used to create a film mask through which washes of colored ink built up a vibrant textural effect.

THE DESIGN OF LETTERFORMS

The legibility of an alphabet form depends upon every letter retaining its most basic identifiable structure - the triangular, crossed shape of the capital A, for example; or the stem and bowl of P; the enclosed and open counters (interior spaces) of O and C, and so on. But this is essentially only the skeleton form of the letter which can be built upon and elaborated by any number of techniques and devices. The calligraphy samples in this book have been specially selected to demonstrate how versatile are these basic forms, and how many formal and decorative possibilities are applicable to the 26 alphabet letters in both their upper-case and lower-case forms.

One of the most significant factors affecting the visual appearance of a calligraphic letter is the writing instrument with which it is described. Brush-written lettering is different in feel from pen-written letters. The actual shape and texture of the pen further affects the appearance of the writing. The responsiveness of a hand-cut quill, still the favored tool of calligraphers, allows rather more fluidity than the relatively rigid metal pens, while the easy motion of a fiber-tip or fountain pen by its nature suggests a relaxed, informal style of script.

It is important to differentiate between calligraphy written with an edged pen, that is, one with a squared tip to the nib, and that executed with a pointed pen, since these tools definitely dictate the basic style of the written letters. There is a historical difference here which for some time caused confusion in the technique and practice of calligraphy. By reference to the writing samples shown in the following pages, it is immediately apparent that the chronologically earlier styles are typically of heavy or medium weight, with a striking modulation between thick and thin strokes and a definite directional balance or pull based upon this weighting of the pen strokes. These are the characteristics of edged pen writing, since whatever the pen angle, its movement naturally produces thick/thin variation according to whether it is the full width, or the fine edge of the pen tip which is travelling on the surface.

Pointed pen lettering is invariably more linear and finely textured. The modulation in pen stroke has to be somewhat artificially created by varying the pressure on the nib which, when heavily pressed, will splay slightly and put down a noticeably thicker line. Pointed pen writing was standard practice from the eighteenth century, and in study of previous calligraphic forms, it was not fully realized that the weight of the letters came from use of a different type of pen. It was thought that the density of the lettering came from drawing the forms in

The hand and whole arm should be free to move

outline and filling the strokes, using a pointed pen or similar tool. It was rediscovery of the vital element of edged-pen writing that stimulated the most recent, and fruitful revival of interest in the calligraphy of the past.

These different intrinsic qualities also give rise to different techniques in writing. A pointed pen can with practice be pushed and pulled in any direction on the writing surface without interrupting the flow of the script. The hand and whole arm should be free to move—the form is not described by the action of fingers and wrist only.

An edged pen, by comparison, is much more easily drawn down the grain of the surface so that the edge and underside of the nib maintain the consistency of the stroke. When pushed upward, and against the grain, the movement is obstructed and the stroke becomes irregular and imprecise,

Much has been written about 'correct' practice of calligraphy, but the most crucial factor is responsiveness on the part of the calligrapher—to the touch and movement of the writing tool on the surface, and to the relationships of letters, and their internal proportions, the weight, spacing, texture and placement on the page. Proportion and balance are not governed by fixed standards; to a large extent the yardstick in calligraphy is simply whether or not the form or design looks right, and this is a judgement with a large degree of subjectivity involved.

destroying control of the linear qualities. In formal calligraphy, the movement of the edged pen flows downward from the top of the letter, and to complete a form it may be necessary to lift the- pen from the surface at the termination of a stroke and return to an appropriate starting point to form the width and direction of the next stroke. This implies a natural order and direction for vertical, slanted and horizontal strokes.

While the purpose of calligraphic practice is generally geared toward the writing of formal and decorative texts, the basic structure and elaboration of the alphabet itself is the starting point. The samples collected here demonstrate that this has been the fascination of calligraphers over centuries. They are intended as a resource for the practice and development of writing skill. Their variety and expertise, from the most restrained and formal to the most curiously inventive, present a pattern of richly instructive elements at any time capable of being invested with new life.

A rhythmic and elegant capital letter alphabet (far left) by modern scribe Robert Boyajian, is enlivened by the use of subtly contrasting colored inks applied from a fine ruling pen.

Gothic black letter elongated and compressed, is the basis of this style (left) the heavy forms cleverly overlaid with a spidery script executed in shimmering blue-grey, an ambitious and highly successful combination of opposites.

This richly textured, symmetrical design (right) demonstrates the continuing usefulness of one of the earliest forms of writing tool: a hollow reed trimmed and shaped to form a broad-tipped pen. The hazily random color changes derive from tile medium used - an ordinary black writing ink which, when diluted, separates into cool blue and warm brown tones.

MATERIALS & EQUIPMENT

The craft of calligraphy does not require a huge outlay: The main requirements are pen, ink and paper, and the main ingredient is a willingness to learn. Don't rush out and buy any old pen. Read these pages carefully and then decide upon your own requirements. There is a tremendous range of materials and implements available to the calligrapher. The craft is currently experiencing a revival, and many companies are entering this market for the first time, especially in the production of writing implements.

Writing Tools

Calligraphic felt-tip pens with broad, chisel-shaped tips are useful for planning layout ideas, but are not normally used for finished work, where accuracy and clear lines are essential. For this you will need to invest in a steel-nibbed pen.

There are two main types of steel-nibbed pens: the pen nib with reservoir and pen holder, which requires constant filling and the fountain-type pen, which has a built-in reservoir. The latter is a better choice for the beginner. It relieves you of the tedious task of constantly filling the reservoir, using a paint brush of pipette which then requires washing out, before continuing to letter; full concentration is needed and so any distraction of encumbrance should be avoided.

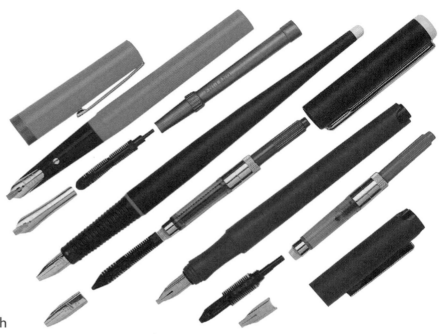

Above: Three kinds of fountain-type pens. The top two have a variety of interchangeable nib units. The third art pen is a complete unit, available in a number of metric sizes. The ink holders, or reservoirs, are either the squeeze or piston type and all three pens have an optional cartridge ink supply.

Left: A left-hand nib unit and a right-hand nib unit.

Top right: A selection of nibs.

Right: Pen nibs and holders with an ink reservoir, and nibs with integral reservoirs and holder.

Whichever type of pen you choose, always inform the supplier whether it is for a right- or left-handed person. There are special nibs for left-handed users where the end of the nib slopes top right to bottom left when viewed from the top. Whichever pen collection is chosen, there will be a variety of nib sizes available, although the size of, say, an Italic fine may vary between different manufacturers, whether it is for a fountain pen or nib holder.

Fountain-type pens

There are various calligraphic pens on the market. Some are purchased as an integral unit (that is, a complete pen); others are

bought as a set and include a barrel, reservoir and a set of interchangeable nib units. Avoid the cartridge refill as it limits the color of ink that can be used. It is better to buy a pen which has a squeeze –fill reservoir so that color can be changed quite easily.

Don't be afraid to ask the local art shop, or stationers to show their entire range. The larger suppliers often have demonstration pens that can be tested finally before making a decision to purchase. The choice of pens available is ever-increasing, and you must ensure that you choose one which is the most comfortable for you.

reservoir and set of nibs. If you do decide to purchase this type of pen you will need to remove the film of lacquer with which the nibs are coated to avoid deterioration. This can be done either by passing the nib through a flame briefly, or by gently scraping the surface.

Checking the Nib Size

You may find reference to Mitchell Nib sizes throughout this book. Mitchell roundhand nibs are widely used by calligraphers. If you a re using a different brand, you will need to convert these sizes to those of your nib. A simple way of doing this is to hold each of your nibs against the size checker below to determine which Mitchell size it most closely matches.

0
1
1^1/$_2$
2
2^1/$_2$
3
3^1/$_2$
4
5
6

Nibs

Once you have confidence and experience with a pen, a pen holder and range of nibs is the next addition to your equipment. The range available is vast, including round-hand, script, poster, scroll and special-effect nibs. These items are sold separately, or can often be bought on a display card which contains pen holder,

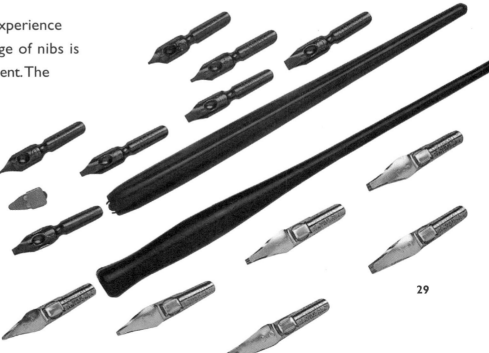

Loading the Pen

If you fill your pen by dipping it directly into the ink or paint, it will be hard to control the amount of liquid in the reservoir, and you may get drips on your paper. It is therefore advisable to use a brush to feed ink or paint directly into the reservoir. Always make sure there is no ink or paint on the upper surface of the nib.

Handmade Pens

It is easy to make your own pens from a fine piece of bamboo. Such pens can produce an interesting and highly individual lettering effect.

Cleaning the pen

Taking care of your tools can become an enjoyable part of the whole craft, not a chore. A pen must be kept clean to perform well. Nibs left with ink, or paint drying in their recesses will clog and rust. Rust will also develop on pen-holders left to soak in water with their nibs attached. When writing is finished, the pen-holder, nib, and reservoir need to be separated, washed and dried.

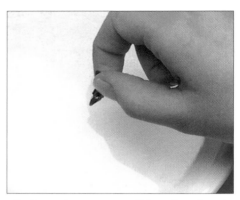

1 *Ease the reservoir off the nib and soak in a bowl of lukewarm soapy water. If it is stuck, do not force it. This may damage the nib. Soak it first to loosen any dried ink.*

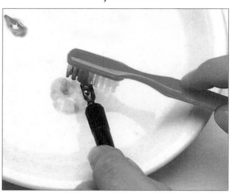

2 *Dip an old toothbrush in the lukewarm water, and gently scrub both sides of the nib and reservoir.*

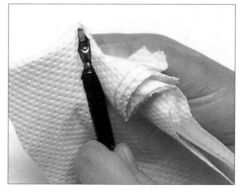

3 *Immediately after washing, dry the nib and reservoir with a cotton rag. Do not use tissues, which leave fibers.*

Left: It is actually possible to produce a brush-stroke effect with a very broad-nibbed pen. There is almost as much scope and skill involved with this tool as with the brush. Here Arthur Baker, an American scribe, has produced a free-style, pen-drawn alphabet, where the heavy forms are legible mostly through familiarity. The texture of the writing surface is often visible when using such a broad nib, particularly where letters are formed quickly. The broken strokes on the ascenders and descenders demonstrate this.

Brushes

There are three main purposes for which a calligrapher may need a selection of brushes. One is for feeding ink into the pen. A medium-sized, roundhair sable brush suits this function. The same type of brush can be used for applying size and color in decoration. It is as well to have at least one fine and one medium for this purpose, and if color plays an important role in the work, it is advisable to build up a good collection of watercolor brushes. The approach recommended by scribes is to keep a separate brush for each color. Experience will tell whether this is necessary, but it may be noted that the bright colors favored in decorative lettering have strong pigments, so it is necessary at least to clean brushes thoroughly when changing from one color to another.

A brush may replace the pen as the calligrapher's writing tool. This is the basis of eastern calligraphic traditions, but is less common in the west. Early forms of brushes were reeds with the fibers beaten out at one end to separate, and make them flexible. This type of brush is still available from some specialist suppliers. More common are Chinese bamboo brushes with hair tips. The body of the hairs in these brushes may be more or less thick, but they are brought to a fine point to allow the greatest variation in the brush strokes. There are many different kinds of oriental calligraphy brushes with hair and feather tips, whose uses are generally unfamiliar to those trained in the tradition of the pen. However, it is possible to acquire these brushes and to experiment with brush-drawn lettering. A study of eastern calligraphy will also help to give a greater understanding of their potential.

The nearest equivalent to the shape of an edged pen is the flat-tipped sable brush, sold for use by watercolor artists. Round hair brushes are also used for lettering. The characteristic changes from thick to thin strokes, natural to the pen, are softened by the flexibility of a brush. It tends to produce more evenly graded forms. A different type of lettering tradition is represented by sign-writers' brushes. These are fashioned with long, narrow, rounded hair tips; the finest are made by fitting the hairs to the shaft of a quill.

Alan Wong, an oriental calligrapher, designed this motif for a greeting card (below left). The modern style Chinese characters were written with a brush. Brush lettering may be produced with a variety of tools (below). A bamboo stem makes a good brush, where the fibers at one end are broken up to provide a bristly tip (1). A duckdown feather provides a very soft-tipped brush (2). An alternative feather, which is popular with the oriental calligraphers, is the peacock feather (3). This can be a very striking brush, with the peacock markings showing clearly; on the one pictured, an eye can be seen beside the brush holder. A hair tip is broad and soft, but fashioned into an extremely fine point (4). Such brushes give great variation in the brush strokes.

Brush-writing techniques, like those of the pen, must be learned through experience, based on a good understanding of the character of different alphabet forms.

Choosing Brushes for Illumination

The artist has used brushes to carry out most Illumination work in this book: small, springy brushes apply the washes; fine pointed ones fashion the intricate outlines; and shorter ones dot around the Celtic initial. For the calligrapher, brushes have a host of other uses, too; they are used in the gilding process and for applying binders. You do not need to buy a vast array of brushes to get started; it is better to buy one or two and then add to your selection as, and when you find you cannot do without a certain brush.

You can start working with only one brush. It needs to be fine, size 0 or 1, and springy, with short rather than long hairs. Sable hair brushes are considered the best, and if looked after well they last a long time. But they are expensive, and the new breed of synthetic brushes control well and produce a fine line. Brushes that are manufactured especially for miniature painting with short, soft, springy hairs for close control, and so-called spotting brushes, used for photographic retouching are also worth considering.

Choosing a Brush

Take your time to find the perfect brush for your illuminations. A good sable brush is so expensive that most stores will not mind if you ask for some water to try it out on some scrap paper or on the back of your hand. Check that it has a good point that springs back into shape, and does not divide when a little pressure is applied. If you find that it is not satisfactory when you try it out at home, you may be able to take it back.

Inks and Paints

To produce the sharp strokes that characterize calligraphy, your pen and your ink must be compatible. The inks used by medieval scribes (often composed of lamp black—a kind of soot—mixed with gum and water) were efficient and durable, as surviving manuscripts testify. However, inks that had been suitable for quills frequently corroded metal pens, and during the 19th century alternative inks were developed. Some calligraphers continue to make inks from old recipes for creative purposes,

USING INK
Fill a medium-size paintbrush with ink. With the brush in one hand and the pen in the other, feed the ink in from one side, between the nib and the reservoir. A dropper may be used instead of a brush to load ink into the reservoir.

but nowadays there are a great number of prepared inks from which to choose, offering a variety of properties.

It is fun to experiment with inks once you have gained confidence, but for now there are only two factors to consider. The ink must flow smoothly and be an intense black, even when dry. Some inks appear black at the time of writing, but dry to a disappointing gray. For smooth flow, the ink must be non-waterproof.

You can buy non-waterproof ink ready for use, or in a thick solution to be diluted with water. Use distilled water, not water from the tap, or the ink will deteriorate.

USING PAINT

1 *Squeeze out about ¼in (6mm) of paint or gouache. Add water and blend thoroughly with a soft paintbrush until the mixture is the consistency of ink.*

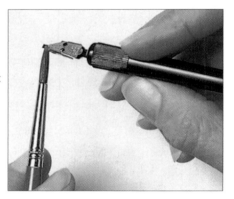

2 *Load the reservoir with the paint using a brush.*

3 *Test the paint flow on a piece of scrap paper. If the paint is too thin, the color will not be strong enough. If the paint is too thick, it will clog the pen.*

4 *Be sure to mix enough paint to complete the job. A change to a new batch of color halfway through is likely to show.*

Remember to keep the lid on, so that the ink does not dry around the top of the bottle and flake into the liquid. Always shake the bottle or stir the ink before starting to write, and if you write for a long period, stir the ink occasionally.

There are many inks available and choice is made difficult by this fact. The main property the ink should have is that it should flow marginally better than waterproof inks and watercolors. The medium should not spread on the writing surface. Unwanted feathering can be attributed either to the paper or to the ink, and you should experiment with both to confirm compatibility.

Density of color is important in finished work and there are inks available which are specifically stated as being calligraphic inks. These are suitable for use in fountain-type pens. There are also inks that are referred to as "artist color", some of which are waterproof; many need a cleaning fluid to clean or flush the pen through after use. (Check with the stockist that such a cleaning agent will have no harmful effects). The range of colors is wide and most of these types of inks are miscible, giving an even wider range.

Some bottles have a pipette incorporated in the cap. This is useful for charging the reservoirs in pen holders, and saves loading with a brush.

The introduction of color in the pen strokes or background opens up a vast range of creative possibilities. The methods used are easily within the reach of the beginner. The paints generally used by calligraphers are artists' watercolors, gouache (an opaque form of watercolor), and some liquid acrylics.

Calligraphers often use watercolor paint for embellishment. This is satisfactory for a pen and holder, but not a fountain pen. Instead of watercolors, pens can be filled with artists' retouching dye, which is translucent and the color is very pure and water soluble. Inks and watercolors vary in light fastness; so check the label for the product's degree of permanence.

Paper

For the beginner, a draughtsman's or designer's layout pad is ideal for roughing out ideas and preliminary pen work. Pads come in various sizes, finishes and weights. Initially, choose a paper that is not too opaque and make sure, when the paper is placed over the sample alphabets in this book, that you can still see the letterforms through it.

There are typo pads specifically made for designers' layouts. This type of pad is ideal, because it is used for tracing letters in studios when laying out work. It has a slightly milky white appearance and is not as transparent as tracing paper.

For finished work a good quality cartridge paper is ideal. Writing papers are produced in many shades and finishes, although they can be a little restrictive due to the sizes available. There are also many drawing papers which can be put to good use. It is as well to experiment with different types of paper, avoiding those with a heavy coating, as they will obstruct the passage of the nib and the flow of the ink. For outdoor work such as

PAPER SAMPLES
Build a collection of samples of papers that interest you, storing them in a folder. Remember to label each paper, and annotate it with observations on how it affects nib movement and how it interacts with ink and paint.

posters, special papers that weather well can be used, but do not forget to use a waterproof ink.

Paper makes a great contribution to the mood, direction and success of the work produced on it. By getting to know some of the many types of paper available, and how they behave with different nibs, you will be able to increase the accuracy of your writing. Medieval manuscripts were written on parchment, or its finer-quality counterpart, vellum—both durable surfaces made from animal skin. Printing brought about the development of paper made from vegetable fibers. Today, calligraphers choose their papers from three main categories: handmade, mould-made and machine-made. Most papers have a range of finishes: hot-pressed (the smoothest surface), Not (which has more of a tooth) and rough (which has a very textural surface).

Different paper types for finished work, available in pads or single sheets

the

SURFACE TOO ROUGH
*Ink flow is impeded and it is
difficult to guide the nib
steadily and smoothly.*

the

SURFACE TOO SLIPPERY
*The nib cannot be controlled.
Ink builds up on the surface
and may run into lower lines.*

the

UNSIZED, OR
WATERLEAF, PAPER
*Absorbs ink or paint like
blotting paper.*

the

TEXTURED PAPER
*Surface bumps may distort
writing, and may contain hairs
that are picked up by the nib.*

the

UNEVEN SIZING
*This causes the letters to
"bleed" in patches.*

the

GREASY SURFACE
*This resists the writing
medium. Grease spots can
cause the same problem.*

Handmade papers are made by dipping a mesh-covered frame, known as a mould, into a solution of fibers. These are held in place on the mould by another frame called a deckle, which gives its name to the distinctive wavy edges of a handmade sheet. The same materials are used to produce mould-made papers, but the process is speeded by a cylinder-mould machine, which produces the paper as a continuous roll. The quality of mould-made paper is close to that of handmade sheets, but there are only two deckled edges, and machine production usually makes them less expensive.

Machine-made papers are mass-produced. Their main advantage is their low cost. Many machine-made papers are suitable for calligraphy and artwork. Machine-made papers are especially useful for practicing and planning, to avoid wasting expensive paper.

Choosing Papers

When choosing paper, you need to consider its weight and its surface. The weight, which indicates the thickness, is especially important when using painted backgrounds.

Paper Problems

Becoming familiar with different types of paper will enable you to choose the best surface for your work. Knowing the cause of paper problems (see illustration, left) can be helpful.

Drawing Board

A drawing board on which to work will of course be required. This need not be an expensive purchase. In calligraphy, work is carried out with the drawing board at an angle. Position yourself in front of the work so that you can see it clearly without stretching. The angle of the board should ideally be about 45°.

However, providing you are in a good viewing position, it may be as low as 30° - whatever suits you. Never work on a flat surface as this necessitates bending over the board and using the pen in an upright position, whereas on a sloping board the pen is at a shallower angle, helping to regulate the ink flow.

A drawing board can be purchased, with or without adjustable angles, from most art shops. Alternatively, laminate shelving board is available at most timber merchants and is quite adequate. A suitable board size is 18in x 24in (450mm x 600mm). Apply iron-on laminate edges to give a clean finish. The board can be supported on your lap and leant against a table or desk, making an angle of about 45° with the desk top. A professional-looking board that adjusts to three angles can be made quite readily. The board illustrated is

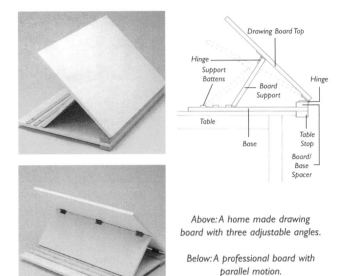

Above: A home made drawing board with three adjustable angles.

Below: A professional board with parallel motion.

approximately one-tenth scale so multiply all measurements by ten.

Cut two laminate boards to the dimensions above, one for the base and the other for the top. In the same material cut a further piece for the board support and some softwood for support battens, table stop and board-base spacer. All these items measure the same width as the drawing board. In addition, six butt hinges and some chipboard screws will be required.

Screw a board spacer to one edge of the base together with a table stop on the opposite side to prevent the board from sliding when in use. Screw the support battens to the base in the positions shown to give three angles from 30° to 45° approximately.

Attach the board support to the drawing board top with three hinges, one in the center

and one a little distance in from each end. It is essential that the support is positioned correctly to achieve the desired angles. Fix the remaining three hinges to the drawing board, underside at the base, with the other side to the board-base spacer. Give all edges a clean finish with iron-on laminate.

Ruler

Choose an 18in (450mm) ruler, preferably with both metric and imperial calibrations. Transparent rulers with grid lines running parallel to their edges can be useful for horizontal alignment in rough layouts, where multiple lines need ruling.

> A ruler with a good bevelled edge is more accurate and when reversed prevents ink seeping under

A ruler with a good bevelled edge is more accurate in transferring measurements and is useful when reversed for ruling ink lines as the bevelled edge prevents ink seeping under the ruler.

Set Square

A 45° set square will be required. Some have millimetre calibrations on the right-angles edges and these are useful when laying out rectangular shapes. The square should be at least 10in (250mm) on the shorter edges. A similar 30° / 60° set square will also be needed.

Pencils

An H or 2H pencil is needed for preliminary guidelines, which need to be fine. The leads are not too soft; so the student won't be spending a lot of time keeping a keen point on the pencil.

An HB will be required for rough layout work as it is sufficiently soft to give a good idea for initial test layouts and can be sharpened to a chisel edge to emulate the size of calligraphic nib to be used.

Propelling or clutch pencils have become very popular in recent times and HB, H and 2H leads are available. A $1/50$in (0.5mm) lead size is preferable, as the smaller leads tend to snap easily.

Eraser

There are many erasers on the market. Choose a plastic one for paper or film.

Cutting Tool

A surgical scalpel is very useful and has an exceptionally keen edge. Replacement blades are sold in units of five per packet. Do be careful when changing the blade, it will be extremely sharp and should be treated with great respect. Always remove the blade by lifting it first from its retaining lug and then with the thumb, push the blade away from the body. Keep the fingers well away from contact with the cutting edge. When fitting a new blade, slide it on to the retaining lug, grip the blade on the blunt top edge and push it home. When the scalpel is not in use, a cork from your favorite bottle of wine will protect both you and the blade.

Additional Requirements

These include masking tape and a few large sheets of cartridge paper to cover the new board and to guard any work. Absorbent cloth or kitchen roll will also be necessary to wipe clean the fountain pen after filling, and the nib when the ink shows signs of building up or clogging.

Some double-sided tape and a substantial weight of card will be required, as may additional lighting if the work areas lack sufficient daylight or good artificial light.

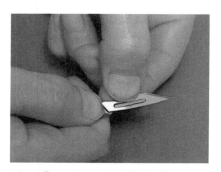

1   *Ease the scalpel blade from its mounting using a thumbnail.*

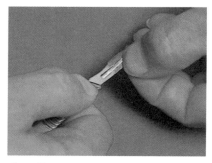

3   *Place the new blade on the handle mounting.*

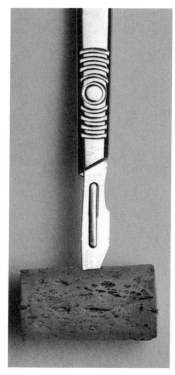

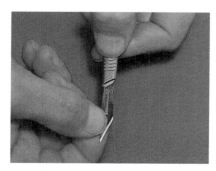

2   *Pull the blade from the handle mounting by gripping the blunt edge.*

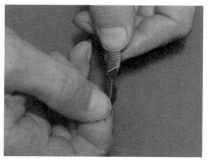

4   *Push the blunt edge of the blade firmly on to the mounting gripping.*

When the scalpel is not in use, use a cork to prevent accidents and avoid blunting the blade

Masking Fluid

Masking fluid is used to conserve areas of white paper which can then be worked on at a later stage. It is usually yellow so that it can be seen on white paper. In the first project, a general area of paper is reserved, but in later projects more precision is required. This will take practice as masking fluid is rather grainy and glutinous. Apply it using a fine, but old, brush, cleaning it immediately in warm, soapy water (a process not recommended for new brushes). Once superimposed washes are dry, gently remove the masking fluid with a soft, clean eraser.

1 Apply the masking fluid with a fine, old brush. The yellow color allows you to see it against the white paper.

2 Paint over the masked area with a dilute wash of color. The paint will not adhere to the masking fluid.

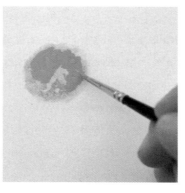

3 Add more opaque color. As it dries, the paint will recede away from the masking fluid.

4 Once the paint is dry, remove the masking fluid with a soft, clean eraser. Rub very gently.

Vellum

Most medieval manuscripts were produced on vellum - the prepared skin of a calf, sheep or goat - because it is both durable and supple, and so could endure centuries of handling. It is still used today, because of its unique surface and properties of durability, but it is extremely expensive. You can buy it in small pieces or, more economically, in whole skins, but you will have to do further work on the skin yourself to get good results.

Types of Vellum

It is worth looking at the various types of vellum available, with their different textures and colors—shades of white, cream, and yellow. All of these treated skins, whether fine or coarse, have their uses and are worth the trouble required to make them workable.

Manuscript vellum is highly prepared and particularly fine; it is thin, smooth, bleached white, and is finished on both sides. Classic vellum is creamy colored, not as highly finished as manuscript vellum, and only treated for writing on one side. Natural vellum is also not so highly prepared and so is darker and coarser. It usually needs quite a lot of work before it can be used. Goatskin vellum is even coarser and again needs a lot of work, but the results are no less beautiful.

The inner side of a piece of vellum is usually rougher and not so easy to work on.

To cut vellum, use a sharp scalpel or knife and a metal ruler on a thick cutting mat.

Buying and Storing Vellum

Suppliers selling calligraphic materials will usually sell pieces of vellum by the square foot, which is the best way of buying it if you are trying it out. The cheapest way of buying vellum, however, is by the skin, and usually by mail. You will find that the size of the skin will depend on the animal from which it comes; for example, the skin of manuscript vellum which comes from a calf is usually about 6-8 feet square. If you have the opportunity to choose your skin, take your time, checking it carefully for blemishes. Storing a skin successfully is not easy. It needs to be stored flat in a cool, dryish place: heat will make it crumple, and dampness will cause it to stretch, but if it gets too dry, it will harden and become unusable.

Cutting Vellum

Vellum has a smooth side (originally the outer hairy side) and a rough side (originally the inner side of the skin). With some types of vellum, such as manuscript vellum, both sides can be worked on, but the outer side is usually regarded as the better of the two.

The problem with cutting a skin is that it is not a consistent thickness, as you will see if you hold it up to the light. Choose the best part of the skin for the work you are doing, and try to keep any variations symmetrical, i.e., keep the thickest part, usually found down the backbone, in the center of your support.

Always cut vellum on a flat surface. Either a piece of wood, the size of a drawing board, or a rubber cutting mat, which can be placed on a table and cut into, is extremely useful. Use a metal edge or ruler to cut against and a craft knife with a clean, sharp, strong blade to cut with. Map out the shape you want first with a pencil, allowing for margins, for stretching and/or for framing.

Once the skin feels smooth, gently brush the vellum surface with a clean feather. Save any excess pounce as it can always be reused.

Prepare your vellum by treating it with an abrasive powder called pounce. Rub the pounce over the surface in a circular motion using a scrap of vellum.

Preparing Vellum

Vellum has a greasy surface which makes it difficult to work on, so you will need to remove the grease. You will also need to give it a nap which will accept the paint or ink and bond it with the skin, as well as providing a surface which is good to work on. You do all this by treating the surface with an abrasive powder called pounce. Pouncing is rather like sanding. The pounce is made by grinding up the following ingredients (available from speciality suppliers) to a fine powder in a pestle and mortar:

Sprinkle a little pounce onto the surface of the skin and then gently rub it around in a circular motion with a scrap of vellum until the skin feels smooth. The amount of pouncing a skin will need will depend on the quality of the skin. Once you have achieved the desired surface, brush off the powder with a soft brush or clean feather. Make sure you have removed all the surface powder, or it may scratch the surface of the gold when burnishing. Do not touch the skin once it has been pounced or you may transfer grease from your hands.

YOU WILL NEED

- **4 measures of cuttlefish bone**
- **8 measures of powdered pumice**
- **2 measures of gum sandarac**

Quills

Quills have been in use for hundreds of years. Although they have been superseded by the widespread use of metal pens, quills are still preferred for writing on vellum, because of their particularly sensitive touch and flexibility. The word pen, in fact, derives from the Latin *penna*, meaning 'feather'. The popular conception of a curly plume, associated with elaborate writing styles, is a more romantic object than the true form of a quill pen. In practice, the quill is cut to a convenient length, about 7-8in (18-20cm) and stripped of its barbs, leaving a plain, stream-lined instrument. Too much length can be a hindrance as a long quill tends to twist in the hand and the rising end may also be uninten-tionally obstructed by the scribe. There is no advantage to keeping the barbs; the stripped quill is cleaner and more easily handled.

The primary flight feathers of a swan, turkey or goose make the best quills; they are slightly curved to left or right, depending on whether they come from the right or left wing of the bird. Left-wing feathers make the best pens for right-handed people.

To render a quill suitable for use as a pen the natural oils must be dried out. This takes from six to twelve months if it is left to dry naturally. Forced drying methods involve cleaning by scraping, soaking or steaming, followed by heat-drying, which makes the quill lose some of its elasticity. In its natural state the shaft of the quill is opaque and relatively soft; it is hardened and clarified by heat. The simplest heat treatment is to hold the quill near a fire or put it briefly in a gently heated oven. One traditional method is to soak the quill, dry it and then plunge it into a tray of heated sand. The quill takes on a more brittle texture after heating and needs only brief exposure to heat. Natural drying is a less risky, if lengthy, process. But some scribes prefer the touch of the hardened quill and it is worth trying both drying methods to discover how they suit individual requirements.

The natural size of a quill obviously limits the width of stroke that it can make. The pointed end is fashioned into a nib shape by shaving away the underside, paring down a double shoulder and slicing across the tip to form the writing edge. The end of the nib is bevelled at an angle and then the whole nib is carefully slit up the center to encourage the flow of ink. Quills are sold cut or uncut. The cut quills may be useful for those learning to handle the tool initially, but most scribes prefer to trim the writing tip to their own specifications.

44

HOW TO MAKE YOUR OWN QUILL
After trimming off all the barbs as described in the text, take a
sharp knife and follow the steps below. Take particular care with
the final step as a square edge is essential. Periodic recutting may
be required to maintain a clean line.

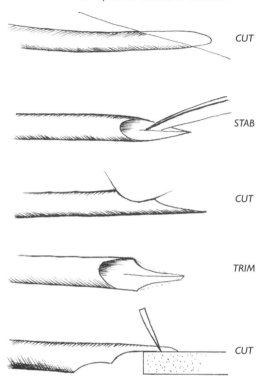

CUT

STAB

CUT

TRIM

CUT

HOW TO FIT A RESERVOIR
Running out of ink slows you down and breaks your rhythm.
Cut a thin strip of soft tin of the right thickness to go inside the stem
of the pen that you have cut. Fold one end to make a hook and push
it into the pen. This makes a little tongue that sits behind the nib
and forms a very satisfactory reservoir.

The quill is, much more vulnerable than a metal nib and will need frequent recutting when used continually. It is important to remember always to cut back the shoulder of the pen as well as trimming the writing edge, so its flexibility is maintained. Trimming is a delicate business that must be carried out properly, as a ragged quill will pick at the writing surface.

A sharp, sturdy knife is needed for quill cutting (the origin of the term penknife, although the present-day version is no longer designed for such). Quill-cutting knives should be available from quill suppliers. A tough surgical scalpel or gardener's budding knife are acceptable substitutes. The knife may also be used to scrape ink from vellum when an error is made. Other necessary items of equipment are an oilstone for sharpening the knife, a small slab with a smooth, rigid surface as a base for cutting, and a magnifying glass for checking the nib quality. The fascination with writing accessories long ago produced quill-cutters that trim, shape and slit the nib mechanically. However, hand-cutting is often preferred, as it preserves the particular shape of the pen chosen by individual scribes to complement the touch and movement of their writing.

Egg Tempera

With egg tempera, the yolk of an egg is used as a binder for pure ground pigment. Water is used to dilute it. Using a good-quality ground pigment, which you can buy in small quantities, produces an intensity of color rarely achieved by ready-made paints. Start with ultramarine blue, cadmium red, scarlet lake, chrome or lemon yellow, zinc white, and ivory black.

1 To mix egg tempera, separate the egg yolk from the white by picking up the sac between thumb and index finger. Dry it on some tissues. Then holding it over a clean container, nick the sac with a craft knife.

Making colors

After cracking an egg and pouring off the white, remove the yolk between thumb and index finger by holding gently onto the sac in which it is enclosed. Dry it off on some tissue—the sac is quite robust, but don't get over confident. Now, holding the sac again, pierce the yolk with a sharp knife so that it falls into a clean bowl or the dried-out shell. Throw the sac away.

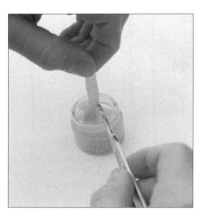

2 Hold the sac so that the yolk drops into the container. You can use a craft knife to ease out the yolk but leave the sac intact.

Make up your colors by spooning a little ground pigment onto a pallete and adding a little water to dilute it. Now add a few drops of yolk with a clean brush—in this way the yolk does not get dirtied. Combine the yolk, water and pigment and add a little more water to dilute (about half yolk and half water). You will find that some pigments mix in more easily than others. For example, ultramarine blue combines with the yolk very easily, whereas white may need to be ground in a pestle and mortar first.

3 Spoon a little ground pigment into a dish and then add a few drops of water to dilute it. Add more water if necessary.

4 Add the egg yolk using a clean brush. Try to keep the ratio of yolk to water about half and half.

Using Egg Tempera

Egg tempera is slightly glutinous in consistency and dries quite quickly, after which it becomes very stable. It cannot be painted on with sweeps of the brush, instead you have to progress across the required area with small, thin interlocking parallel strokes. This produces an area of even, translucent color through which the vellum shines, adding greatly to the richness of the hue.

More color can be added in successive layers until the required intensity of color is reached. Mistakes are more easily rectified with egg tempera than with other media because the layer of paint remains on the surface and can be removed by gentle scraping with a knife.

5 Use a different brush for mixing. Continue to add water and egg yolk until you have achieved the right consistency.

6 Paint on the tempera with a fine brush using small, interlocking parallel strokes. You can build up the strength of color by adding more layers.

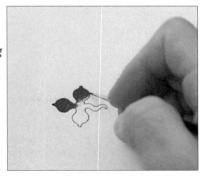

Full Fathom Five
Thy Father Lies;

Of his bones are coral made,
Those are pearls that were his eyes
Nothing of him that doth fade
But doth suffer a sea change
Into something rich & strange
Sea nymphs hourly ring his knell
Ding Dong
Hark how I hear them
Ding Dong Bell.

LAYOUT & DESIGN

Layout is the arrangement of the text (and any illustration) on the page. The aim is to bring together the visual and textual content of the work in a way that is attractive, harmonious and legible. To some extent, layout will be dictated by the purpose of the work, the degree of formality or freedom involved, and the mood that is sought. No single format will suit every case. Creative decisions always depend upon individual judgment. This is an exciting area for discovery, but there are formulae and guidelines to help you.

LAYOUT BASICS

Layouts can have a vertical or horizontal shape, and text may be aligned left, aligned right, justified, centered or asymmetrical. Deciding which arrangement to choose means considering the overall texture of a piece of work in terms of positive and negative shapes—marks on the page and the spaces between them. Accustom your eye to looking for weak features when planning your layout, and aim for positive rather than understated contrasts, such as large and small, dark and light, strong and weak.

The choice of layout also depends on the sense and mood of the text, and the way it divides into lines. For a poem, line endings need to be kept as the poet wrote them. In interpreting prose, line breaks can be planned to enhance the meaning of the text. It is usual to have lines of eight to nine words in a relatively lengthy text. In short texts, just one or two words per line can provide an interesting layout. Line spacing and the style of script—tall or laterally spreading letters—will also affect the shape of the text area. It is useful to begin by making thumbnail sketches—small, quickly delineated inspirational drawings that play with design ideas.

Sizing Up

To convert your thumbnail sketches to full-size layouts, draw a diagonal line from the bottom left corner of the thumbnail to the top right of the larger sheet as shown in the diagram. If the measurement is twice the size of the original, for example, all measurements should double, including the nib size. An alternative method is to use a photocopying machine that records the percentage of enlargement.

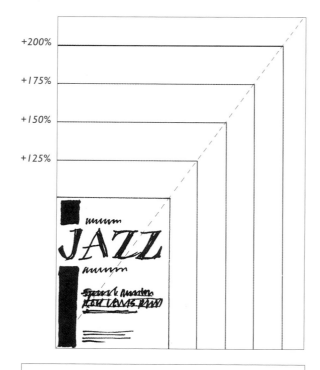

FACTORS THAT AFFECT YOUR CHOICE OF LAYOUT:

- **Who is the text for?**
- **Where will the text be displayed?**
- **How much text is there?**
- **Are there other components— heading, subheading, author, title or date, for example?**
- **Is the text poetry that must retain its line scheme?**
- **Is the text prose, and where should line breaks come?**
- **How long are the lines?**
- **What is the meaning of the text?**
- **What is the mood of the text— lively, static, formal or informal, for example?**
- **Does the text need decoration, and of what kind?**

Types of Layout

Centered

The writing lines are balanced equally on either side of a central line (drawn faintly in pencil for guidance and erased when writing is complete). This symmetrical layout is often useful when balancing long and short lines. A centered layout is most suitable for poetry or short prose pieces.

Aligned Left

All writing lines begin from a straight vertical left margin. This gives a strong left edge and a softer right-hand effect. Avoid marked variations in line length and split words. This is a versatile layout, used for both poetry and prose.

Aligned Right

The lines are aligned vertically on the right. This layout can be effective in giving a degree of tension to a design, although it takes practice to achieve the necessary accuracy of letter widths and spacing. This layout is often seen in short texts such as letterheads.

Asymmetrical

This is a layout that does not conform to an established alignment and yet maintains a sense of balance. A key feature is the non-alignment of most or all line beginnings and endings. The informality of the layout lends itself to texts of all kinds where a feeling of movement is appropriate.

Justified

Both right and left edges are vertically straight. Skill is needed to calculate word spacing to achieve this effect. Justified layouts produce a formal effect that is useful for prose work.

CUTTING AND PASTING

Planning a layout and making a draft version to guide your final work is best done by the method known as "cut and paste". This avoids the process of repeatedly re-writing a text in a particular format each time a problem arises. Cutting and pasting enables you to reassemble the text quickly and accurately in numerous alternative layouts. It allows you to "play" with the text and in this way, to discover a range of approaches. Begin by writing your text on layout paper.

Cut this into lines or words, and on a clean sheet of paper large enough to allow the text to be moved around and with adequate surrounding space for the calculation of margins. Move the strips around freely to evaluate different arrangements. It is a good idea to write the text twice, or to photocopy it, so that you can try alternative layouts and compare them side by side.

When you have finalized your decisions about overall shape, line length and spacing, rule writing lines at the chosen height and paste the text in place. You now have a rough paste-up from which to copy your finished work. A step-by-step demonstration of the cut-and-paste method is shown on the facing page.

To center text during the cut-and-paste stage of layout planning, fold each cut line of writing in half, so that the first and last letters cover each other. Then align this center fold with the vertical line at the center of your page and paste it down. When writing the final version, take careful measurements from the centered draft layout, marking each line beginning and ending with a pencilled dot. Alternatively, use a photocopy of the centered layout text, cut and fold it line by line, and keep it directly above your work for reference while you write the text in its final version.

Cutting and Pasting Equipment

For cutting and pasting you will need a craft knife and glue. Rubber cement, which allows you to re-position the text until you are happy with the result, is the best glue for this purpose.

Assessing Your Layouts

Having cut and pasted your text into a provisional layout, you need to be able to make a judgment on its merits. Train your eye to look for balance and variety in the distribution of text within your chosen margins. The illustrations in this box show examples of the types of faults for which you should be on the look-out in your own paste-ups.

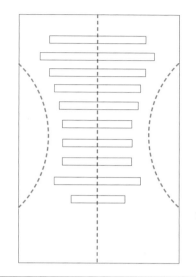

Top heavy layout

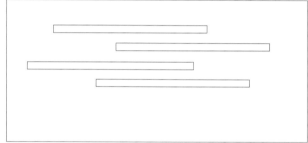

Third line too long, leaving insufficient left margin

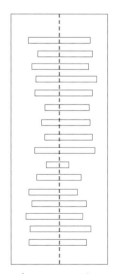

Inaccurate centring

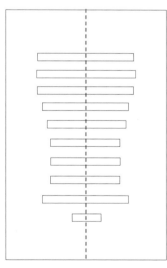

Line lengths too similar, bottom line too short

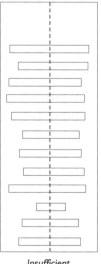

Insufficient bottom margin

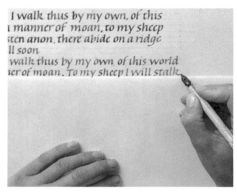

1 Write your text in your chosen script and size. This is italic script, written at an x-height of 4 nib widths.

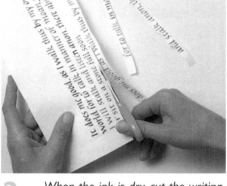

2 When the ink is dry, cut the writing into lines using scissors, or a craft knife and metal ruler.

3 Rule a vertical line in pencil on a sheet of layout paper, approximately 2in (54cm) from the left edge.

4 Assemble the strips of writing on the sheet, beginning against the pencilled line. Move the lines to various positions across the sheet to observe the effect on shape.

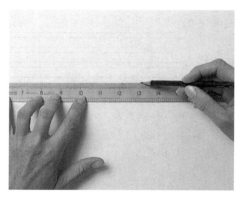

5 Once you have decided on your preferred layout, mark and rule the lines on the layout paper.

6 Apply rubber cement along the writing lines.

Cutting and pasting a layout

The materials needed for cutting and pasting are a sheet of layout or drawing paper measuring at least 11in x 17in (27.5cm x 42.5cm), scissors, a ruler and glue such as rubber cement, which will allow you to re-position pieces of text.

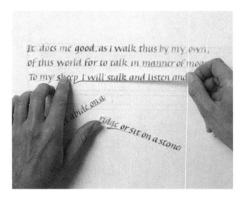

7 *Position the strips of text and press them into place. Re-positioning is possible if necessary.*

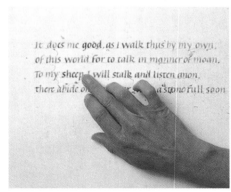

8 *When the rubber cement is dry, rub away any excess with your fingers to leave a neat and securely glued rough paste-up of your script.*

USING COLOR

The introduction of color into a calligraphic work instantly adds substance and gives another dimension to the piece. In past centuries, as now, the use of color was dictated first by the availability of materials and second by the requirements of the work. Pellucid, uncomplicated color decoration was applied initially to draw attention to specific information and to contrast with the dense blackness of the text.

Color made from rubrica, a red earth, was commonly applied to manuscripts not by the scribes themselves, but by rubricators, experts at employing the pigment. The 'rubric' which they applied might be the title, a heading or an initial letter in the manuscript, notes of instruction in the margin of a text, or an entire paragraph.

The opportunities for including color to some degree paralleled the development of the scripts that they both accompanied and utilized. The Versal letter, for example, heavily ornamented, blossomed on the pages of broad-pen scripts, creating immediate interest and contrast.

The range of color applications remains largely unchanged since the time of considered and glorious ornamentation of illuminated manuscripts. Color can be included as an entire pictorial piece, as a single capital letter at the beginning of the text, or as individual letters throughout the work.

There is an extensive range of materials supplying color for the calligrapher. The two most useful sources of color to be laid down for finished work are colored inks and paints. Some consideration needs to be given to selecting the right medium for the work. The medium must be suitable for application with the intended writing instrument, giving sharp edges and hairline serifs, or decoration as required. You must also consider the permanence of the work. Inks with an inherent transparency will have a tendency to fade, unlike opaque designer's colors or gouache.

The paper must also be chosen carefully. If you are using watercolors, a paper that can absorb the added moisture will be necessary.

Applying Color

When working with any color system, always mix more than the job will require and keep a note of the colors you use and their proportions in the mixtures. You will need to practice mixing colors to a good working consistency so that the paint flows in a manner that will achieve the intended results.

Do plenty of rough workings and test the substrate for absorbency. Always have a sample of your selected paper or board to

USING A LARGE BRUSH

1 Working with color and a large brush is an adventure, and one from which much can be learned. The freedom of movement afforded by the brush, combined with the search for an interesting layout and arrangement of color, is also good for developing personal concepts for use in later works.

2 Placing a second color over a first, while the latter is still wet, can produce exciting results.

3 Occasionally this wet-into-wet technique results in a muddy mess; but the enjoyment experienced and the discoveries made through your experiments are, initially, more important than achieving a perfect result everytime.

4 Experience will tell you how much time to allow between applications of color to achieve a more controlled result.

hand on which you can test the color, for both consistency and color match. Mix the colors well, check that you have the required color, and keep on checking and stirring so that the colors do not begin to separate out.

There are two agents that you can use to improve paint consistency. The first is gum arabic. Most designer's colors use this as an ingredient. It aids the handling or flow of the paint and slightly increases the gloss of its finish. The other agent is ox gall. Both agents improve the adhesive quality of the paint. When using gum arabic or ox gall, add them to the paint mix very care fully and only one drop at a time. Use a toothpick or matchstick to apply the drops, not a brush.

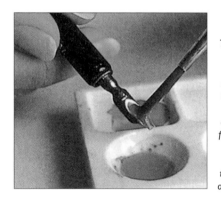

PREPARING TO USE PAINT WITH A NIB
The paint is prepared in a palette. Water is carefully added with a brush or eyedropper so that the paint does not become too thin. It is always advisable to test for consistency and color match on a scrap of paper. Use a brush to transfer a small amount of the paint onto the nib.

If you are using a pen, load the nib with a brush, then check that it is not overloaded either by flicking the pen (well away from the final piece) or by writing a small stroke on a scrap sheet.

Working with paint, in particular, necessitates cleaning the nib or brush frequently. This should become a habit and be done even if the tool does not seem to require cleaning. It is better to do so before a disaster mars the work.

When the medium is mixed with water, the liquid tends to collect at the bottom of the letter strokes. This may be the intention, and can be exploited to the advantage of the work. However, if this is not what is required, you need to lower the angle of your work surface toward the horizontal.

Understatement, deliberately limiting the amount of color, can result in a superior finished work as compared to a piece where color is overstated and the impact is lost. Color intended to provide contrast and draw attention to the work must also supplement it; but if the lettering is not well executed, the color cannot save the work.

USING A NIB

 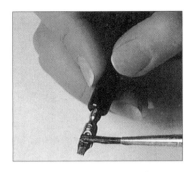 

1   Hairline extensions to letters are often easier to form with paint than with ink. Paint takes longer to dry and so enough residue of liquid is available to pull down with the corner of the nib. Load the nib carefully with a brush before starting to work.

2   When executing fine lettering with paint, the nib will require frequent cleaning. This is best done between letters to prevent clogging and to maintain the crisp edge required of the lettering style.

3   When working with color, care must be taken to maintain an even distribution of color tone, unless an irregularity is being exploited. The hairline extensions are made by lifting the nib, and dragging wet paint with one corner of it. This can be easier to achieve with paint than with other media because paint takes longer to dry. A pool of liquid, ready to be pulled into an extension, remains at the beginning or end of the stroke for longer.

PREPARING A COLORED GROUND

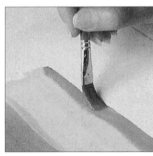  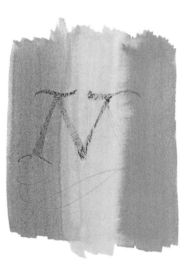

1   Although most calligraphy is done on white or cream paper, a colored ground can often add an extra dimension to a work. To create a delicate wash of color, use thinly diluted watercolor paint applied to pre-dampened paper with a broad flat brush. Color-washing works best on heavy or absorbent papers. Be sure to mix plenty of paint so you don't run out half way through, and apply the wash quickly to avoid streaks and runs.

2   Allowing different drying times between the application of adjacent colors will permit some of the colors to merge into each other. In well planned and more complicated works, this can add background interest and suggest visual ideas that can be exploited.

3   Make sure the paint is absolutely dry before attempting to write on the sheet.

FLOURISHING

Flourishing, the ornamental embellishment of a letter or letters, requires some study before it can be used effectively. There are innumerable examples that you can refer to, in books, manuscripts held in museum collections, and the work of engravers on glass or metal. In all these examples, a wealth of challenging ideas can be confronted. Look for common elements and develop a personal working language for flourishing. Make sketches, and, where possible, put tracing paper over the flourishing and trace the flowing lines. Discover the shape formed by the flourishing, what space it occupies, how thick lines cross thin lines and diagonals run parallel.

The most obvious context for flourishing would seem to be as an extension of formal scripts, but this is not its only place. There are plenty of opportunities, but proceed with caution. When learning to apply flourishing, bear in mind that the basic letters of the work must be well formed.

In work that technically could form the basis for splendid flourishing, the nature of the words, or of the job itself, may dictate otherwise. Studying the text together with the guidelines of the brief will quickly reveal whether the work should be treated to a subtle or elaborate amount of flourishing - if any at all. There are occasions when a measure of controlled flourishing is quite sufficient and the result is more effective for the restraint applied. Other situations provide a challenge that should be met with flourishing that is innovative and inventive.

Begin with simple solutions, always remembering that the strokes must be perceived as a natural extension of the letters, not as additions. They should flow freely and be naturally incorporated into the whole design. They should not bump into or obscure the letters of the text. Always plan flourishing well in plenty of rough workings.

JOHN SMITH
The choice of a dark colored paper adds an extra dimension and depth to this work. The gouache. with its excellent opacity, sits well on the colored ground. The contrasting colors used for the words by PB Shelley work well together, especially in their arrangement of broken lines. The grouped lines, with color overlapping, add movement to the work, designed to a circular format and transformed visually into a spiral.

USING A POINTED BRUSH

1 Successful flourishing requires practice so that the strokes can be accomplished in a relaxed manner and flow naturally. Flourishes should blend with the work and not appear too contrived. A pointed brush is an excellent tool to assist in developing a rhythmic and fluid style.

2 The brush moves with great agility to create expressive arcs and lines. Varying the pressure on the brush produces lines that vary from thick to thin in one continuous stroke.

3 Flourishing exercises can be interesting pieces in their own right. Here the addition of red dots, made with the tip of the brush, provide a finishing touch.

4 Practice making traditional flourishing shapes and simple marks before attempting to apply the lines as letter extensions.

USING A SQUARE-CUT BRUSH

1 A small square-cut brush will mimic the thin and thick lines of a broad nib, but not create too much resistance in its movement.

2 A large square-cut brush is used here to add red dots as a finishing touch.

3 Exercises like these will demonstrate how thick and thin strokes evolve, especially when using a square-cut brush. They will also help develop your ideas on layout.

JEAN LARCHER
An exuberant display of flourishing using copperplate~style lettering. The final piece was produced by silk screening one color in reverse. The artwork was prepared in black on scratchboard.

USING A SQUARE-CUT BRUSH

1 *Employing double points to make flourishes provides an opportunity to introduce letters to the exercises. The double points are treated in the same manner as a square nib, but can be manipulated with greater freedom of movement across the page.*

2 *Double pencils allow an energetic flourish to emerge and be applied as an extension to a letter. The flourish on the italic 'h' is drawn to resemble a ribbon unfurling.*

IEUAN REES
An energetic but controlled flourish which adds great interest and balances the work. Note how the bold lines which form the basis of the flourishing are parallel.

Practice with a relaxed arm movement, using whatever instrument feels most comfortable. A fine pointed nib works well. Experiment with taking thin strokes upward and working the down strokes with more pressure applied. Applying pressure on upward strokes is disastrous - the nib digs into the paper and ink splatters on the work.

Accomplished and elaborate flourishing can look wonderful, but needs much study and practice. As you gain confidence, flourishing will become quite a logical extension to much of your calligraphic work. Sign writing, memorial inscriptions, civic documents, certificates, letterheads and single-letter logos, and delicate personal messages all provide potential for flourishing.

Margins

When you use your writing for a finished piece of work, the margins that you choose will make an important contribution to the overall effect. To show your writing to best advantage, you need to balance the text against the space around and within it. The amount of space between the lines, between areas of text and between heading and text helps to determine the proportions of the outer margins. Too much space makes it look cramped. Generous margins are generally preferable to narrow ones, because surrounding space gives the text unity.

Many designs use the traditionally proportioned margins found in printing and picture framing, and these are easy to calculate (see right). Others may flout convention to achieve a particular effect. Each piece of work has its own requirements. Your ability to assess margins will gradually become intuitive.

Side margins should be equal, but the bottom margin should be larger than the top, so that the work does not appear to be slipping off the page. If a title or author's name is used, this should be considered as part of the text area when measuring margins.

As well as the more traditional margin proportions shown here, there are many other possibilities, where less-conventional margins would be appropriate to the mood and layout of the text. These include placing the text high or low on the page with exaggerated space above or below, or placing it to one side of the page. Such margins are more intuitively assessed than "traditional" margins.

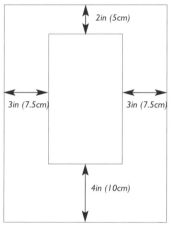

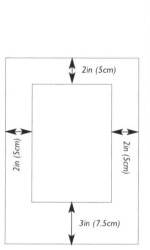

Calculating Margins: Vertical Layout
For a vertical panel of text, the top margin is gauged by eye and doubled for the bottom margin. A measurement between these two is used for the sides. In the example above, the top is 2in (5cm), the bottom 4in (10cm) and the sides 3in (7.5cm). An equal measurement for the top and sides, with a deeper margin at the bottom, is sometimes appropriate (left).

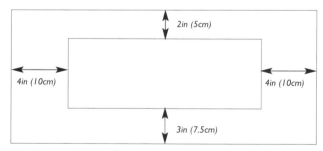

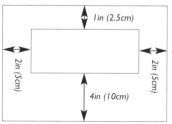

Calculating Margins: Horizontal Layout
For a horizontal panel of text, the widest space needs to be at the sides. In the example above, the measurements are 2in (5cm) at the top, 4in (10cm) for the sides, and 3in (7.5cm) for the bottom margin. An alternative formula is shown at left. Side margins should be equal.

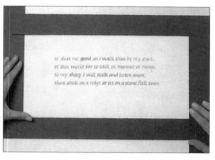

Assessing Margins Using Cardboard Strips
Cardboard strips can be used as a framing device to help you determine the most suitable margins for your work. Make a collection of strips in varying sizes from 2-4in (5-10cm) wide: four of each width at different lengths (two long, two short). L-shaped pieces of cardboard or mountboard can also be used. You may be able to obtain scraps from a picture framer, or you could use old mounts cut into L-shapes that will, placed together, form an adjustable rectangle.

1 Place the strips, or L-shaped mounts, like a frame.

2 Here, the text is "lost" within overly wide margins. Experiment by moving the strips toward and away from the edges of the text.

3 Take care not to cramp the text between narrow side margins, as occurs here.

4 When the balance between text and white space looks right, mark the chosen margins with a light pencil point in each corner.

The hours when the mind
is absorbed by beauty
are the only hours
when we really live,
so that the longer
we can stay among
these things, so much
the more is snatched
from inevitable time

Horizontal Layout
In this piece (above), the space on either side of the text is filled with pale flourishes, which extend the width of the layout. The bottom margin is slightly greater than the top one, thereby "supporting" the text.

Vertical Layout
This panel of poetry (left) achieves visually equal margins at the top and sides by the top margin being measured from the tops of the flourished ascenders and the side margins from their narrowest point.

Ruling Writing Lines

Ruling your own lines for writing will give you more precise results than guide sheets with pre-ruled lines placed under your paper. It will also provide useful practice in judging letter heights and vertical spacing. Draw the lines lightly, using a well-sharpened pencil and a metal ruler or T-square.

> A large t-square can assist in the ruling of guidelines. As this enables you to draw parallel lines, you need only mark the line depths along one margin.

There are several ways to rule guidelines for writing with the edged pen, and each person usually has a preferred method. None of these is complicated, but, whatever method you choose, it is important to be accurate.

The key factor is the x-height. This is measured in terms of nib widths to ensure that letter proportions remain correct for the size of nib being used. The measurement is made by marking the nib widths in a series of small blocks that form a "staircase" or "ladder" of the required height. Therefore, if you are using a script written with an x-height of 4 nib widths, you will build a "staircase" of four blocks to represent the height of the writing line. It is helpful to use dividers to "hold" the measurement of the x-height for transfer to

your writing sheet. Alternatively, you can mark it in pencil on a strip of paper.

The spacing between writing lines, called interline (or simply line) spacing, is a multiple of the x-height. Take it from your first set of nib-width measurements to your writing sheet by means of small pencilled lines—marked down both sides of the sheet to ensure accuracy. You can then rule your lines from these marks, using a ruler and set square aligned with the edge of the paper.

Measuring by Nib Width
Write the nib-width blocks by holding the nib vertically and pulling it briefly to the right (or to the left, if you are left-handed). You can create a vertical "ladder" (right) or a "staircase" (far right).

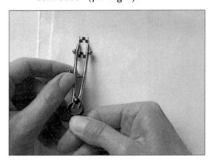

1 *Set the dividers to the height of your "staircase" of nib widths.*

2 *Place the dividers on a previously marked guideline indicating the top of your first line, and mark the baseline at each margin. Rule the baseline.*

Ruling your writing sheet

The method of measuring writing lines in nib widths is the best way of ensuring accurate letter proportions. Save time by making a collection of marker strips for different scripts and nib sizes to re-use when ruling writing lines.

1 Line up a strip of paper with the top edge and left margin of your paper, and mark the position of the top of the x-height on both the paper and strip.

2 Mark the right margin in the same way, using the same marked paper strip as a guide.

3 Use a ruler to draw a line between the two marked margins.

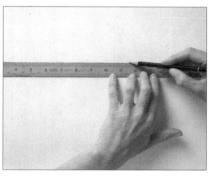

4 Use your chosen nib to create a "staircase" or "ladder" guide for the x-height—in this case 3 nib widths - on a piece of scrap paper.

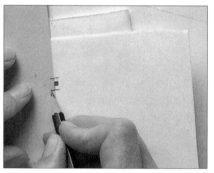

5 Place the paper strip used above against the ladder, aligning the marked point with the top. Mark the base of the x-height on the strip.

6 Place the strip on the paper with the top mark aligned with the line you previously ruled. Mark the baseline on the left and right margins, and rule a line across.

7 Mark the interline space on the strip beneath the x-height guide. Try measuring multiples of the x-height you have already marked.

8 Using the interline space mark on your paper strip, mark the top of the x-height for the next line on both margins and rule this on the paper. Continue marking the x-height and the interline spaces for the required number of lines.

WATERCOLOR WASHES

Many writing surfaces, including those which can be cut into like wood, glass and stone, have inspired the calligrapher. Finding a good-quality surface that will take ink and is not too rough or too smooth is a constant problem. Flecks of fiber in paper and pore marks and different coloring in vellum make good backgrounds for calligraphy. In Anglo-Saxon times vellum, was frequently stained purple to set off the lettering or gold. But vellum is expensive to buy and requires considerable skill and patience to prepare. However, in an exciting combination of calligraphy and painting, you can create your own backgrounds by using color washes over the coarse surface of water-color paper.

Good-quality watercolor papers are made by machine, mainly from cotton. They are evenly white and are a little too rough for writing very fine lines. Handmade papers are often tinted and some contain an interesting amount of fiber from flax, which is made into linen, or other papermaking plants. Most handmade papers have a pattern of "laid" lines, which come from the mesh or "deckle" on which they were made. Wove papers do not have these lines.

Most modern papers have size added to the pulp, rather than being sized later as completed sheets, or tub sized, as handmade papers traditionally used to be. To prevent the watercolor wash from affecting the sizing in the paper some modern watercolor papers are tub sized as well. Even so, in order to write over a layer of watercolor pigment, this new surface has to be sized by a dry method using ground sanderac to stop the ink from bleeding into the pigments.

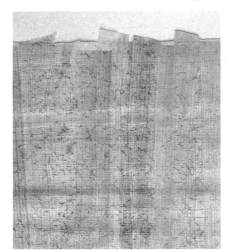
Papyrus, made from an aquatic plant, was used as a writing surface by the ancient Egyptians, Greeks and Romans.

Vellum for calligrphy is usually a calfskin which can beprepared as a writing surface.

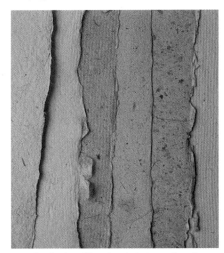
A selection of handmade papers of varying colors and textures, showing the deckle edge.

Watercolor pigments

It is useful to understand something of the chemistry of watercolor pigments. Those mentioned in the list below divide into two groups: soluble stains and insoluble, sedimentary colors. By understanding this principle and mixing the different kinds of pigment, you can achieve a variety of effects. A huge range of colors are available to dazzle the unsuspecting student. In fact, all the colors you need can be mixed from a few basic pigments. These are: Alizarin, Burnt Sienna, Burnt Umber, Cobalt, French Ultramarine, Phthalocyanine Blue, Raw Umber, Sap Green, Viridian, Winsor Yellow, Yellow Ochre. Additional useful colors are: Aureolin, Cadmium Red, Cadmium Yellow, Cerulean, Chrome Lemon, Hookers Green, Oxide of Chromium, Scarlet Lake.

It is essential when buying watercolors that they should be artist quality. Only with these will you be sure of obtaining true pigment. Student-quality watercolors, or anything which is described as a hue, should be avoided. A hue is often an imitation of an expensive pigment which is quite unlike it in its effect. It will not behave in the same way in terms of solubility or insolubility. The washes described here can be achieved only by using the best-quality artist's watercolors in tubes.

Pigments which are largely soluble include: Alizarin; Phthalocyanine Blue (variously named Winsor, Monestial, Hoggar, Thalo, Phthalo, Helogen); Sap Green; Winsor Yellow (a good primary which is reasonably soluble). These pigments stain the surface of the paper evenly to make staining washes. They mix with each other in water.

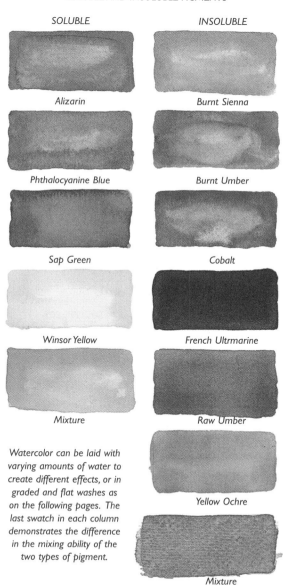

SOLUBLE AND INSOLUBLE PIGMENTS

SOLUBLE   INSOLUBLE

Alizarin   Burnt Sienna

Phthalocyanine Blue   Burnt Umber

Sap Green   Cobalt

Winsor Yellow   French Ultrmarine

Mixture   Raw Umber

Yellow Ochre

Mixture

Watercolor can be laid with varying amounts of water to create different effects, or in graded and flat washes as on the following pages. The last swatch in each column demonstrates the difference in the mixing ability of the two types of pigment.

Pigments which are largely insoluble include: Burnt Sienna; Burnt Umber, Cobalt; French Ultramarine; Raw Umber, Yellow Ochre. These pigments are sedimentary and used for texture washes. They do not mix with one another. If you mix two sedimentary colors together in a wash, they will precipitate differently. For instance, Yellow Ochre and Cobalt will separate when they are mixed together, with the Cobalt sinking to the bottom of the well and the Yellow Ochre remaining on top. These pigments, when used together in a wash, give an interesting textured surface because the pigments will precipitate before the wash dries, emphasising the texture of the paper surface.

Basic equipment

In order to use watercolor washes as backgrounds to calligraphy you will need: Artist-quality watercolors in tubes; 2 round water-color brushes, size 8, containing at least a proportion of sable; 1 palette with 6 deep wells for mixing washes; a block of water-color paper such as Bockingford 300gsm (140lb). The advantage of a block of paper is that the sides of the block are firmly glued, which controls the cockling when the wash is applied. Loose sheets of paper are more inclined to curl up, making it very hard to achieve a smooth and regular

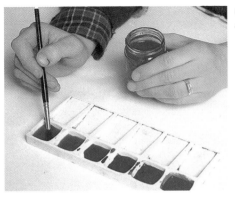

1 To mix a graded wash, transfer a brushful of pigment from the first well, add 5 brushfuls of water and stir

2 Repeat until you have 6 wells of pigment.

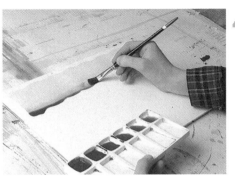

3 Start laying the wash at the top of the page using the most dilute well of pigment

4 Use a flat watercolor brush and apply pigment in a wavy line, massaging it down over the paper.

5 *The pigment and water pool into a bead at the bottom of the stroke.*

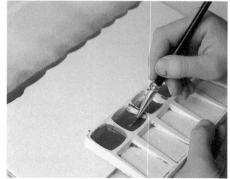

6 *Each stroke should pick up the bead of color and draw it down and across the page.*

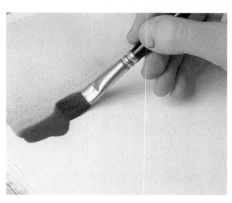

7 *Having applied a full brushstroke from the weakest well, transfer a brush of color from the fifth well to the sixth. Add a stroke to the paper before moving on to the fifth well. When the wash has been completed, the bead of color must be removed from the paper.*

8 *Place a dry, flat brush along the bead. This will absorb the excess color. If the bead is left it will make an unsightly blemish (above).*

wash. The advantage of a sable brush is that it holds a wash and allows it to flow on to the paper surface. Nylon brushes do not hold the water properly and they flood.

Preparation

Interesting effects can be achieved by applying the staining colors in a graded wash. Using Phthalocyanine Blue as an example, a wash which starts off very light in color and gradually moves through stronger and stronger tones to a much darker version of the color can be built up.

Put a small amount of Phthalocyanine Blue in the first of the six wells of the palette. Using the round watercolor brush, add five brushfuls of clean water by stroking it on the side of the well. A brushful is when the brush is put into the water and allowed to take up as much water as it will. Mix the pigment and water together thoroughly. This then becomes the darkest element of the wash.

Taking a brushful of the strong pigment from the first well, transfer it to the second. Add five more brushfuls of water to the already diluted pigment. Mix thoroughly and then take a brushful of pigment from the second well to the third and add another five brushfuls of water. Repeat this process until you have six wells of pigment, each more dilute than the last. The final well will be very pale mixture indeed.

make a sharp line of color rather than allowing for the gradual color change through the wash.

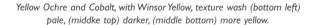
Yellow Ochre and Cobalt, with Winsor Yellow, texture wash (bottom left) pale, (middke top) darker, (middle bottom) more yellow.

Left: Texture wash showing the circular movement of the brush across the paper. The bead of color must be drawn across the dry paper as for graded washes.

Alizarin Crimson graded wash and a Winsor Blue graded wash (bottom right).

Laying a graded wash

The graded wash is laid onto the paper on the block. Working on a drawing board at a fairly flat angle, begin at the top of the paper with the most dilute well of pigment. This wash is applied in a wavy line with the flat watercolor brush. The wavy stroke allows the pigment to be massaged down over the paper surface, moving the pigment around more effectively than if a simple straight stroke were used. The water and pigment pool at the bottom of the stroke in a bead of color. It is very important to maintain this bead of color throughout the wash. If the pigment is allowed to remain on the dry paper without enough water, it will

Each stroke that is added to the wash should pick up the bead of color and draw it down and across the page. Having applied two full brushstrokes from the sixth, or weakest, well, take a brushful of paint from the fifth well and place it in the sixth well. This allows for a very gradual mixing of color from one well to the next. A stroke is then made from the sixth well with the pigment from the fifth added to it, before you move on the fifth well itself.

Each time a stronger color is required, ad a brushful of the stronger pigment in the next well. This allows for the most gradual movement of color possible, moving from the very palest color at the top of the page to the darkest at the bottom.

When the wash has been completed the bead of color must be removed from the paper. This can be done by placing a dry, flat brush along the bead. This will absorb the excess color and water from the paper surface. If the bead is allowed to remain on the finished wash, the moisture will move back up the wash through capillary action as it dries. This will leave unsightly blemishes on the wash and ruin it.

The staining pigments give a wonderful variety of color and can be used alone or mixed to give a wide range of graded washes. They color the paper evenly and do not take advantage of the qualities of the paper surface in the same way that the texture pigments do.

Laying a textured wash

Insoluble sedimentary pigments create wonderful textured washes. Because of their chemistry, they will not mix. They precipitate on the paper, leaving one color in the hollows or the pitted surface of the paper while another is distributed over the whole surface. This can give a feeling of depth to the wash.

A simple texture wash can be made up by mixing two pigments, such as Yellow Ochre and Cobalt. A large amount of the basic wash can be mixed in one well. The amount of water that should be added is a matter of personal choice

and depends on how dark a background you want to achieve. When using these washes in conjunction with lettering, it is important to bear in mind that the background should not be so dark that it detracts from the lettering. Take a round watercolor brush, and apply the wash on to dry paper. Use the brush in a circular motion to agitate the pigment across the paper surface. Each new stroke should pick up the bead of color, adding to it and drawing it across and down the paper.

Stains add color to the wash. Top: Winsor Yellow, Winsor Blue and Alizarin have been added separately to a wash of Yellow Ochre and Cobalt Blue (left) light, (right) dark. Bottom: Burnt Sienna and Ultramarine (left) Burnt Sienna, Ultramarine and Sap green (right).

Texture and stains

The basic texture wash can be made more interesting through the addition of stains. These simply add color to the wash. Take a large amount of Yellow Ochre and Cobalt mixed I a wash and divide it into three wells. Add a small amount of Winsor Yellow to one, Winsor Blue to the second and Alizarin to the third. This will give three very different, colored texture washes from the one basic mixture.

The three colored texture washes can be combined on the page by first laying some of the yellow mix, then some of the red mix and then introducing some of the blue mix. The results are both varied and exciting.

Once you have grasped this basic principle, the possibilities for different colored texture washes are infinite. Try some of the following: Alizarin (graded wash); Alizarin (graded wash with Yellow Ochre); Cobalt, Hookers; Burnt Sienna, Ultramarine; Burnt Sienna, Ultramarine and Sap Green; Burnt Umber, Ultramarine; Burnt Umber, Ultramarine and Sap Green; Raw Umber, Cobalt (dark); Raw Umber, Cobalt (light).

Combinations

It is possible to combine two wash techniques. For this you lay a graded wash made with the

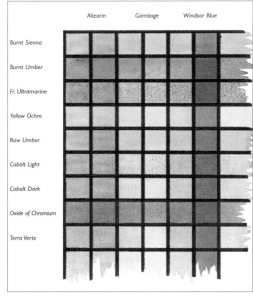

Watercolor wash techniques by Bob Kilvert Chart showing staining colors in vertical stripes with texture washes of pigments laid over them (above).

Diana Hoare—Xanadu 11in x 10in (29cm x 25cm) Graded wash in Sap Green, Winsor Blue and Alizarin (below).

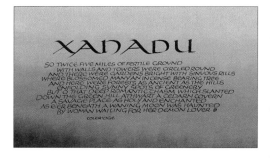

staining pigments, over which you put a wash of a sedimentary pigment.

Take a pale, graded wash of Alizarin and put this down on the dry paper with a flat brush. When this is thoroughly dry take a pale flat wash of a sedimentary such as Yellow Ochre and apply this with a round water-color brush over the top of the first wash. The soluble Alizarin pigment allows the white paper to reflect through it, giving the wash a wonderful, luminous glow. The Yellow Ochre wash allows the light to reflect back from itself. The combination of the two gives a glowing trans-parency to the page.

When using two washes together, it is essential to remember that the staining pigments must be used first. These stain into the surface of the paper and, once dry, they will not move when the second wash is added. However, the sedimentary pigments remain on the paper surface. If a second wash is added to them, they will lift off the surface and mix with the second wash, making an unpleasant muddy color.

The way in which the pigments work together can be best understood in chart form. The soluble staining pigments are put down first and painted in strips down the page. When these washes are dry, the insoluble texture pigments are painted in strips across the page so that they cover the staining pigments.

Writing on a wash

The watercolor washes should be completely dry before any calligraphy is started. Once dry, the surface of the paper should be prepared with finely ground sanderac in a linen bag. Rather than rubbing the paper surface, the bag should be banged down vigorously. This will discharge the sanderac without discoloring the watercolor. When the whole writing area has been treated in this way, the paper should be dusted well with a feather to remove any surplus sanderac, as this would repel the ink and make the writing less sharp.

Chinese stick ink works well, rubbed down to a fairly thick consistency so that it is very black. The use of colored letters on the colored ground is also possible but less legible. To make them richer and more visible, egg tempera can be used. Mix one egg yolk with two pints (one litre) of water, stir thoroughly and use this to dilute the watercolor paints instead of just water. A pencil can be used to

rule up if necessary, but do not press hard into the surface or you will cause unsightly score marks. The pencil needs only to stroke the surface of the paper lightly. It is not possible to erase the lines afterwards since this disturbs the wash and leaves lighter patches on the work. The lines should be accurately measured so that the writing fits exactly on them and no ruling remains visible.

The washes described here can only hint at the exciting possibilities of leaning how to paint in watercolor. Experience and experimentation will open up new avenues to explore.

Bob Kilvert—Reeds in the Wind
10in x 7in (30cm x 18cm)
Background wash of mixed Cobalt and Raw Umber, colored with Alizarin and Pthalo Blue. Reeds lifted out with edge of flat brush and repainted in.

THE WHOLE LAND, EVERY DALE & GLEN, WEEPS ITS LONG SORROW AFTER THE GRACEFUL SUMMER; NO TREE-TOP CAN DO MORE, NOR WEEP LEAVES AFTER THAT

NINETEENTH CENTURY WELSH ENGLYN · THOMAS NICHOLSON · ART ST/SCUBE · STAN KNIGHT 1985

CALLIGRAPHY ON WASHES

Stan Knight
AUTUMN
16in x 10in
(40cm x 26cm)
One of four panels representing the season. Based on photographs and sketches, written and painted on Arches Aquarelle paper in watercolor (left).

Stan Knight
WINTER
16in x 10in
(40cm x 26cm)
The fourth panel of a series representing the seasons. Written and painted on Arches Aquarelle paper in watercolor (right).

WHITE FLOUR
EARTH-FLESH,

A COLD FLEECE ON THE MOUNTAIN

SMALL SNOW OF THE CHILL, BLACK DAY

SNOW LIKE A PLATTER,
BITTER COLD PLUMAGE.

A SOFTNESS SENT
TO ENTRAMMEL ME

HEADINGS AND SUB-HEADINGS

Many factors combine to make a calligraphic design successful. One is the presentation of the work as a whole, and an important contribution to this is the treatment of the heading or title.

The role of the heading is multifaceted. The word or group of words has to attract the attention of the viewer-to the whole work and to the title itself. Having captured the focus, it must allow the reader to read the text. It has, therefore, to standout and be emphasized in some way. Bold lettering, contrasting colors, good letter spacing, and careful use of rules or decoration are all effective devices for catching the eye, but in so doing they must not render the information illegible.

The position of the heading is important. In order to make a visual impact on the reader, the words need to be placed slightly apart from the main body of the text. This does not mean that they stand in total isolation; there are several solutions to creating this space apart from just physically separating the title and text.

The first considerations are the size, weight, style and color of the letters. Then, although the name suggests that a heading should beat the top of a page, this is certainly not the only place, nor, for some works, the best place visually.

The information given by the title is important and must be seen to relate to the whole design. A heading is not an appendage. However, you can experiment with headings in different positions on the page. A single-word title could run vertically down one side of the page. If the text is composed of individual verses or independent pieces of information, the heading could be located in the middle of the page and centered.

Alternatively, it could run across the base of the work, be placed at an oblique angle, or aligned at one side. Look for the solution that offers the most visual impact without loss of meaning.

PAUL SHAW
The red words of the title of this work are ranged right, an alignment method that requires good planning. The letters of the alphabet have been placed centrally to the work. Here, they are both an illustration and a heading. The names of the authors are treated as sub-heads in size and position of lettering.

Positioning Headings

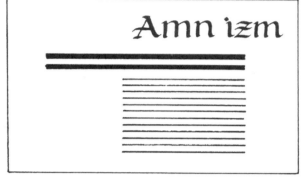

Headings serve many purposes and their design and placement deserve careful consideration. Experiment with different arrangements on the page to find the most suitable and aesthetically pleasing solution. It may be useful to use a grid system to assist in working out the layout of the page. Most printed matter - books, magazines, and newspapers - is designed using a grid, enabling the designer to align the work in a clean, legible manner, both horizontally and vertically. Look at some examples and see how the text and images are laid out on the page, often in columns of a specific width. Rough sketches are initially sufficient for working out the position of a heading. Once an idea has evolved, begin to work some of the text into the sketches.

Study early and modern examples of calligraphy to see how the problem has been solved before. Observe the variety of solutions and do lots of roughs, working thoroughly through as many options as possible. Mark in the body of the text with lines, ruled if necessary, to indicate the area it will occupy, so you can better perceive the balance of space.

If a heading has not been supplied and one is required, you must give careful thought to the wording. The heading should be thought of as a descriptive statement of the contents of the text, expressed both precisely and succinctly.

If you have to include the name of an author, a date, or a reference relating to the text, consider this at the same time as the heading. Often it is this important data that can create a balanced feel to the work. Do not neglect it; like the heading, it is not an afterthought.

Sub-headings

It was a relatively common practice of the early scribes to include in their manuscripts one or more lines of words with letters of a smaller size than those of the title, but larger than the text. The words would appear below a heading or after a decorated letter. Usually, they simply formed the beginning of the text, on occasions extending to quite a lengthy introduction. The concept can be most effectively employed and often works particularly well combined with a decorated or dropped capital.

Expert scribes used numerous variations of this arrangement and the best way to understand them is to spend some time looking at the manuscripts. Keeping reference notes and sketches of unusual layouts will help you to expand your repertoire.

Although some difficulty may arise in working out the letter size to fit the available space, this practice can make a good contribution to achieving a finely balanced work.

USING A RULING PEN

The ruling pen is an excellent instrument for drawing up rules of various widths. It can be used with ink or paint, so is versatile for introducing or enhancing color work. The pen consists of a handle to which two stainless steel blades are attached. One blade is straight and flat, the other bows slightly outward. The tips of the blades almost meet: space between them forms a reservoir for ink or paint. By adjusting a thumbscrew on the bowed blade, you can alter the distance between the blade tips, which dictates the thickness of the line made by the ruling pen.

The medium is loaded into the pen with a brush, or using the dropper supplied with some ink bottles. No ink or paint must be left on the outer edges of the blades, as this could flood the paper if it comes into contact with the the ruler used to guide the pen. The pen must be operated with both blades resting on the paper. Its movement discharges the fluid held between the blades.

Although the thickness of the line can be considerably varied by adjusting the pen, some rules may be of a thickness that is best achieved by drawing two parallel lines and filling in between them with a small brush.

A ruling pen attachment is often found in a standard compass set. It can be used in place of the pencil lead normally inserted in

Using a ruling pen

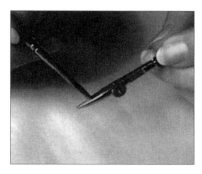

I   Use ink, or paint mixed to a fluid consistency. Insert the color between the blades of the ruling pen with a dropper or brush. Wipe off any excess medium from the edges of the blades.

2   Place the ruler flat on the surface with the bevel edge sloping inward and hold firmly. The thumbscrew on the curved blade of the pen should face outward. Hold the pen at a slight angle to the ruler to avoid paint or ink flooding underneath the edge. Keep the drawn stroke light, smooth and steady, with the points of both blades on the paper to ensure an even flow of medium. It may be necessary to do a 'dummy run' to check that the width of the line is correct.

Using a Compass

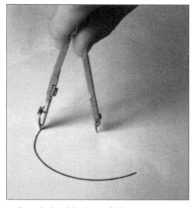

Load the blades of the compass attachment with liquid medium, place the center pin of the compass onto the paper and draw the blades over the surface.

Brush Ruling

When using a brush to rule lines, avoid smudging by holding the ruler at a 45° angle to the paper so that the edge is not actually touching the paper. Gently draw the brush along the ruler, keeping the ferrule against the ruler's edge to ensure a straight line. When the line is completed, remove the ruler carefully to avoid smudging.

the compass, so that you can draw perfect circles of ink or paint.

For fine work, the ruling pen has perhaps been superseded by the technical drafting pen, also available as a compass attachment, but for the ability to produce rules of different weights and colors, the ruling pen remains unsurpassed.

EDGED-PEN PRINCIPLES

The edged pen builds up a letterform stroke by stroke, in the way that you have practiced in pencil.

However, a pen-made letter is composed of thin and thick strokes made by keeping the nib edge at a constant angle to the writing line. The width of the stroke varies according to the direction in which you move the pen while maintaining that fixed nib angle. Pen angles are specific to each script and an essential part of its individuality. A script written with a pen angle of 45°, for example will look different from one formed mainly at 30°. Some scripts use a single pen angle and others call for changes.

Key Characteristics

Pen angle is not the only feature that helps to define a script. Listed opposite are eight characteristics that define and distinguish all the scripts in this book. At the start of each script you will find a panel that profiles the script in terms of these characteristics. The eight principles are therefore your key to understanding each set of letterforms.

Height and Weight
Letter height is measured in nib widths of the chosen nib size. The size of the nib and number of nib widths determine the density (or weight) of the script. There are recommended letter heights for each script based on historical examples. It is advisable to gain experience with these before exploring alternatives.

Pen Angle
The edged pen is held at a constant angle to achieve thick and thin lines. A recommended pen angle for each script, based on historical precedent, gives the correct distribution of weight to the letters. It may be helpful in the beginning to measure and draw the main angle of a script with a protractor.

Slant
All the thick downstrokes of a script, except diagonals, must slant consistently at the correct angle for that script, or letters will appear unmatched. Writing with a consistent slant is achieved by matching each successive down-stroke to its predecessor, and requires practice. The correct pen angle and the correct slant must be maintained simultaneously.

ITALIC SCRIPT
Gareth Colgan

I HAVE AN ORCHARD
THAT HATH STORE OF PLUMS
BROWN ALMONDS, SERVICES
RIPE FIGS AND DATES
DEWBERRIES, APPLES
YELLOW ORANGES
A GARDEN WHERE ARE
BEEHIVES FULL OF HONEY
MUSK ROSES AND
A THOUSAND SORT OF FLOWERS
AND IN THE MIDST
DOTH RUN A SILENT STREAM
WHERE THOU SHALT SEE
THE RED-GILLED FISHES LEAP
WHITE SWANS AND
MANY LOVELY WATERFOWLS

CHRISTOPHER MARLOWE

ROMAN CAPITALS—Liz Burch

Serif Forms

Serifs are small introductory or finishing strokes made during the construction of a letter. Their shape can vary, but must harmonize with the script. They are sometimes termed "roof and root" lines because of the repeating pattern they create along the top and bottom edges of the writing line. This pattern determines the uniformity of letters within the word shape.

O Form

In many scripts, 'o' is the key letter shape because the formation of the other letters is related to it. For example, in foundational hand, the arch structure of 'm', 'n' and 'h', and the curved parts of letters such as 'a', 'b', 'c' and 'd', show the roundness of the fully circular 'o'. The same rounded shape is used for serifs. In contrast, italic is based on an oval 'o'.

nthemum o

Stroke Order and Direction

This is the sequence in which you write the component strokes of a letter, and the direction in which the pen travels, being either pulled or pushed. It is important to follow the stroke sequence, which has evolved as a natural consequence of writing from left to right and gives optimum spacing, rhythm and flow to emerging letters.

Arch Shape and Structure

One of the main features of a lowercase (or minuscule) script is the arch structure in letters such as 'm', 'n' and 'h'. The arch shape often reflects the form of the key letter 'o', and stroke direction and sequence are vital to accurate arch formation. The details of arch structure are explained along with the relevant scripts.

Speed

Certain scripts, such as foundational hand, are written slowly with many pen lifts and few push strokes, giving a characteristic formality and elegance. Others, such as italic, are written at greater speed with the pen being pulled and pushed, rarely leaving the paper, which produces a rhythmic, flowing quality. You will need to write most scripts slowly at first to get used to producing the letterforms accurately, but you will develop the right speed with practice.

Foundational Hand

The Arts and Crafts Movement of the late 19th and early 20th century, with its rejection of industrial methods, generated a renewal of interest in illuminated manuscripts and formal calligraphy. William Morris revived the handmade-book arts, inspired by Renaissance manuscripts, while at the turn of the century Edward Johnston based his early formal penmanship studies on the 10th century Ramsey psalter (now in the British Library). Johnston's analytical studies of letterform, and his teaching and inspiration, were responsible for bringing edged-pen calligraphy back into current usage in the 20th century. The Renaissance manuscripts and the Ramsey psalter were also very influential on other calligraphers of this period.

Today's calligraphers still find historical scripts a useful resource on which to base their own adaptations. The letter heights and pen angles recommended for the edged pen are based on those that produced the balanced proportions of traditional writing.

Pencil skeleton forms reveal the underlying structure of letters and enable you to practice stroke sequence and spacing. When you make letters with the pen, you incorporate variations of stroke weight and thickness. These are determined by the angle of the pen and the direction of your stroke. If your pen is at a 30° angle to the writing line, a straight stroke will only be as wide as the nib can make it at that angle. This will become obvious with practice, but it is essential to hold the pen at the required angle and to follow any changes in pen angle necessary for particular letters; otherwise the thick and thin parts of the letters will not have the correct width and may not be in exactly the right place.

PEN, BRUSH AND INK
For your first script with the broad pen use a good quality black calligraphy ink loaded into your pen with a brush.

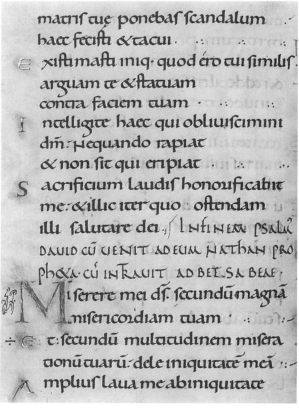

THE RAMSEY PSALTER
This text is from an English manuscript of the late 10th century. It is one of the chief sources for modern roundhand lettering.

Ausculta, o fili, praecepta magistri,
  et inclina aurem cordis tui
et admonitionem pii patris libenter excipe et
efficaciter comple; ut ad eum per obedientiae'
laborem redeas, a quo per inobedientiae desidiam
recesseras ▾ Ad te ergo nunc mihi sermo dirigitur,
quisquis abrenuntians propriis voluntatibus,
Domino Christo vero Regi militaturus, obedientiae
  fortissima atque praeclara arma sumis ✚

THE RULE OF ST BENEDICT
Joan Pilsbury

This panel, written on vellum, shows the suitability of round-hand scripts for formal work. The versal initial letter and the use of two sizes of text provide added interest. The generous interline spacing contributes to the legibility of the whole. Dimensions: 8in x 5in (20.5cm x 12.5cm).

Characteristics
Foundational hand is characterized by its rounded forms, based on a circular 'o', and vertical stems.

Letter Height
4¹/₂ nib widths x-height.
Ascenders and descenders: 3 nib widths

Arch Shape and Structure
Based on a segment of a circle, emerging high from the stem.

O Form
Circular

Pen Angle
30° for most letters; 45° for left-hand diagonals of 'v', 'w', 'x' and 'y'. 0° for 'z' diagonal.

Stroke Order and Direction
Letters are formed with frequent pen lifts and use mainly pull strokes. These characteristics help to give this script a formal quality.

Speed
Moderate and rhythmic.

Slant
None, keep letters vertical.

Serif Forms
Round hooks, echoing the circular 'o', are the most suitable.

Double Pencils

One way to make the transition from pencil to pen-made forms is to practice the basic letters with double pencils. The two pencil points act like the corners of the broad nib, producing the same strokes in weighted outline form. They will help you see how thick and thin strokes form naturally as a result of the angle of the writing edge on the paper and will give you a clear demonstration of letter construction. A carpenter's (chisel) pencil can also be used for your first work with weighted letters.

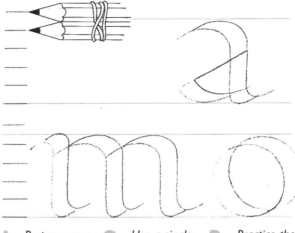

1 *Prepare your pencils as shown. The points should be ¹/₄in (6mm) apart.*

2 *Use a single pencil to rule lines 1¹/₈in (27mm) apart.*

3 *Practice the letters shown. Hold the double pencils at 30° to the horizontal.*

Foundation Pen Strokes

The nib used in the foundational-hand pen exercises is a Mitchell No. 1¹/₂, which is large enough to show letter details clearly.

1 *Rule lines at an x-height of 4¹/₂ nib widths of a Mitchell No. 1¹/₂ nib.*

2 *Following the diagram at right, practice the thick vertical downstrokes. Keep the pen angle at 30° and try to achieve vertical strokes with sharp edges. All your strokes should be the same width. The width will vary if you change the pen angle or if your strokes are not vertical.*

3 *Repeat the exercise for diagonal, horizontal and curved strokes, changing the pen angle to 45° for the left-to-right diagonals. These will be used later to write 'v', 'w', 'x' and 'y'.*

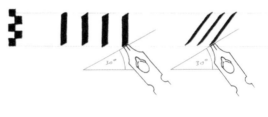

Arches

Arch structure is a defining feature of all lower-case scripts.

1 *Rule lines at 4¹/₂ nib widths of a Mitchell No. 1¹/₂ nib.*

2 *Make a vertical downstroke.*

3 *Place your nib completely inside the vertical as you begin the arch stroke.*

4 *Move the nib uphill to the right, keeping it almost straight until it leaves the stem. Once outside the stem, move the nib horizontally to the right, then around and down to form a circular arch with a hint of squaring at the right side where the arch and downstroke join. Make sure that your arches follow the arc of a circle.*

5 *practice the letters 'n' and 'm' until you are satisfied with the result.*

Letter-formation Groups

Begin practicing weighted letters in their formation groups, so that you get used to the movements needed to make related strokes.

1 Leave two lines blank between each writing line.

2 *Practice each group several times, following the model closely. The arrows indicate stroke order and direction. Use a 30° pen angle for all strokes except the thick diagonals of 'v', 'w', 'x', 'y' (45°), and the 'z' diagonal (0°),*

3 *Check your letters against the model after each attempt. Make sure that the letters within each group relate, exhibiting the details common to the group.*

Spacing

The principle of even spacing is the same for weighted as for skeleton foundational letters. However, if you compare skeleton letters and weighted letters of the same height, you will notice that the weighted letters are spaced slightly closer. This is because weighted strokes take up some of the counter space (enclosed space) within letters, and so slightly less space is needed between letters.

1 *Rule lines at an x-height of 4¹/₂ nib widths of a Mitchell No. 1¹/₂ nib*

2 *Write a foundational-hand 'h'.*

3 *Place an 'i' next to it, slightly closer than the width of the 'h' counter.*

4 *Place an 'o' slightly closer to the 'i'.*

5 *Write a 'c' alongside the 'o', even closer but not touching.*

Watchpoints

Once you are familiar with the letter groups and spacing, you are ready to write the foundational letters in alphabetical order on paper ruled at an x-height of 4½ nib widths of a Mitchell No. 1½ nib. Write the alphabet in sections: 'a-f', 'g-n', 'o-u', 'v-z'. Repeat each section several times, checking pen angle, letter shapes and spacing each time before re-writing. Use the Rule of Three to help you verify spacing.

Slightly flattened curve

softened front of bowl

crossbar on x-height

Arches based on 'a' form

Top counter circular, lower counter oval

Right angle at joint

Arch based on a form

Slightly squared-off join

Slightly flattened curve

Aligned vertically at right of letter

Slightly squared-off join

0° pen angle for diagonal

Vertical 'v' elements

Straight right-hand diagonal

YOU WILL NEED

- **Keep your letters vertical.**
- **Keep your pen at an angle of 30° to the writing line, except for the thick left-hand diagonals of 'v', 'w', 'x' and 'y' (45°) and the 'z' diagonal, written with a flat pen (0°).**
- **Make sure that the bodies of your letters fill the double line (except 'g').**
- **Check that the arches form an arc of the circular 'o'.**
- **Make sure that stroke joins occur at the same height in letters of the same formation group, such as 'h', 'm', 'n' and 'r', or 'q' and 'd'.**
- **Make sure that the base curves of 'l', 't' and 'u' relate to the circular 'o'.**
- **Check that the crossbars of 't' and 'f' coincide with the top writing line. The base curve and crossbar of 5 should align on the right.**
- **Ensure that the two halves of 'm', and 'w', are equal.**
- **Keep ascenders and descenders 3 nib widths above and below the line.**

j k r t x y

tt tt ff ff ry fl

Alternative Forms and Awkward Joins

Some letters have alternative forms. If you choose an alternative, it is usually preferable to keep to it throughout a piece. Also shown are some letter combinations that sometimes cause difficulty with spacing.

1 Rule lines at an x-height of 4½ nib widths of a Mitchell No. 1½nib.

2 practice each of the letters shown in the second line.

3 Then practice the letter combinations shown in the second line.

Word practice

Once you are able to write and space the alphabet accurately, begin writing words. Trying the letterforms in new combinations will consolidate your knowledge of their shapes and extend your experience of spacing. It is best to concentrate on writing the same few words repeatedly at first. The area between words should be consistent: leave space for a foundational-hand 'o'.

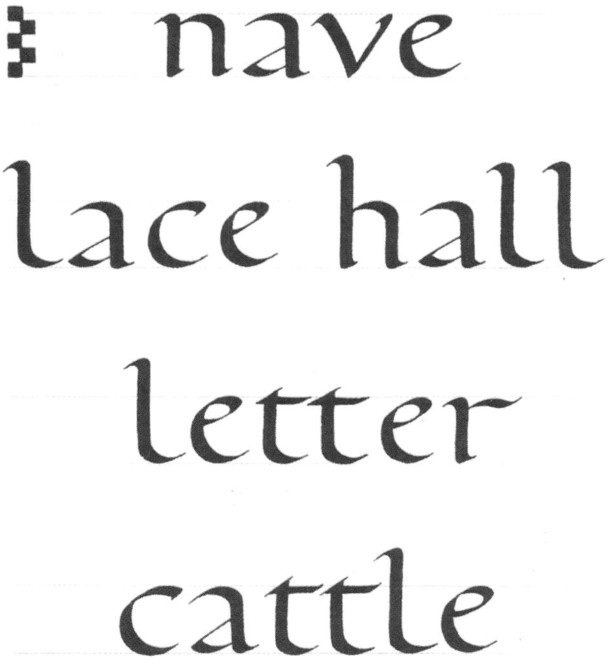

nave

lace hall

letter

cattle

1 Write at an x-height of 4½ nib widths of a Mitchell No. 1½ nib.

2 Leave the width of an 'o' between words.

3 Warm up by writing a line of "nini", treating it as if it were a word. Straight-sided letters are written equidistantly and are therefore easier to space.

4 Practice each of the words shown at right several times, checking each time for accuracy of letterform, pen angle and spacing.

5 Apply the Rule of Three spacing check to each word.

Foundational-Hand Greetings Card

Now that you have mastered the essentials of foundational hand, you can begin to use your skills in simple decorative projects such as this attractive greetings card, written with a Mitchell No. 1½ nib and decorated with gouache applied with a pen and a brush.

Writing a Short Quotation

Planning and writing a short quotation will give you practice in rhythmic writing, spacing and design. Use a Mitchell No. 1½ nib. Write the final version over a watercolor wash in colors that echo the text.

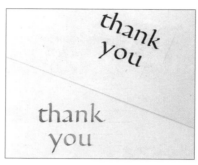

1 Write out the words on lines ruled to 4½ nib widths. Cut and paste the lines into a centered layout. Copy carefully on to folded paper.

2 Rule margins on to the pasted-up version, and try out a simple border decoration in gouache. Copy the border on to your final version.

1 Write out your text on layout paper between lines ruled at 4½ nib widths. Do not worry about making decisions on layout at this stage.

2 Cut the text into individual words, and experiment with different layouts. When you have decided on a layout, paste the words into position. This then acts as a guide for the final version. A centered layout has been chosen here.

3 The next stage is to prepare the background. Apply a mixed watercolor wash with a large soft brush. The watercolor paper used here is heavy enough not to require stretching.

4 Allow several hours for the wash to dry. Dust with gum sandarac, and lightly rule writing lines. Write the words in blue/grey gouache.

5 Finished piece: The final text is an attractive piece of decorative calligraphy.

Scaling Down

The smaller the script, the less contrast there is between thick and thin strokes. Great precision is therefore needed when writing with small nibs. When you start to practice using small nibs, work your way gradually down the nib sizes, so that you do not lose pen control. Keep your letters at $4^{1}/_{2}$ nib widths.

Writing Large

Large writing gives you practice in moving your whole arm and therefore encourages rhythmic writing. It is also helpful for detailed study of letterforms. Above all, it is fun and so encourages the flow of creative ideas. Automatic pens are ideal for large-scale writing. Large nibs devour ink and may need filling every letter, but ink can be diluted for the sake of economy when practicing, or diluted paint can be used. It is usual to write with the grooved side of the nib uppermost, which gives the best flow, but writing with the grooved side down often ensures sharper strokes.

Try your pen both ways, because results vary. Make sure that no ink or paint dries in the nib after use. This could impede subsequent ink flow.

The best way to begin is to repeat a simple word, concentrating on forms and spacing. An interesting texture can be built up by such repetition and used later for a design. You may want to explore color changes in the pen.

No. 1 1/2   o abcde
No. 3   o abcde
No. 3 1/2   o abcde
No. 4   o abcde
No. 5   o abcde

1 *Begin with the largest nib and practice each size in turn, writing the foundational alphabet several times, followed by words and then a short quotation.*

2 *Correct the letterforms and spacing, re-writing as necessary.*

3 *Move down a nib size only when your writing is reasonably sound.*

Combining Large and Small

Combining large and small-scale writing can create effective contrast, but sizes must harmonize. The example below consists of the main word written with a Mitchell No. 1 nib and subsidiary text written with a No. 3 nib. The lettering is written in gouache on a Conte-crayon background.

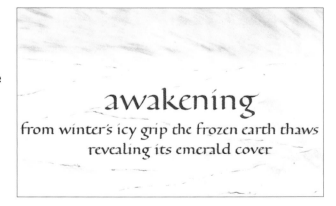

awakening
from winter's icy grip the frozen earth thaws
revealing its emerald cover

like a man cros

MASTERING LETTERFORMS

In order to fully understand letter construction, you will need to understand the terminology used to describe the constituent parts of letterforms. When analysing a particular style, this nomenclature is used to define the various elements in a concise manner. There is no standard nomenclature to define constituent parts of letters, but many of the terms are self-explanatory. The terminology used here is based on that employed by letter designers and therefore may differ from that found in calligraphic references. Many descriptions are repeated from letter to letter as these terms are used generally throughout the alphabet, and are not necessarily confined to a specific letter. The parts and names illustrated refer to the Quadrata capitals (majuscule) and a complementary lower-case (miniscule) alphabet although most of the terms can be employed to define other forms.

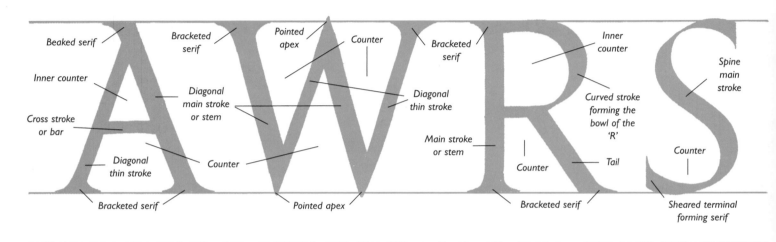

Beaked serif

Bracketed serif

Pointed apex

Counter

Bracketed serif

Inner counter

Spine main stroke

Inner counter

Diagonal main stroke or stem

Diagonal thin stroke

Curved stroke forming the bowl of the 'R'

Cross stroke or bar

Main stroke or stem

Counter

Diagonal thin stroke

Counter

Counter

Tail

Bracketed serif

Pointed apex

Bracketed serif

Sheared terminal forming serif

INTER LINEAR SPACING

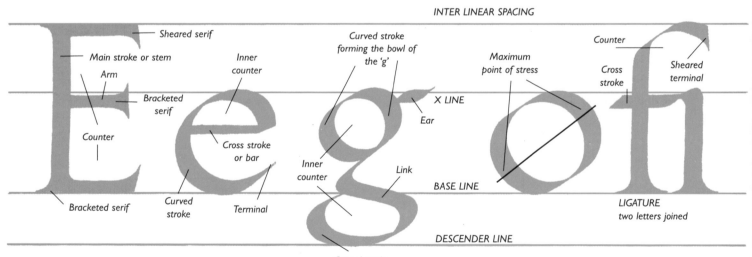

Sheared serif

Curved stroke forming the bowl of the 'g'

Counter

Main stroke or stem

Inner counter

Maximum point of stress

Cross stroke

Sheared terminal

Arm

Bracketed serif

X LINE

Counter

Cross stroke or bar

Ear

Inner counter

Link

Bracketed serif

Curved stroke

Terminal

BASE LINE

LIGATURE
two letters joined

DESCENDER LINE

Curved stroke forming the loop

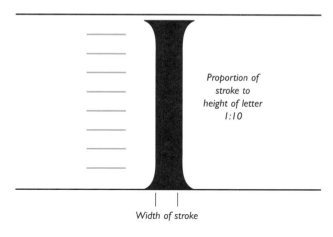

*Proportion of
stroke to
height of letter
1:10*

Width of stroke

Understanding Letter Construction

Quadrata is the criterion on which all subsequent styles are based. It is therefore most important for you to understand this fine, proportioned alphabet.

Roman is not just the name of the country of origin, but is used more generally to describe any style appearing in a vertical attitude. The capital alphabet contains more straight lines than curves, and many letters have a combination of both vertical and horizontal strokes giving a squarish appearance, hence the word quadrata. There is an architectural, geometric quality within the style which would account for the harmony created when lettering is used on buildings in stone.

Capital letters can be defined as having a uniform height throughout; that is, they are written between two parallel lines.

The letters are contained without a capital or cap line (top line) and a base line, with the exception of the letters 'J' and 'Q' which break the base line in some styles. The lines are also marginally broken by minor optical adjustments to certain letters where pointed apexes and curved strokes slightly overlap.

There are now two fixed points, the capital and the base lines, between which to construct the letters. There is, however, a problem as you will need to decide how far apart the lines should be drawn. Consider the proportions of the letters opposite. There is a definite relationship between the capital height and the width of the main stroke. In Quadrata, the stem divides into the capital height 10 times, giving a ratio of 1:10. It is important to evaluate this ratio, as misinterpretation will result in an untrue reproduction of the style.

Once the height and weight ratios have been established, give consideration to the construction of individual letters. The Romans were a practical and efficient race, and their ability to rationalize and organize is reflected in the formal appearance of their design. The alphabet which follows has been produced with a pen and is based on formal Roman characters. If the forms are analysed, it will be noticed that there are similar characteristics between certain letters, the E, F and L for example.

It is also apparent that the widths of letters are not identical and that each character occupies a given area in width while retaining a constant height. This width is known as the unit value of the letter, the 'M' and 'W' being the widest and the 'I' and 'J' the narrowest.

When letters are placed on a gridded square, an immediate visual comparison between the letterforms is possible. The grid illustrated has been divided into units of stem width for convenience, giving an initial square for the capitals subdivided into 10 units of height by 10 units of width. The lower blank portion is for the lower-case letters, which appear after the capitals. The lower portion will then be used to accommodate the descenders.

Incidentally, the words 'lower case' are a printers' term, now in common use to describe minuscule letters. It derives from the typesetters' cases which contained the metal or wooden letters. The capital letters of an alphabet were stored in the upper case and so are sometimes referred to as such, with the small letters stored in the lower case. Although concerned with calligraphy here, the common terms for majuscule and minuscule letters - capitals and lower case - are better employed and this is the terminology used from now onwards.

When analysing the construction of individual characters, fix their images firmly in your mind. The proportions of this style will be found to be indispensable as you become more involved with letterforms, and the ability to draw on your experience of the classical Roman style will help you when analysing other letterforms. The letters fall into six groupings, from the widest to the narrowest characters.

This alphabet has been lettered with a pen to illustrate proportion; it also shows that a classical Roman style can be achieved calligraphically. It is not necessarily helpful for you to begin lettering with this style for the construction of the letterforms is difficult in as much as they are not easily reproduced with a square-ended nib.

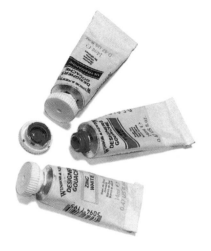

Roman Capitals

Group 1

The 'M' is one of the widest letters of the alphabet, occupying slightly more than the square with the diagonal strokes breaking the grid at both sides. The true Roman 'M' has pointed apexes, along with the 'A' and 'N', which are easily cut with a chisel; but when a pen or brush is employed, other forms of ending the strokes are more natural.

In order to achieve a pointed apex, the pen strokes end short of the cap and base lines and are then brought to a point. The apexes project beyond capital and base lines in order to obtain optical alignment with letters ending in square terminals or with beaked or bracketed serifs. Because the apexes of the 'M' in the example alphabet end in a beaked serif, this will naturally be carried through to the 'A' and 'N' to give continuity. The straight, thin strokes in the 'M' and similar letters are approximately half the thickness of the main stroke, but these strokes do alter because of the fixed lettering angle of the pen in relation to the direction of the strokes.

The 'W' is perhaps the widest letter of the alphabet. It does not appear in Roman inscriptions but is a medieval addition to the alphabet. In Latin inscriptions 'V' stood for both the 'U' and 'V' sounds - hence the name 'double U', drawn as two 'V''s virtually joined together, with minor adjustments. The 'U' symbol was a later development, perhaps to avoid confusion.

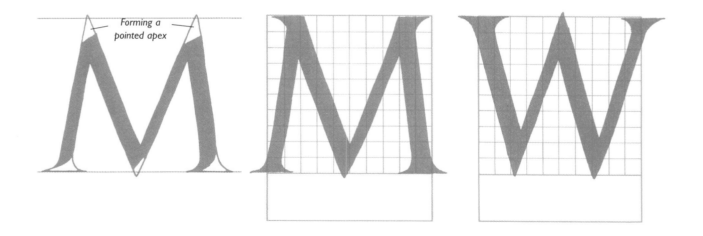

Forming a pointed apex

Group 2

The '0' sets the standard for all curved letters and the 'Q' can be said to be an '0' with an added tail. It is advisable to make note of the point at which the tail joins the curved stroke. Some letters, unfortunately, have a tail which appears to emanate from the lower left-hand curve of the letter, as an extension. This is undesirable as the tail is most definitely a separate stroke.

The widest point of the thick stroke of the '0' is marginally wider than that of the stem of the 'I'. In a free-drawn letter, that is, a letter drawn and then filled in, this is an optical adjustment made to compensate for the tapering or thinning of the stroke toward the thinnest part of the letter. Without this alteration, the curved stroke would appear optically thinner than the stem of the 'I'.

In calligraphy, the adjustment to thicken the curved strokes is automatic because of the oblique angle of the pen to the direction of writing. The thin strokes are substantially thinner than half the width of the main stroke, due to this same action of the pen. If desired, these thin strokes can be thickened to compare more favorably with the straight, thin strokes.

The widest point of the curved stroke is known as the 'maximum point of stress', and in this example it can be said that the letter has diagonal stress with oblique shading. There are many styles which have horizontal stress with vertical shading.

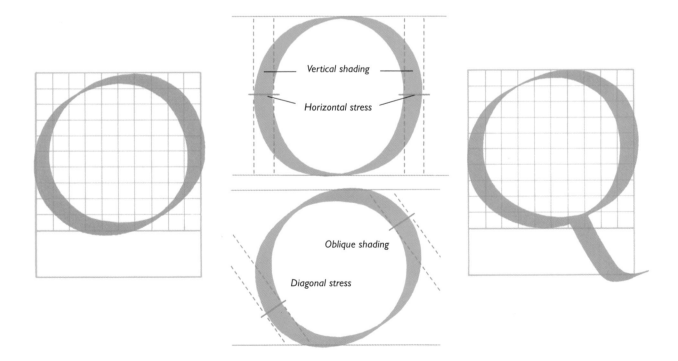

Vertical shading

Horizontal stress

Oblique shading

Diagonal stress

Group 3

The 'C', 'D' and 'G' take up about nine-tenths of the width of the gridded square. Because they are all rounded forms, -the top and bottom curves project slightly over the cap and base lines. This is to ensure that the round letters appear the same height as those ending in flat serifs. Without this refinement they would appear smaller.

The 'C' follows the left-hand curve of the '0', but the upper and lower arms are somewhat flattened. The upper arm ends in a sheared terminal which is slightly extended to form a beak-like serif. In Quadrata, the lower arm also ends similarly. This serif is extremely difficult to produce with a pen.

'G' follows the lines of the 'C', with the stem of the 'G' rising from the lower arm to within five-tenths of the letter height, and terminating in a bracketed serif.

'D' follows the right-hand curve of the '0' with the upper and lower curves extending from the initial cross-strokes, so slightly breaking the cap line and base line. The stem appears slightly thickened toward the base cross-stroke where it is joined with a curved bracket. The serifs are bracketed on the left hand of the stem.

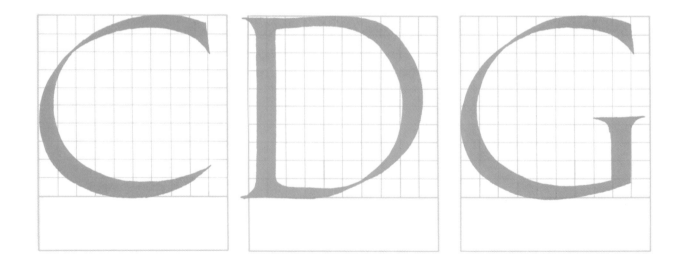

Group 4

This is the largest group of letters and includes 'A, H, K, N, R, T, U, V, X, Y' and 'Z', all of which occupy approximately eight-tenths of the gridded square. The 'A, V, X' and 'Y', being letters formed from triangular elements, should appear almost symmetrical. The 'V' and inverted 'V' shapes should be balanced, not leaning to right or left. The cross-stroke of the 'A' is positioned midway between the apex and the base line. The cross-bar of the 'H' should be slightly above the center line; otherwise it seems to be slipping down the main stems. The two diagonal strokes of the 'K' meet at a point which, too, is slightly above the center, making the lower counter fractionally larger than the upper counter.

The pointed apex of the 'N' should

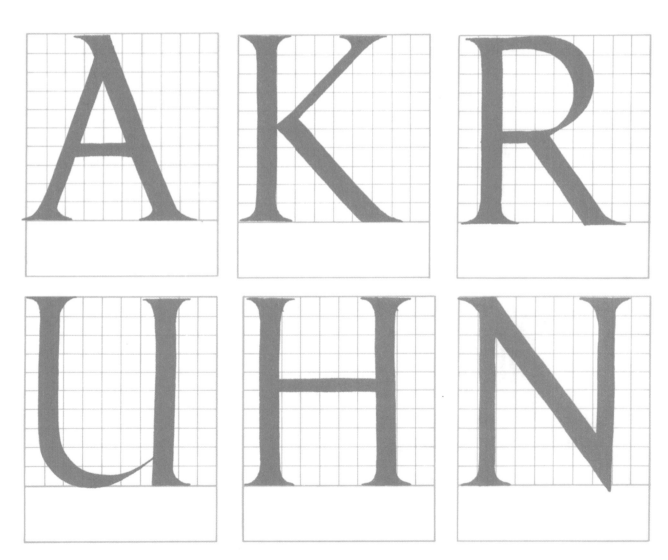

protrude below the base line with the upper left-hand serif being beaked. Both the upper part of the bowl of the Rand the curved stroke. Of the 'U' project above the cap line and below the base line respectively. The top of the lower cross-stroke which joins the bowl of the 'R' is positioned on the center line. A careful note should be made as to where the tail of the 'R' meets the bowl.

The cross-bar of the 'T' is sheared to the lettering angle on the left and right sides, ending in a slight serif. The spurs added to the serifs protrude above the cap line.

The 'Z' is a problem letter as the main diagonal stem requires a change of pen angle to thicken the stroke. Otherwise the stem would appear as a hairline-thin stroke. This makes it difficult to execute with the pen.

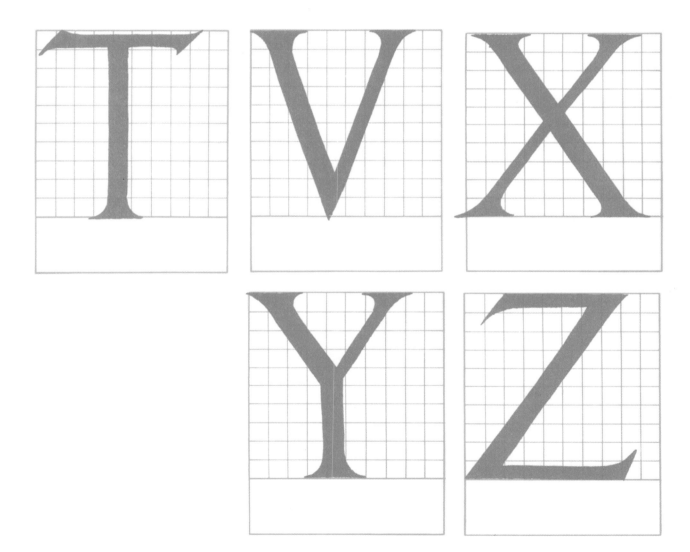

Group 5

Within this group are the letters 'B, E, F, L, P' and 'S', each letter occupying about half the width of the gridded square. The upper bowl of the 'B' is smaller than the lower and therefore the intersection is above the center line. This is intentional: if both bowls were equal in size the letter would appear top-heavy.

The upper arm of the 'E' is slightly longer than the middle arm, which is placed high on the center line, making the upper counter smaller than the lower. Again this is optically necessary. The lower arm projects a little beyond the upper arm with both ending in sheared, bracketed serifs.

The 'F' may be regarded as an 'E' minus the lower arm. The 'L' is an 'E' without the upper arms. The stem at the cap line has the addition of a bracketed serif on the right.

The letter 'P' at first glance resembles a 'B' minus the lower bowl. Closer inspection will show that the bowl is larger than the upper bowl of 'B'. The cross-stroke joins the bowl to the stem below the center line.

The upper counter of the 'S' is smaller than the lower counter, with the letter sloping

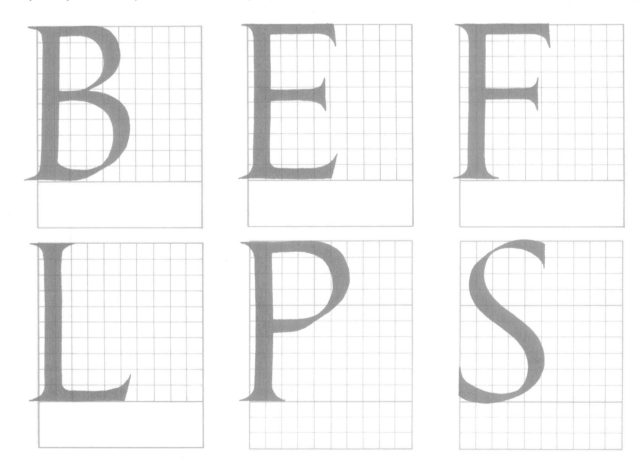

slightly to the right. The diagonal spine is of uniform thickness until it tapers to meet the curved arms. The 'S' is a diagonally stressed letter, having this characteristic in common with the 'A, K, M, N, R, V, W' and, in this alphabet, the 'Z', which is the only letter with a thick diagonal stroke running from top right to bottom left. The upper and lower arms end in sheared terminals and fractionally extend to form beak-like serifs. Being the only letter with diagonal stress it is important for balance that the lower counter is slightly larger than the upper counter. This gives the 'S' a slight forward tilt, making it one of the hardest letters in which to achieve a good poise.

Group 6

The 'I' and 'J' take up approximately three-tenths of the gridded square. The 'I' is a simply constructed letter. Nevertheless, it is important because it sets the standard for the alphabet in height and stem width.

The 'J' does not appear in the inscription on the Trajan Column where its present-day sound is represented by an 'I'. 'J' is written like an 'I' minus the base-line bracketed serif, where the stroke continues through the base line and curves to the left, ending in a pointed terminal. The length of the stroke is contained within the descender area.

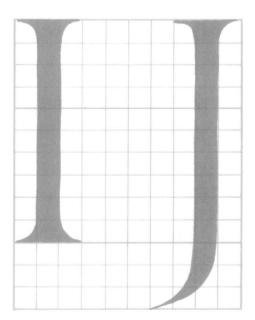

The Development of Lower-case (Minuscules)

The Ouadrata and Rustic capitals were followed by uncial, born of the need to write more quickly while still maintaining a formal style. Uncial is a true pen form with a simple construction and comparatively clean finishing strokes. Uncial was the literary hand for fine books from the fifth to the eighth century. The letterforms were more rounded than traditional Roman capitals. The chief characteristic letters within the style were the 'A', 'D'', 'E', 'H' and 'M' and, although they were still written between the capital and base lines, certain letters, namely the 'D', 'F', 'G', 'H', 'K', 'L', 'P', 'O', 'X' and 'Y', began to have longer stems which marginally broke through the cap and base lines.

Uncial was followed by half-uncial and here some letters are seen predominantly to break through the writing lines forming ascender and descender areas. Letterforms were modified, notable the 'a', 'b', 'e', 'g' and 'l', with the remaining letters receiving only minor amendments, if any at all.

Toward the end of the eighth century, with the revival of learning, came a reform of the hand in which works of literature were to be written. The emperor Charlemagne, who governed a vast area of Europe, commissioned the abbot and teacher, Alcuin of York, to rationalize and

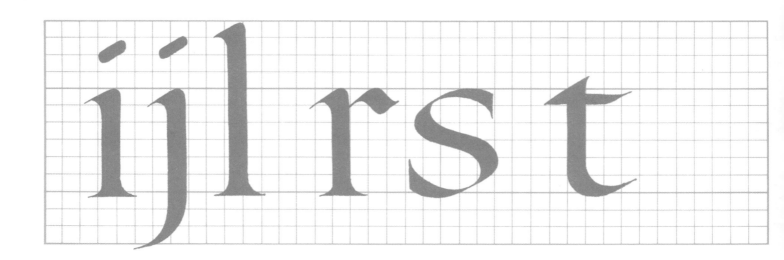

standardize the various minuscule scripts which had developed. Alcuin studied the former styles of Ouadrata, Rustic, uncial and half-uncial and developed a new minuscule as a standard book style. This has become known as the Carolingian minuscule after its instigator, the emperor Charlemagne. Calligraphy now entered a new era.

Although the Romans used mainly capital letterforms, a classical lower-case alphabet has been included, together with Arabic numerals, to complement the capital forms previously described, and to give the student an insight into their construction. The letters and numerals that follow are of classical proportions and, once their relative widths and construction details have been mastered, knowledge of them will stand the student in good stead for lettering the sample alphabets in this book.

The letters have been placed on a grid which consists of squares of stem width: thirteen units deep, with four units allocated for the ascenders (those letters which reach the cap or ascender line, the 'h' for instance), six units for the x-height (that portion of the grid which contains letters such as the '5') and three units below the x height (to accommodate

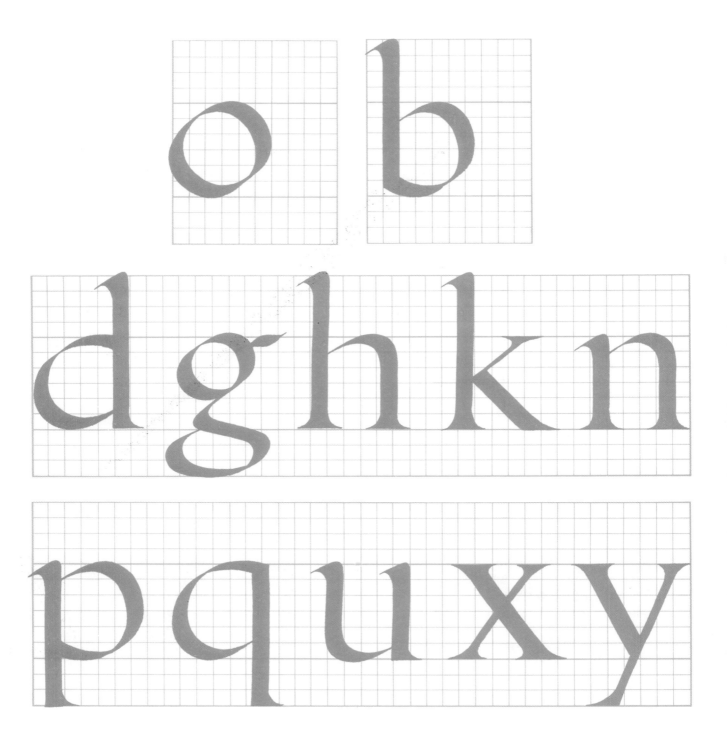

the descenders of letters such as the 'g' and 'y'). The characters have been grouped together with common widths, starting with the narrowest and ending with the widest.

The first, and narrowest, group comprises the letters 'i', 'j' and 'l'. They are easily constructed, with the humble 'i' and 'l' setting the pattern for straight letters. The dot over the 'i' and 'l' can be round or flat and is usually positioned about midway between the x- and ascender lines. The 'l' initially follows the 'i' but extends below the base line where it curves to the left, ending in a pointed terminal.

The next grouping contains three characters, about five units wide: the 'r', '5' and 't'. From the main stem of the 'r' there is a small shoulder stroke which should not be overdone. The '5' is constructed in the same manner as its capital.

The main stem of the 't' starts obliquely, a little way above the x-line, moving to the right before reaching the base line and ending in a pointed terminal. Like the 'f', the cross-stroke is finished with a slight upward movement.

The third group contains the 'a', 'c', 'e', 'f', 'v' and 'z' and, with the exception of 'f', they are all contained within the x-height.

The 'a' starts from a pointed, curved arm which leads into the main stem. The bowl starts from the stem above the center line of the x-height and moves to the left before the downward curve. It rejoins the stem above the base line, leaving a triangular shape. The 'c' follows the left-hand stroke of the '0', the upper arm being slightly straightened and ending in a sheared terminal which is extended to form a beak-like serif. The lower arm ends in a pointed terminal. The 'e' follows the 'c'; the upper arm, however, is not straightened but flows round. The bowl is formed by a cross-stroke above the x-height center.

The 'f' is an ascending letter, starting its main stroke below the ascender line with the arm projecting to the right and ending in a sheared beak-like serif. The cross-bar is positioned just below the x-line. The 'v' and 'z' both follow the same construction as their capital counterparts.

The two letters in the subsequent group take up approximately six-and-a-half units in width. The 'b' is an ascending letter, the main stem swinging to the right before it meets the base line. The '0' is contained within the x-height with the exception of minor optical adjustments at the x- and base lines.

Each letter in the penultimate group occupies about seven units. The group comprises 'd', 'g', 'h', 'k', 'n', 'p', 'q', 'u', 'x' and 'y'. There are three letters with ascenders ('d', 'h', and 'k'), four letters with descenders ('g', 'p', 'q' and 'y'), and three contained within the x-height.

In the 'd', at the point where the lower curve of the bowl meets the main stem, there should be a triangular space formed by the upward movement of the curved stroke. The upper serif of the main stem projects slightly above the ascender or cap line.

The old-style 'g' is very difficult to master. In this style the bowl does not take up the whole depth of the x-height: instead it occupies just over three units. It then joins the link which carries down to the base line and then turns sharply to the right and ends forming the right side of the loop. The loop is accommodated within the three-unit descender area. The ear is attached to the bowl at the right side, leaving a v-shaped space.

The 'h' and 'n' are formed in a similar fashion, although the 'h' has the first stem lengthened to form the ascender, with the serif extending over the ascender line. The letter 'n' can be taken as an 'h' without the ascender. The ascender stem of the 'k' is like the 'h' and the diagonal thin stroke, and the

tail intersect just above the center of the x-height.

With the 'p', the join of the lower part of the bowl to the stem is somewhat flattened. A serif is attached to the bowl at the top left-hand corner. The 'q' is not a 'p' in reverse, but is totally different in character, having no serif at the x-line and with the upper stroke of the bowl being straightened to meet the stem.

The 'u' is not an inverted 'n'. The upper serifs protrude beyond the x-line and a space is left where the curve makes its upward movement to meet the second stem. In the 'x', the point of intersection of the thin and

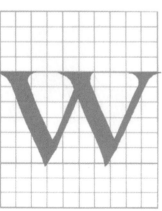

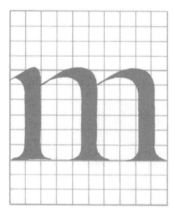

thick strokes is above the x-height center, making the lower counter larger than the upper. The diagonal thick stroke of the 'y' does not reach the base line but is intersected by the thin stroke, which follows through to the descender line where it ends in a flat, bracketed serif.

The final grouping, containing the widest letters, again comprises only two. The lower-case 'm' and 'w' occupy approximately 10 units, and both letters are contained within the x-height. In the 'm', observe the point at which the curved shoulder of the second stroke meets the stem of the first—the second shoulder intersects at the same height. The serif of the first stroke and both shoulders, because they are curved, are positioned so that they break the x-line to give optical alignment with the letters 'v', 'w', 'x', 'y' and 'z'; their tops are either bracketed serifs or, in the 'z', a cross-stroke.

The 'm' is not two 'n''s joined, as the inner counters of the 'm' are narrower than that of the 'n'. The apexes of the 'w' extend slightly below the base line and the inner apex is the x-line. This shows that the diagonal strokes are positioned correctly.

Other Characters

Within our written language there are of course many other symbols such as parentheses, exclamation marks, and question marks, to name but a few. These will become natural enough to create once the student starts practicing calligraphy.

The character '&' is known as the ampersand. This is possibly a corruption of the mixed English and Latin phrase 'and *per se* and'. It is an ancient monogram of the letters 'e' and 't', the Latin word *et* meaning 'and'. The *et* in this instance is not reflected in the character on the grid, which occupies nine units in width. The upper bowl is much smaller than the lower with the angle of the diagonal stroke cutting through to form a semicircular counter and the tail ending in a bracketed serif. The upward tail to the bowl ends with a bracketed serif above the center line.

Numerals

The Romans used letters of the alphabet for their numeric reference. We are all familiar with the Roman-style numerals when applied to a clock face, but perhaps not so with 'M' = 1,000, 'D' = 500, 'C' = 100 and 'L' = 50. It takes little imagination to see that mathematical calculations could be made easier by changing the symbols. The Arabs did exactly that, and based their system on 10 numeric signs, the 'Arabic numerals' we use today. They can be either of uniform height ('lining numerals') or of varying height ('old style' or 'hanging numerals'). In the latter style the '1', '2' and '0' appear within the x-height, the '6' and '8' are ascending numerals, and the '3', '4', '5', '7', and '9' are descending characters.

The main characteristics of the numerals need little explanation, but a few points should be noted. For example, if numerals are not constructed carefully they can appear to be falling over. This is probably because they are mainly asymmetric in form, with the exception of course of the '0', '1' and '8', which are basically balanced.

If the curve of the '2' is allowed to project beyond the base cross-stroke, it will appear to be leaning to the right. If the tail of the '9' is not carried sufficiently far to the left, the figure will appear to lean to the left; if too far, it will look as if it is leaning to the right. The '9' is not an inverted '6'. The join of the small curved stroke to the main curved stem alters in each case, making the inner counters slightly different in shape.

The upper counters of the '3' and '8' should be smaller than the lower; otherwise the characters will be top-heavy. The cross-bar of the '4' is fairly low on the stem so that the inner counter does not appear too small. The diagonal stroke of the '7' cannot extend too far to the left:

Once it goes beyond the alignment of the upper stroke, it makes the letter look as if it were leaning backwards. If the cross-stroke of the '5' is too long, it too can appear to lean to the right. Finally, it would be noted that the numeral '0' is compressed and not by any means the same as a letter 'O'.

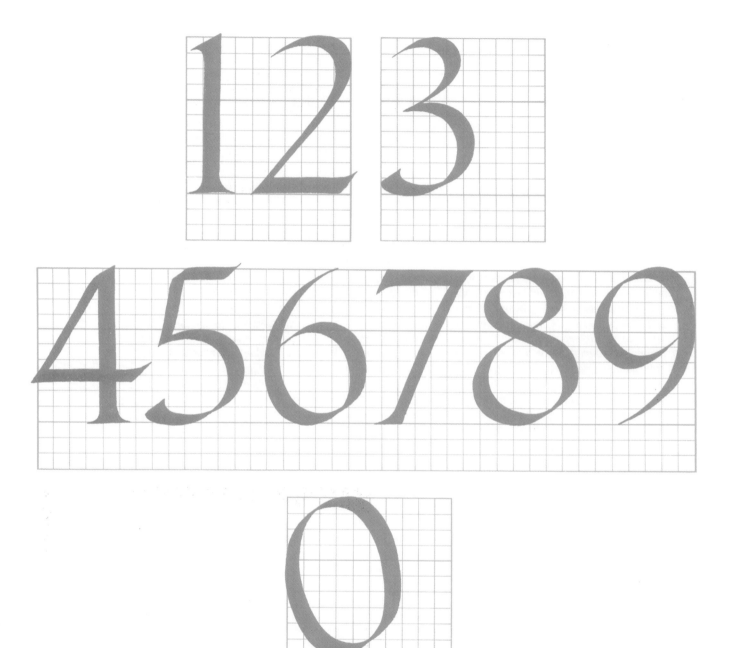

FORMAL ITALIC

With its rhythmic movement and its flowing qualities, italic epitomizes the 'dance of the pen'. Writing this script on a good surface can be an exhilarating experience. Italic evolved in the early 15th century and owes its name to its Italian origins. Inspired by the Carolingian minuscule scripts of 9th century France, Renaissance scribes developed a formal script called Humanist bookhand. Seeking a faster style to meet their increasing workload, papal scribes copying documents for the Roman chancery developed the chancery script. More quickly written than the Humanist book-hand, with narrower, forward-slanting letterforms, this script exhibited the flowing qualities characteristic of italic.

In the 16th century a number of writing instruction manuals were printed from calligraphy cut on wood block. The first and most famous was *La Operina* by the Venetian Ludovico Vicentino Arrighi, published in 1522. The manuals show a wealth of italics with many subtle variations. Some have few or no ligatures (connecting lines); others are emphatically cursive (joined and flowing); some have rounded letterforms; others are angular.

RENAISSANCE MANUSCRIPT
This fine example of Renaissance italic, with its flowing rhythm, narrow letterforms, sparing flourishes and wide interline spacing, has an elegance that is typical of the best formal italics. The marginal capitals are a type of versal.

MARY MAGDALENE AT THE SEPULCHRE
Joan Pilsbury
This manuscript book written in ink on vellum shows a double-page opening in an elegant formal italic. Dimensions: 13in x 9¹/₂ in (32.5cm x 23.75cm).

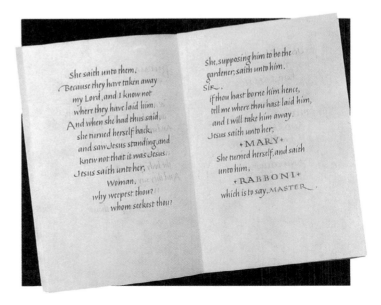

However, all exhibit the key features of the italic script: rhythmic, compressed letterforms, springing arches, forward slant, and a relatively steep pen angle of approximately 45°.

Experience with italic handwriting can help promote the fluency needed for all calligraphic work. The contemporary calligrapher uses two basic italic scripts: formal and cursive. The formal script is an easier one for beginners. A more controlled writing method, it enables the analysis of individual letter-forms, providing a sound basis from which to develop the rhythm and flow of the cursive form.

Italic is a versatile script, offering ever more opportunities as you progress. The basic formal and cursive scripts described in this book can be applied in a variety of ways and contexts, as well as providing the basis for many later experiments.

Italic is an excellent script for encouraging rhythm in writing. This is one of the key qualities of calligraphy, and it is important to develop this aspect.

CHARACTERISTICS
Italic is based on the elliptical 'o', with lateral compression. It has a constant slight forward slant of the downstrokes, and arches that spring from the letter stem.

Letter Height
4 nib widths x-height. Ascenders and descenders approximately 3¹/₂ to 4 nib widths more.

Pen Angle
45°

'O' Form
Elliptical, showing the lateral compression characteristic of italic. The 'o' width is about two-thirds of the letter height in skeleton form.

Arches
Springing arches also contribute to the flow of the script. They are asymmetrical and start from the letter stem between half and two-thirds up the letter body height.

Serifs
Simple oval-hook serifs that are integral to the stroke are suitable for a basic italic. Triangular serifs will add a more formal look.

Slant
Letters may slant forward between 5° and 10° from the vertical, but 5° is sufficient for formal italic.

Stroke Order and Direction
The many upward 'push' strokes and few pen lifts help to give italic its flowing quality.

Skeleton Italic

Before writing italic letters with an edged pen, you need to learn the essential skeleton form. Remember that, because italic script consists of compressed forms, all letters (except 'i', 'j', 'm' and 'w') are virtually the same width— many faults in italic are due to incorrect widths. The oval 'o' is shown in a parallelo-gram with sides slanting 5° from the vertical. The 'o' is a key to letter width, although not to shape; 'c' and 'e' relate to 'o', but most italic letters relate to the arch shape.

Letter-Formation Groups

Italic letterforms are easiest to learn in groups of similar formation, as shown in the geometric diagrams (right).

Clockwise arched letters: 'h', 'n', 'm', 'r', 'b', 'p', 'k'. The group also includes 'l', which is the beginning stroke of the other letters. The arches spring from half to tow-thirds up the x-height.

Counter-clockwise arched letters: 'l', 't', 'u', curved 'y'. Base curves relate to the shape of clockwise arched letters.

Diagonal letters: 'v', 'w', 'x', 'y', 'z'. The first strokes of 'v', 'w', 'x', 'y' and the third stroke of 'w' must be relatively vertical, so that the axis of the 'v' part of the letters has the same slant as the downstrokes of the script.

Oval letters: 'c', 'e', 'o'. The 'c' and 'e' are the only italic letters whose shape relates directly to the elliptical 'o'.

Triangular letters: 'a', 'd', 'g', 'q'. These are softened triangles. The curve joins the straight stroke on the right side, half to two-thirds down the x-height.

Letters with related top and/or tail curves: 'f', 'j', 's'. The tail curves of 'f' and 'j' mirror the top curve of the 'f'.

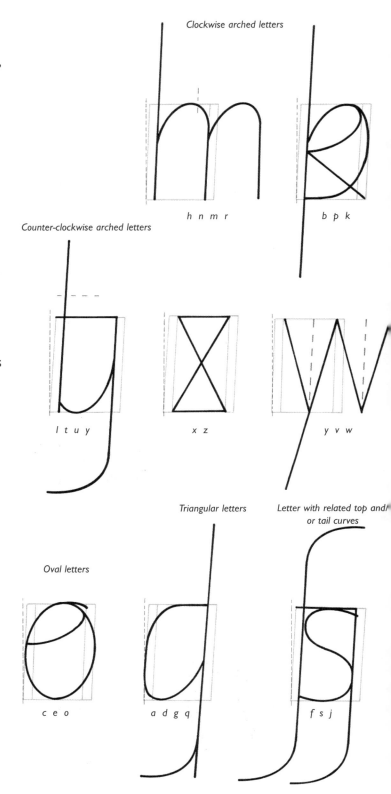

Clockwise arched letters

h n m r

b p k

Counter-clockwise arched letters

l t u y

x z

y v w

Triangular letters

Letter with related top and/or tail curves

Oval letters

c e o

a d g q

f s j

Skeleton Practice

Practicing in pencil is the simplest way to get the feel of the script and fix the letter shapes firmly in your mind. Spending as much time as you can to acquire accurate information at this stage will make the learning of edged-pen italic easier and more successful.

1 Rule lines ⁷/₁₆in (11mm) apart.

2 With an HB pencil, write the letters in formation groups, working on alternate lines and setting out your work as shown to avoid collision of ascenders and descenders.

3 Follow the stroke order and direction shown in the diagrams.

4 Aim all straight and curved downstrokes just to the left of six o'clock to give the right amount of forward slant (about 5in).

5 Subtly flatten curves such as the sides of 'a', 'd', 'g', 'q': otherwise they may become too circular.

6 Do not lift the pencil off the paper unless indicated by the stroke sequence.

7 Draw the letters lightly with the pencil until you begin to feel the form, making alterations along the way as necessary. Write each group several times before moving on to the next.

Spacing and Word Practice

When you feel confident with the letterforms, begin to practice writing words. To do this you will need to consider the letter spacing. Maintain equal space between all letters to achieve a balanced appearance.

Weighted Italic

The versatility of italic makes it an essential part of the contemporary calligrapher's repertoire. Once you are able to write a sound basic italic, you can then create your own variations in letter slant, writing speed, letter width, weight, and other aspects—the possibilities are virtually limitless.

LARGE-SCALE ITALIC Formal italics written with an edged pen produce lively calligraphic effects.

The edged pen is a fascinating challenge for calligraphy beginners. Thorough practice of the skeleton letterforms in pencil will have familiarized you with the letterforms and spacing considerations. However, there is one more step that will help you succeed with the pen. Double-pencil italic letterforms will reveal the principle of the two overlapping skeleton shapes that produce the weighted forms.

Stroke Practice

As you first practice with the pen, concentrate on achieving uniform thick and thin diagonal and horizontal strokes and straight downstrokes. Practice curved strokes last.

Arches

Flowing asymmetrical arches are a key characteristic of italic. Creating smooth arches with consistent shapes will help you to achieve a rhythmic, even script. The springing arch leaves the letter stem between half and two-thirds up the x-height, and, because the nib is being pushed uphill to the right against its front edge, there is some thickness at the beginning of the springing stroke. It is important to lighten the pressure on the nib on all uphill (push) strokes to enable the nib to move smoothly.

Practicing arches will help you acquire the rhythm and flow of italic script.

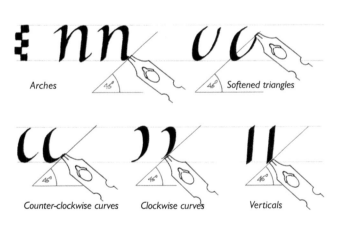

Arches   45°   46° Softened triangles

Counter-clockwise curves   Clockwise curves   Verticals

1   Write between lines ruled at 5 nib widths of a Mitchell No 2 nib, holding the nib at a constant angle of 45° for all strokes.

2   Make sure that the straight downstrokes have a slightly forward slant.

3   Variations in stroke width mean that you have changed the pen angle or altered the slant of the strokes.

1   Rule writing lines at 5 nib widths of a Mitchell No 2 nib

2   Following the diagram, write a line of repeating 'i's, 'n's and 'm's'.

3   Re-write the line, alternating the 'n' and 'm' with 'i'. As these are straight-sided letters, they should be easy to space, and this will allow you to concentrate on the arches.

Serifs

Oval hooks, which reflect the script's elliptical 'O', are a good choice for your first italic serif. In formal italic, the serifs are restrained, but a less formal, more rapidly written version will have increasingly pronounced serifs.

When you have mastered the hook serif, vary the effect by adding a sharp-line serif on ascenders only (see stroke order, right), ending the descenders with a hook, a sharp line or a slightly uphill light slab.

Hook serif and bottom

Sharp-line serif top and bottom

Built-up triangular serif top, sharp line bottom

SONNET—Gareth Colgan
This passage from a sonnet by John Donne is taken from a larger work. The quill-written italics rendered in Chinese ink and watercolor on watercolor paper display rhythm and finesse. Dimensions: 24in x 11in (60cm x 25.5cm).

Letter-formation Groups

Weighted letters are best learned in groups according to their shape and mode of formation. The groups are the same as for the skeleton forms.

1 *Write the groups as shown between lines ruled at an x -height of 5 nib widths of a Mitchell No 2 nib, but leave two x -heights clear between each line of writing to accommodate ascenders and descenders.*

2 *Keep the pen angle at a constant 45°.*

3 *Practice each group several times, following the model closely. The arrows indicate stroke number, order and direction.*

Spacing Edged-pen Italic

As Italic is a compressed script with letters of approximately the same width (excepting 'm' and 'w'), it is more or less equidistantly spaced. Practice with the edged pen to get the feel of weighted spacing. Remember that curved letters are placed slightly closer than straight letters to create the impression of equal spacing.

Watchpoints

The italic alphabet has been labeled with important details to help you write it as accurately as possible. Look at the alphabet as a whole, and take note of these before you begin writing the alphabet.

CHECKLIST

- The top of the crossbars of 't' and 'f' coincide with the top writing line, but can be slightly lower on 'f'.
- The 's' and 'z' align at the right and left with the slant of the script.
- The axis of 'v', 'x' and diagonal 'y', as well as the two axes of 'w', should have the same slant as downstrokes such as 'i' in order to relate them to the slant of the rest of the script. See the 'v' in the alphabet above as an example.
- All serifs are smooth, oval and restrained.
- The tails of 'f', 'g' and 'j' have smooth follow-through curves of identical shape.
- Check that the top and bottom curves of the 'o' mirror each other.
- The curves of 'b' and 'p' are subtly flattened. Base curves should join the stem in a slightly downhill direction to avoid an over-heavy join.

Left and top curves blend

Top of crossbar is on or slightly below the line

Curved and straight strokes join half to two-thirds down the x-height

Right and base curves blend

Enclosed top counter is kept above halfway

Tail and straight stroke blend

Oval serif

Branch relates to oval 'o'

Tail projects beyond top arm

Two halves are of equal width

Gentle curves

Rounded counter spacious and oval

Base curve relates to arch shape

Follow through curve

Top of crossbar on the line

Keep second stroke straight

Top counter minimally smaller—align letter at right with slant of script

Maintain forward slant—central axis has same slant as script

Cross minimally above halfway to give balanced letter

Align at right and left with slant of script

Joins and Alternative Letterforms

Double 't', 'f' and 'ft' may be written separately or joined by the horizontal stroke. Double 'f' combinations may consist of two identical 'f's' with extended descenders, joined by their horizontal bar, or a linked combination of two forms (right). Take care when writing 'r' followed by diagonal 'y': the shape of the 'y' may cause over-spacing.

1   *Use lines ruled to 5 nib widths of a Mitchell No 2 nib.*

2   *Copy the letterforms and combinations shown at right.*

Word Practice

As soon as you feel sufficiently familiar with letterforms and spacing patterns, move on to words, which will extend your skills. Continue the practice of writing a word several times and checking the spacing and letterforms each time. Assessing your own writing gives you independence; it means you learn through understanding rather than copying. Although good writing develops gradually with practice, it requires understanding of letter-form construction, which comes from adopting a critical approach from the moment that you begin to learn calligraphy.

1   *Write between lines ruled at 5 nib widths of a Mitchell No 2 nib.*

2   *Repeat each word several times, leaving room for an 'o' between words.*

3   *Correct letters and spacing as necessary.*

Creating Texture in Color

Repeated writing of the same word enables you to concentrate on letterforms, spacing and rhythm. At the same time, you can create a close-knit texture on the page, incorporating a subtle range of colors. You can use the same techniques later for exciting work with texts.

For this piece of work, the calligrapher used a Mitchell No 2 nib and watered-down gouache with color changes in the pen. An interesting texture and pattern is produced by the graduated color effect and the pattern of the lettering.

Capitals and Weighted Italic

In Renaissance times, plain Roman capitals were commonly used with italic. At line beginnings these were often set with a noticeable gap between capital, and following italic, lower-case, letters. However, a rich variety of flourished italic capitals can also be found in Renaissance manuscripts, and the choice of capitals depends on the context, and, on the writer's preference. You can use Roman capitals, plain italic capitals, or flourished italic capitals, alongside italic minuscules.

Plain italic capitals are the easiest to write, although they need accurate letter-width judgment. However, the flowing lines of flourished italic capitals encourage rhythm in writing.

1 Write a word on alternate lines ruled at 5 nib widths of a Mitchell No 2 nib. At this stage, decisions on the use of color and an asymmetrical layout have already been made.

2 A review of the first draft shows that standard spacing allows too much white space between the lines, which distracts from the textural effect desired. Your next option is to try closer line spacing.

3 A closer line spacing allows the ascenders and descenders to blend into the adjacent lines of text.

4 The final version can form part of a larger work.

California,

Iowa, Ohio

Quotation in Italic Minuscules

Color and design are important and rewarding areas to cultivate. Designing a layout for a short text will help you blend good lettering with creative ideas.

Think about the word meanings and jot down any ideas that come to mind about color, layout and illustration. Satisfactory layout is a matter of individual taste, but there are techniques for achieving the qualities you seek.

1 *Use a 20-30 word quotation so that it can be re-written several times if necessary without becoming too trying. Write with a Mitchell No 2 nib.*

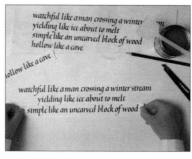

2 *Past up the layout using photocopies. Center the lines to avoid the square and static look of an aligned block.*

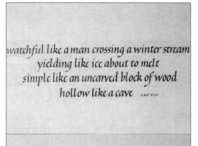

3 *The finished paste-up acts as a model for the final writing.*

4 *Try colored gouache on a word or two. "Winter stream" and "ice about to melt" suggest blues and purples.*

5 *To give the quotation a colored background, scrape Conté colors with a craft knife and blend the powder on the paper.*

6 *Gently rub the color into the paper with a tissue. Spray the background color with a fixative and dust with gum sandarac.*

7 *The credit is added to the final draft in Roman capitals with a Mitchell No 4 nib.*

Working with Large Pens

Practicing any script with large pens loosens writing and encourages rhythm, because the entire arm is used, and the rest of the body is more involved. It is also useful for seeing the details of letterforms, such as arch structure, and for studying any letters that seem difficult. The scale enables you to "feel" the letter more as you write, because every slight change of direction is magnified. It is also fun to play with letters and design on a large scale, allowing ideas to flow freely.

Using Large Pens

Large lettering has many uses—for example, it can be used for headings and as a focal point in a panel of calligraphy. Writing large is a useful skill to master and gives you plenty of scope to be creative. With large lettering, you can really let your imagination run free with innovative uses of color and layout.

1   *A variety of Coit pens is useful for experimentation. Here, several different ¹/₂in (13mm) nibs are tried.*

2   *The nib selected is used for the whole word, and the color is changed in the pen. The effect is too static.*

3   *The word "dance" should really dance. Cut up the lettering and try a layout with some vertical movement to the letters.*

4   *Move the letters until the right effect is achieved. Paste up the layout and transcribe the finished word.*

Using Large and Small Italics

Combining large and small lettering is an effective way to add emphasis. When practicing, choose a short text so that you can maintain a good standard of writing and spacing.

Read the text and decide which words you want to emphasize. In the example, the first two words are selected because they represent a complete thought.

1 Write the quote using a Mitchell No 4 nib. It is easier to assess where a larger nib may be needed if the whole text is written in the same nib first.

2 Paste up the small lettering using pencil marks on the edge of a separate piece of paper to judge line spacing.

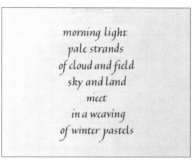

3 Complete the layout. Where line lengths vary, centering the lines is an effective way of adding movement.

4 Write the large lettering in a variety of nib sizes, from Mitchell No 3^1/$_2$ up to No 1 on a sheet of layout paper.

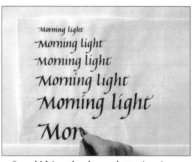

5 Try each size. Here, No 2 is used for the large lettering. Other good contrasts are 1^1/$_2$ and 3^1/$_2$, 2^1/$_2$ and 5, and 1, and 3.

6 Paste up the complete layout, adding flourishes to the last line to give a softened effect

7 The illustration was drawn with colored pencils, crossed by white lines made with an eraser.

8 Finished piece. In the final work, the lettering and the illustration are harmonious.

121

ITALIC CAPITALS

The italic script was used with classical Roman capitals during the Renaissance. These were gradually modified into Humanistic square capitals and flourished italic capitals. Humanistic square capitals remained closely akin to pen-made Roman square capitals. They were often used for text written entirely in capitals, as well as for line beginnings.

Flourished italic capitals were a more compressed and slanting form based, like the lowercase script, on the oval 'O'. Inventive and often exuberant, they were used for line beginnings and within italic text. Even among italic capitals, however, Renaissance scribes often retained the wider Roman 'D'.

It is best to learn the compressed italic capitals without flourishes at first, in order to establish accurate letterforms and see the relationships between the letters more clearly. Unadorned italic capitals are useful in their own right, especially for text that is to be conveyed entirely in capitals. They are suitable for formal purposes, such as presentation documents, or for the expressive interpretation of prose and poetry. You will find italic capitals versatile, and flowing letterforms that offer many design opportunities.

Once you can write the plain capitals well, it is a relatively simple step to create flourished versions.

THE PLOVER—Louise Donaldson

Written over a wash background, this calligraphic interpretation of a passage from a poem by Robert Louis Stevenson is written in three weights of italic capitals. The larger capitals are written with an Automatic pen with color change in the pen. The light-weight letters were written with a ruling pen.

Characteristics

Italic capitals are written with the same pen angle throughout. Like italic lower case, they are based on the oval 'O' and have a constant forward slant.

H F O P l

LETTER HEIGHT	PEN ANGLE	'O' FORM	SLANT	SERIFS
8 nib widths	45°	The 'O' is oval and in proportion to the lower-case italic 'o'.	Approximately 5° forward, as for lower-case italic.	Oval hooks relating to the oval 'O' for a basic version, but other serifs, such as those described for Roman capitals, may be used.

STROKE ORDER AND DIRECTION
These characteristics are the same as for Roman capitals.

SPEED
Moderate

PROSE PANEL—Liz Burch
This panel (right) of strong, well-spaced italic capitals demonstrates that high-quality calligraphy can make an attractive statement without the assistance of additional decoration.

THE GRAND WAY TO LEARN
IN GARDENING, AS IN ALL THINGS ELSE IS TO WISH TO LEARN AND BE DETERMINED TO FIND OUT
THE REAL WAY IS TO TRY AND LEARN A LITTLE FROM EVERYBODY AND EVERY PLACE
THERE IS NO ROYAL ROAD
IT IS NO USE ASKING ME OR ANYONE ELSE HOW TO DIG I MEAN SITTING INDOORS & ASKING IT BETTER GO AND WATCH A MAN DIGGING AND THEN TAKE A SPADE AND TRY TO DO IT AND GO ON TRYING TILL IT COMES AND YOU GAIN THE KNACK THAT IS TO BE LEARNT WITH ALL TOOLS OF DOUBLING THE POWER AND HALVING THE EFFORT
YOU WILL FIND OUT THAT THERE ARE ALL SORTS OF WAYS OF LEARNING, NOT ONLY FROM PEOPLE AND BOOKS BUT FROM SHEER TRYING
FROM 'WOOD AND GARDEN' BY GERTRUDE JEKYLL

JAPANESE POEM—Liz Burch
This delicate panel (left) is rendered in large italic capitals alongside small heavy-weight Roman capitals. Thoughtful placing of rubber-stamp decoration creates a harmonious finished result.

THE PEACH BLOSSOM POOL IS A THOUSAND FEET DEEP BUT NOT SO DEEP AS THE LOVE IN YOUR FAREWELL TO ME

ALTHOUGH I AM SURE THAT HE WILL NOT BE COMING IN THE EVENING LIGHT WHEN THE LOCUSTS SHRILLY CALL I GO TO THE DOOR AND WAIT

THINKING ABOUT HIM I SLEPT ONLY TO HAVE HIM APPEAR BEFORE ME HAD I KNOWN IT WAS A DREAM I SHOULD NEVER HAVE WAKENED

Skeleton Letterforms

Like Roman capitals, italic capitals can be groups according to their width, although, being more compressed letterforms, the width differences are less marked. However, it is useful to recognize the width differences that do exist before writing out the italic capitals in their weighted form.

Letter-Formation Groups

Italic capitals fall into the same formation groups as Roman capitals, but, based on the concept of the oval within the parallelogram, instead of the circle within the square. The letters have a 5° forward slant.

Skeleton Practice

Practice writing the letters in pencil in their formation groups, paying particular attention to their relative widths. Numerals and arrows show the correct stroke order and direction. Remember to check spacing according to the Rule of Three.

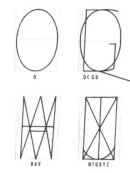

Oval letters: 'O', 'Q', 'C', 'G', 'D'. The 'C', 'G' and 'D' are seven-eighth-width letters.
Three-quarter-width letters: 'H', 'A', 'V', 'N', 'T', 'U', 'X','Y', 'Z'. These fit into a parallelogram that is three-quarters the width of the original one. The width has been reduced by one-eighth on each side to give an area approximately equal to that of the oval. The letters in this group are shown in two diagrams for clarity. They are all equal in width at their widest point.
Half-width letters: 'B', 'P', 'R', 'K', 'E', 'F', 'L', 'S', 'I', 'J'. These are about half the width of the original parallelogram, except 'I' and 'J', which are single-stroke letters. Most of the letters in this group are two-tier letters, based on two ovals inside parallelograms, with the top tier slightly smaller than the bottom in height and width. 'S' aligns at the right with the slight forward slant of the script; it is shown with 'J', which has the same base curve.
Wide letters: 'M and W'. 'M' fits into the original parallelogram. The central axis of the 'V' part should have the same forward slant as the script. 'W' consists of two 'V's' of equal width, with the same slant.

1 Rule double lines ¹/₂in (18mm) apart.

2 Write the letters in group order, as shown below, using an HB pencil. Follow the stroke order and direction indicated, and write on alternate lines.

3 Repeat each group as often as necessary, checking letter widths after each writing.

4 Try the alternative stroke order and direction shown for certain letters. Push strokes add continuity to 'V', 'W' and 'M', and make a neater follow-through from curve to base in 'B' and 'D', but they are harder than pull strokes.

Writing Words

Begin word practice to promote fluency as soon as you feel confident with the italic capitals in alphabetical order.

1 Write words in pencil between lines ruled at ¹/₂in (18mm). Copy letter-form and spacing with care.

2 Re-write words as often as necessary.

Weighted Letterforms

Once you have mastered the skeleton forms, move on to the weighted versions of italic capitals. As with other scripts, you will find it useful to do some work at the beginning with double pencils, which clearly show the construction of the weighted letterforms. You will also need to give some attention to learning the serifs, which are responsible for much of the rhythm and fluidity of this particular script. They help the eye flow naturally from letter to letter along the line. Italic capitals make a very useful script for texts written entirely in capitals where formality is not implied in the words.

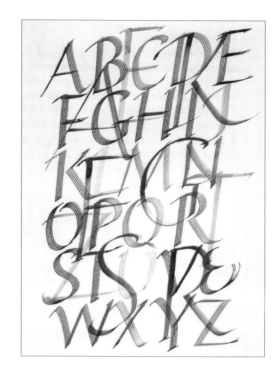

ITALIC CAPITALS ½in (13mm) single and Coit pens were used with gouache color changes in the pen for this decorative piece.

Pencil Letterforms

Your first use of the weighted form could be with either double pencils or a carpenter's (chisel) pencil as shown here. Pay particular attention to stroke joins as you practice.

1 *Sharpen your pencil to a width of ³/₁₆in (5mm).*

2 *Rule lines 1½in (4cm) apart.*

3 *Keep the pencil edge at an angle of 45°, steepening further for the first stroke of 'M' and uprights of 'N'.*

4 *Copy the letters shown.*

Serifs

A number of serifs are suitable for use with italic capitals, as shown at right. Oval hooks are simple to write and encourage flow and rhythm—unlike built-up serifs, which require pen lifts. Note that the built-up top serifs shown at right are constructed before the downstroke is added, providing a clean line from top to bottom, as well as completing the serifs.

Oval hook serif　　*Built-up triangular serif*　　*Built-up slab serif*

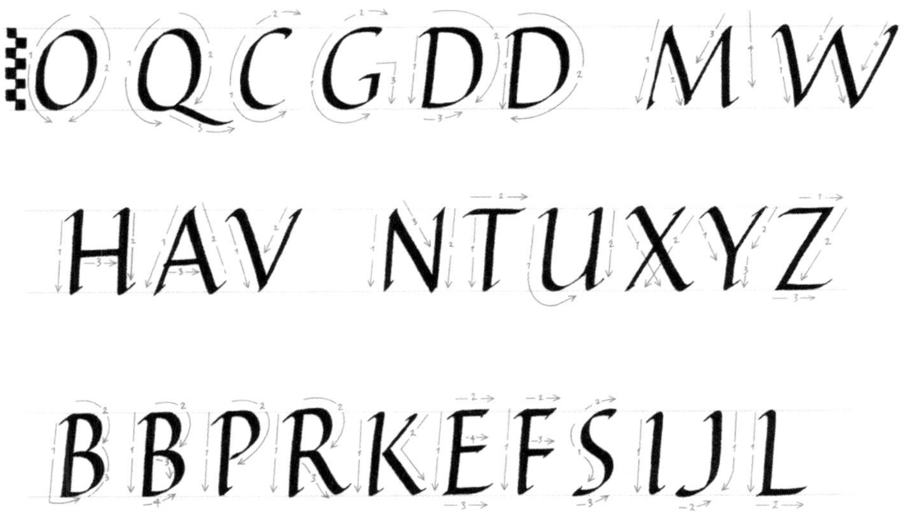

O Q C G D D M W

H A V N T U X Y Z

B B P R K E F S I J L

1 Write the groups as shown below between lines ruled at 8 nib widths of a Mitchell No 2 nib.

2 Use a pen angle of 45°, steepening to 50°-60 for the first stroke of 'M' and the vertical strokes of 'N'.

3 Practice each group several times, following the model closely.

4 Check the letters after each attempt, paying close attention to widths.

Spacing

Establishing the space between the letters in the 'H I O C' diagram will guide you toward even spacing with the edged pen. The spacing practiced here sets the pattern for all the italic-capital work that follows.

HIOC SPACING

1 Write the italic-capital 'H' and place an 'I' alongside it at a distance of two-thirds the width of the 'H' counter.

2 Place an 'O' slightly closer and a 'C' even closer. Equal spacing requires two straight-sided letters to be furthest apart, and two curved letters to be closest together.

Letter-Formation Groups

Practice weighted letters first in their formation groups to establish accurate letter widths. Look at the alphabet details and checklist before writing the formation groups, and check your letter-shapes closely against the examples as you practice.

Word Practice

Begin writing these words as soon as you feel confident with the alphabet. Repeating the same few words at first will enhance your accuracy and readiness for unfamiliar letter groupings.

NAVE

CATTLE

1 Write at a letter height of 8 nib widths of a Mitchell No 2 nib.

2 Repeat each of the words shown several times, checking letterforms and spacing before re-writing.

3 Practice as many times as you need to achieve accuracy and rhythm.

The italic-capital alphabet has been labeled with key points for accurate writing. Take note of these and read the checklist before you begin to write the alphabet. Rule your paper at 8 nib widths of a Mitchell No 2 nib, and write the alphabet in sections: 'A—F', 'G—N', 'O—U', 'V—Z'. Repeat each section several times, checking letter shapes and spacing each time before re-writing.

Central axis aligns to forward slant of script

Curves enclosing counters relate to oval 'O'

Curves relate to oval 'O'

Curve relates to oval 'O'

Curve enclosing counter relates to oval 'O'

Curve enclosing counter relates to oval 'O'

Final stroke almost vertical

Steepened pen angle for verticals

Central axis aligns to forward slant of script

Right aligns to forward slant of script

Right and left align to forward slant of script

Two halves of letter are equal

Diagonals intersect above halfway

WATCHPOINTS

- Check that the three-quarter-width letters ('H', 'A', 'V', 'N', 'T', 'U', 'X', 'Y', 'Z') are equal in width at their widest point, and not wider than 'O', 'Q', 'C', 'G' or 'D'.

- Make sure that the pen angle is steep enough for the first strokes of 'M' and 'N', or the thin strokes will be too heavy.

- Letters containing diagonals must have the same 5° slant as the rest of the script—achieved by slanting the 'V' part of the letters.

- Maintain the correct forward slant in letters containing diagonals, especially 'M'. Remember that the 'V' part of these letters should have the same slant as the thick downstrokes of the script (i.e. 5°).

- Do not allow the final stroke of 'M' to project too far to the right of the vertical, or the letter will look too upright.

Using Italic Capitals

Plain italic capitals have a formal feeling, but this effect can be softened with the creative use of color. Here, the lettering is written over a wash, giving the background the effect of a rainy morning. A Mitchell No 2 nib is used, and the finished lettering is in gouache.

1 Write the entire text in ink on layout paper. Cut up the words, finalize the design and then paste up the words.

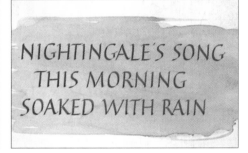

2 Write the quotation on hot-pressed paper using gouache. This leaves a plain white background.

3 Alternatively, add a wash to the paper. Once dry, cover with gum sandarac. This will help to sharpen the writing.

4 Write the lettering in gouache on top of the prepared wash, again following the original paste-up.

5 The result looks formal, but the slight forward slant of the capitals gives a hint of movement, echoing the driving rain.

Scaling Down

It is best to begin learning italic capitals in a large nib size, such as Mitchell No 1 or 2, so that all the details of the letters are seen clearly. Once you have achieved accurate lettering and spacing at this size, move down in scale, but do so progressively, adjusting to each size in sequence. The diagram (right) shows some sample letters written in successively smaller nib sizes.

$O A B C D E$
$O A B C D E$
$O A B C D E$
$O A B C D E$
$O A B C D E$

1 Rule writing lines at 8 widths of the nib you are using.

2 Write the alphabet in progressively smaller nib sizes (Mitchell No 2$^1/_2$, 3, 3$^1/_2$, 4, 5).

Using Italic Capitals and Lowercase

An interesting contrast can be made by using areas of text written in capital letters alongside those in lowercase. Here, both sets of words are written with a Mitchell No 4 nib. With capitals, the lettering looks more dominant, lending weight to the words. The words in lower case have a lighter effect.

1 *Try various designs in pencil thumbnail sketches. This will help you work out which words should be in capitals and which in lower case.*

2 *Write the words in ink on layout paper, then cut them up for use in making paste-ups.*

3 *Lay out individual words following the layout of the thumbnail sketch. Select appropriate line breaks and paste up the design.*

4 *Write the final version of the text following the paste-up.*

5 *Using textured paper for the final piece lends a richer feeling to the work.*

Large and Small Italic Capitals

It is appropriate to write some texts entirely in capitals, and using more than one nib size will give you good practice in balancing different scales of writing. Ensure a standard letter height for each nib size you use, as shown in the example at right. You can also practice varying the standard letter weight to produce either light or heavy-weight versions of this script with different nib sizes.

MIST SHROUDED HILLS
MUTED COLOURS
STILL AIR OF AUTUMN AFTERNOON COOL
AND SILENT WEAK RAYS OF SUNLIGHT

Using Large and Small Italic Capitals

One way to give emphasis to a piece of calligraphy is to use more than one nib size. Some experimentation is required to find suitable contrasts, in this instance, between two sizes of capitals. Here, the small capitals are written using a Mitchell No 4 nib and the large capitals are written using a Mitchell No 2½, both at 8 nib widths x-height.

1   *Write the two parts of the quotation in different nib sizes. Select contrasting sizes and paste them up.*

2   *Lay down a background wash on a heavy-weight paper. When this is dry, apply gum sandarac before writing.*

3   *Rule lines over the wash and write the lettering with gum ammoniac, using the paste-up as a guide.*

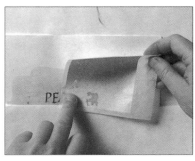

4   *Apply gold leaf and burnish with a silk cloth. Gently brush off any additional gold.*

5   *The gold lettering contrasts sharply with the background.*

Writing Large

Large writing calls for sweeping hand and arm movements. It is a pleasure to feel large letters glide swiftly over the page.

1   *Practice a few words with a ⁵⁄₁₆in (7mm) Automatic pen.*

2   *Keep the letters well-proportioned at a height of about 8 nib widths.*

3   *Practice first with ruled lines and then try writing freely, judging the height by eye.*

4   *Add color changes in the pen to vary the effect.*

Using Large Italic Capitals

Large italic capitals can look very attractive. The pen used is a ³/₈in (9mm) Coit pen that produces just two lines—one thick and one thin. Using a split pen prevents large lettering from becoming too heavy. The space created between the two pen lines adds lightness.

1 *Write the entire text in ink on layout paper. At this stage it is possible to experiment with several Automatic or Coit pens.*

2 *Lay out the words, decide the design and line breaks, then paste up the text.*

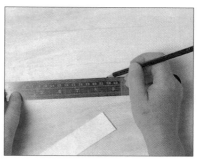

3 *Create the background with Conté crayon. Spray with fixative, rule up the paper, and then dust with gum sandarac.*

4 *Write the lettering with gum ammoniac. Apply the gold-transfer leaf and burnish with a silk cloth.*

5 *Gently brush off the excess gold to leave he letters sharply distinct.*

6 *The combination of gold lettering over blue and yellow gives an impression of sky and grass.*

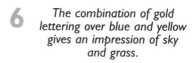

CURSIVE ITALIC

Cursive means joined and flowing, and can refer to any script written with few or no pen lifts. The letter joins, known as ligatures, are the product of writing with speed. In italic, they are diagonal or horizontal. The addition of ligatures is an important consideration, and in some cases, alters the letter construction. For these reasons, cursive italic is treated as a separate script.

individual scribe. It is one of the pleasures of calligraphy that each writer can bring a personal interpretation to the most familiar script. It is essential, however, to build such enhancements on a thorough knowledge of the basic features of the script.

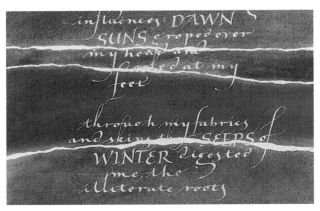

BOG QUEEN—Julia Vance
This detail of a panel of poetry by Seamus Heaney shows a dancing cursive italic with flourishes and subtle italic capitals, written in silver gouache, over a pastel background. The thin horizontal lines are gilded. Dimensions: 51in x 11in (127cm x 27.5cm).

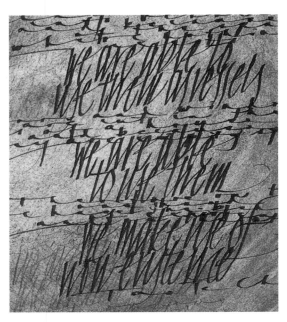

TAO TE CHING—Paivi Vesanto
This lively piece of cursive italic shows the use of contrast between narrow and extended letterforms, and between heavy, and light-weight, characters. The swirling colors of the pastel background add to the movement of the piece. Dimensions: 22in x 14in (55cm x 35cm).

During the Renaissance many cursive italics were written, each subtly different, depending on the style or choice of the

The rich variety of Renaissance italic continues to provide today's calligraphers with a rich source of reference and experiment. To learn the essential characteristics of cursive italic, you must look at a script as free as possible from personal features. A cursive italic, with the same basic characteristics as formal italic but with the letters linked by ligatures, is the best starting point. For this script you will need to master two key strokes: the thin diagonal and the weighted horizontal.

Weighted Horizontal Strokes

The weighted horizontal stroke is important for the tops of letters such as 'd', 'g', 'q', 'a', 's', 'f'. Some of these letters may start with the top stroke, unlike formal italic. For speed and continuity, the stroke is pushed from right to left. In Renaissance times, these "lids" were often written with a pull from left to right, followed by a push from right to left exactly over the first stroke. This was to avoid lifting the pen off the paper. It is a movement that can still be used in some letter combinations, such as 'ma'. At word beginnings, however, it is sufficient to start with a right-to-left push stroke. The alternative is to use the formal-italic stroke order. The exercise below enables you to try three different methods of writing horizontals and to decide which suits you.

1   *Following the example above, try the three methods of writing the letter 'a'.*

2   *Repeat each method of writing several times, and then use each of them in words of your choice.*

3   *You will probably find the first two methods more difficult. These involve push strokes against the front of the nib, but they eliminate pen lifts and ensure writing flow.*

Thin Diagonal Ligatures

The diagonal ligature is a thin uphill push stroke, shown as a broken line joining the serifs in the example below. It is produced by moving the thin edge of the nib uphill diagonally to the right at a 45° angle. All diagonal joins are parallel.

    Following the examples at right, practice the thin diagonals until you have achieved accurate, flowing letterforms.

1   *Rule your lines at 5 nib widths of a Mitchell No 2 nib.*

2   *Write the letters shown, incorporating thin diagonal joins which are formed by pushing the nib uphill at an angle of 45°.*

3   *Check your writing, making sure that all diagonal joins are parallel.*

Using Letter Joins

The various types of joins are shown at right and below.

Diagonal joins (type 1): These occur between letters with a lead-in or lead-out serif. These must be kept thin, straight and parallel.

Diagonal joins (type 2); These lead from the base of letter bodies. Horizontal joins: The ligature usually looks less heavy if it is written with a slight curve.

Double letters: These letters can be left unjoined, or joined with preceding diagonal ligatures.

Letters with descenders: Letters ending in a tail to the left are usually unjoined. A join may be added after lifting the pen to give continuity.

acdehí

Diagonal joins (type 1)

klmntu

beps

Diagonal joins (type 2)

forvwx   ff tt ff tt

Horizontal joins   Double letters

gj qyyy   gy gy

Letters with descenders—unjoined   Letters with descenders— join after pen lift   Letters with descenders—continuous join

Practicing Letter Joins

It is a good idea to practice cursive italic first by writing the alphabet with an 'm' between each letter. Use lines ruled at an x-height of 5 nib widths of a Mitchell No 2

(Note: the model below is reduced in size).

1 *Repeat the alphabet at least twice.*

2 *Check your letterforms, joins and spacing, but concentrate on rhythm.*

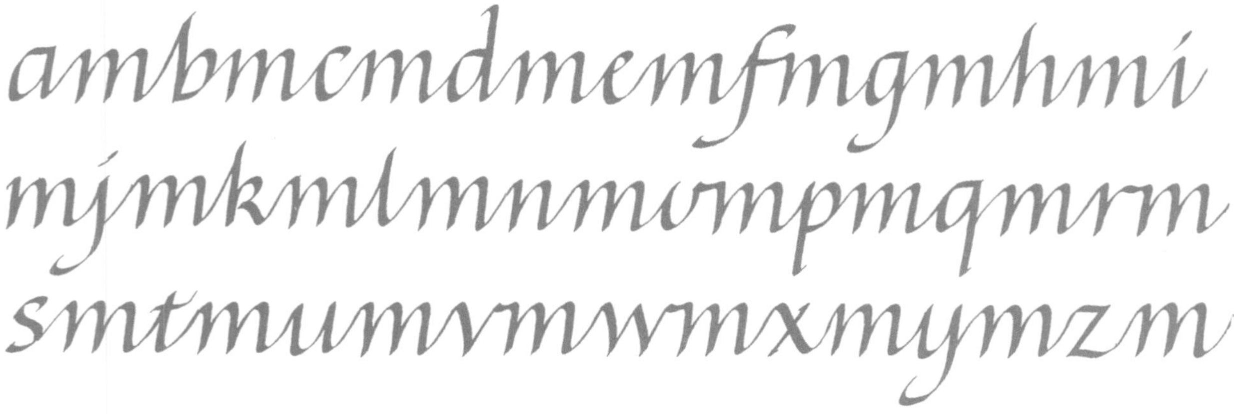

ambmcmdmemfmgmhmi

mjmkmlmnmompmqmrm

smtmumvmwmxmymzm

Writing Small

The first exercises for cursive italic use a fairly large nib (Mitchell No 2), so that details of joins and letterforms can be seen clearly. However, smaller nibs are better adapted to the flow of this script. You may find it easier to develop a rhythm using a smaller nib.

Using Cursive Script

Although cursive italic is often used for handwriting, it is also suitable for a wide range of calligraphic uses. Here it is used to render a quotation in gouache over a colored wash. A Mitchell No 4 nib is used throughout. The cursive hand is written at greater speed than formal italic, the joins drawing the eye naturally from letter to letter.

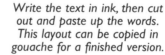

bergamot chervil

fennel garlic basil

coriander lovage

1 Use a Mitchell No 4 nib at an x-height of 5 nib widths.

2 Write the words shown at right in this size.

3 Repeat the exercise until you feel at ease with the smaller nib.

1 Write the text in ink, then cut out and paste up the words. This layout can be copied in gouache for a finished version.

2 An alternative version enlivens the design with flourishes to some letters in the main text.

3 Cut out and add the trial flourishes to the layout. The exact positioning of flourished ascenders and descenders can be critical.

4 The effect of the layout should be balanced and harmonious.

5 The finished work uses gold-transfer leaf lettering over a watercolor wash.

PATER NOSTER
qui es in cælis
sanctificetur nomen
tuum. Adveniat regnum tuum.
Fiat voluntas tua, sicut cælo
et in terra
panem nostrum
quotidianum danobis
hodie. Et dimitte nobis
debita nostra, sicut et nos
dimittimus debitoribus
nostris.
Et ne nos inducas in
tentationem.
Sed libera nos a malo.
AMEN.

THE ALPHABETS

Roman Alphabets

The great legacy of the Romans includes fine letterforms of splendid proportions and sublime elegance. In keeping with other developments in Roman culture, the letterforms matured over several centuries. The shapes of the letters have a strong connection with the introduction of the rounded arch and vault into architectural style.

To record an event, Roman capitals were extensively used incised in stone or marble, on monuments, tombs, and arches. Many fine examples of this alphabet, executed by Roman master craftsmen, can still be found. The execution of the letters was not confined to the chisel. Reed brushes and pens and quill pens also produced the perfect proportions and balance of elegant thick and thin strokes.

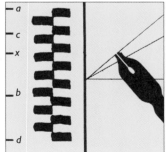

Where appropriate, a symbol indicating the suggested nib width, letter height, and pen angle accompanies each alphabet: use this as a guide only. Whatever size nib is used, the height of the letter is always determined using a "ladder" of nib widths.

'a' refers to the ascender height

'c' refers to the height of the capital letter

'x' refers to the x-height, that is the height of the body of the letter

'b' refers to the baseline, where the body of the cap sits

'd' refers to where the descender finishes

pen angle: *hold your pen over the nib to ensure that it is the right angle before you start: when more than one angle is shown this indicates there is a range of angles for that hand*

nib width: *the correct width of the pen is shown ladder to determine letter height*

The Roman square capitals incised in stone were called *capitalis*. When practiced with a square-cut reed pen or quill, they were known as quadrata. The quadrata required exceedingly painstaking execution to achieve the forms correctly. Quite quickly, the rustic forms succeeded the round forms for use in manuscripts. These were letters of a style that could be written at greater speed and with some economy of materials. The square capitals continued to be well represented in headings, initial letters and special applications, as they are to this day.

In the classical Roman alphabet of 23 letters lie the origins of modern letterforms in the western world. The letters 'J', 'U' and 'W' were added during the Middle Ages.

Close study of the letter shapes reveals adherence to basic geometric principles. The letters are carefully constructed using the square and subdivisions of it. The rounded letters 'C', 'D', 'G', 'O' and 'Q' can be represented by a circle or part of a circle within the square.

The pen angle for this vertical hand varies from 5° for the serifs to 20°-30° for most of the strokes. An angle of 45° is needed for the majority if diagonal strokes. A steeper angle is used for the slanted strokes of 'M' and 'N' and a flat pen (0°) for the diagonal of 'Z'.

The pen moves from the top to the bottom of all vertical and diagonal strokes.

1 *Holding the script pen at the correct 30° angle, draw the first downstroke.*

3 *The second cross stroke is drawn in, making sure that the pen remains consistently at a 30° angle.*

2 *The first cross stroke is then drawn in, incorporating the correctly angled serif on the left.*

4 *The base serif is then added. The height if the completed letter should be exactly 10 nib widths.*

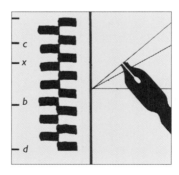

The letter height is 10 nib widths. Meticulous attention must be paid to the height and width of the letters to achieve and maintain their elegant proportions.

Roman letters can be written with a broad pen, held at an angle of 30° for most of the strokes. Diagonal strokes require a steeper pen angle (45°) and the middle stroke of the 'Z' is made with a much flatter angle. The serifs require further manipulation of the pen, including using only the corner of the nib to complete their fine endings. The height of the letters is 10 nib widths.

There are variations in the style and application of serifs and some are more difficult to execute than others. The simplest serif is added as a single separate stroke—a hairline formed by turning the pen to the flat angle (0°) for the horizontal stroke. A bolder serif can be executed as a precursor to or an extension of a stroke.

The classical Roman form has a considered

A Q X

A B C D E F G
H I J K L M N
O P Q R S T U
V W X Y Z

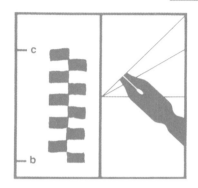

Above: The construction of Roman letters depends on good pen control and achieving and maintaining elegant proportions. Begin and end the vertical stroke with a small hook, which provides the foundation of the serif. To complete it, the pen is turned to 0° to the horizontal writing line.

serif extending on both sides of the upright stroke. There is an almost imperceptible flaring of the upright stroke before it comes to rest in the serif. These elegant endings involve much turning of the pen. Apart from in 'C', 'G' and 'S', all serifs are parallel to the writing line. A concise four-stroke is the vertical, the second the hairline—in some styles this is slightly concave toward the middle. The third and fourth strokes are identical but reversed on either side of the vertical, joining the extremes of the hairline serif to the upright with a gentle curve. The procedure is the same for serifs at the top and bottom of the letters.

Right: Monumental inscriptions were carefully planned and executed, as shown by this example from the arch of Septimus Severus in Rome.

The annotated letters show the order and direction of the strokes forming the alphabet. Not all serifs are formed naturally with the pen; they have to be manipulated with the top or corner of the nib, as seen in 'D' and 'K'.

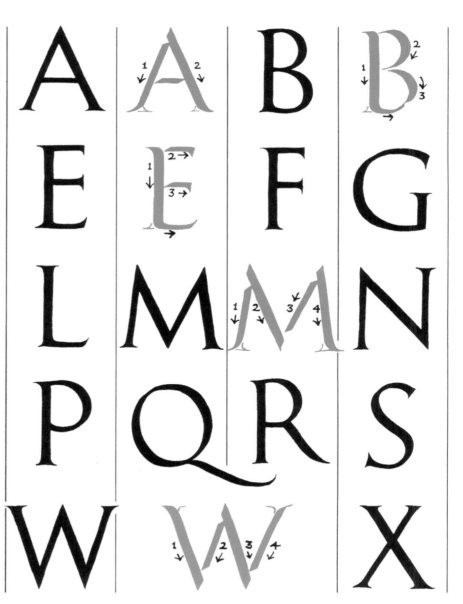

Classical Roman Capitals Alphabet

The elegant style of classical Roman capitals survives most clearly in the stone-carved inscriptions of imperial architecture and monuments. This alphabet is a modern pen-written version based on those carved forms. The accompanying diagrams show the order and direction of the pen strokes by which the character is formed: the square-tipped pen is drawn across the paper, never pushed against the grain. The serifs, or finished strokes, are modeled on the style originally typical of chiselled lettering; they are not natural pen forms and they require a delicate touch and some dextrous manipulation of the pen.

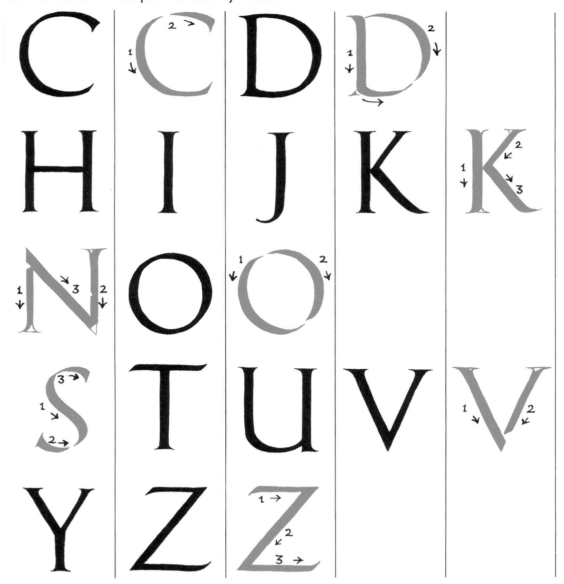

Roman Lower Case Letters

This alphabet is designed as a complement to the preceding capitals; the flat Roman serifs are seen in 'k', 'v', 'w', 'x', and 'y', and at the base of each letter, while the verticals have slanted serifs formed by a slight sideways and upward movement in beginning the stroke, before the pen is pulled smoothly downward. There was no directly comparable contemporary form of what are now called, 'lower case' letters, corresponding to the original Roman capitals. The shorter, more rounded forms, with ascending and descending strokes, were fully evolved in early minuscule scripts, which in turn were re-adapted by later writing masters and type designers, to an overall style and proportion corresponding to the classical squared capitals.

These Roman minuscule letters are formed directly with the pen. Angle of pen is 30° except for the base serif formation.

Compounded Roman Capitals

Delicate proportions and finely varied strokes create a sophisticated modern adaptation of the Roman squared capitals. In this case, the thick and thin stroke variations do not correspond to the actual pen width: the heavier vertical stems and swelling curves are created by outlining the shape and filling on with solid color, in the manner similar to the traditional tendering of decorative Versals. Fine hairlines are used to terminate the individual elements, cutting across the width of the vertical and diagonal strokes with a delicate yet subtle emphasis. There is no attempt to round out the serifs as in the classical Roman capitals.

Built up letterforms are almost always in color. The skeleton of the letter is drawn and filled with fluid color. The fine serif is in lieu of the Roman serif.

ABCD
EFGH
IJKL
MNOPQ
RSTU
VWXYZ

Modern Pen-Drawn Roman Lettering

This freely worked lower-case alphabet written by the American Scribe Arthur Baker employs unusual elongation of extended strokes, although the body of the forms is rounded. Exaggerated thick/thin contrasts weight the bowls of the letters at a low angle. The slashing verticals and flourished tails cut through the solid, even texture, which is created by the use of interlocking forms and repeated letters. All these elements have been carefully thought out in the arrangement of the alphabet as a complete design form. The fluid tracks of the broad-nibbed pen show how the practiced

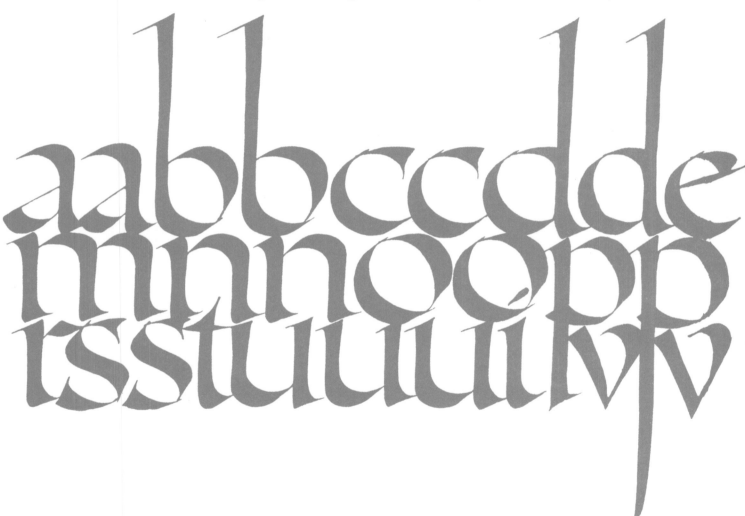

calligrapher can invest simple letterforms with
a lively spontaneity while preserving an
overall balance.

*This lively Roman lower-case letter emphasizes the
pattern value of letterforms, drawn very freely.
although designed en bloc.*

UNCIALS

Uncials followed the Roman square and Rustic capitals and were the result of the need to write in a formal style, but more quickly than is possible using the stately, deliberate capital forms. Uncials are bold, upright, and rounded. They are natural pen letters, having simple constructions and finishing strokes, fluidly contained within the fixed angle of the pen and the direction of strokes.

of formal calligraphy; although Edward Johnston commended them as typical pen-made letters and adapted them for his own use, they were not promoted as enthusiastically as other forms of lettering such as italic, and Johnston's own Foundational hand based on tenth-century script. More recently, uncials have found favor as a highly decorative and vigorous alternative to straightforward capital and lower case forms. Despite their association with some of the finest early Christian manuscripts, they seem to have a curiously modern flavour, which is well-suited to contemporary ideas of design.

A regular, even-height script such as uncials can be used to good effect in a repetitive pattern. Here, basic uncials give a textured, woven look in a design for florist's wrapping paper.

If you have difficulty making the first stroke, divide the task into two strokes. The stroke diagram above shows the delicate nature of the second stroke of Uncial characters, in this case the letter 'A'.

To form the 'G', below, make the long horizontal stroke first, and then add a small stroke on the left-hand top edge. The main stroke of the letter may need some practice to acheive the correct balance of open and closed counter strokes after the application of the final stroke.

Uncials were the standard book hand of scribes from the fifth to the eight centuries, later superseded by the half-uncials and the rapid development of minuscule scripts. They were somewhat neglected during the revival

Uncials are a straight-pen written form, where the pen is held with the edge of the nib parallel to the writing line. The thinnest strokes are precisely horizontal and the thickest vertical. Uncials are naturally quite heavily textured, although they are also pleasantly open as a result of their rounded constructions. The uncial 'O' is a round character, but because there is a pronounced thickening of the curves on either side, the pen form extends across the circular skeleton. The inner space follows the curve of a circle more closely than does the outline of the overall form.

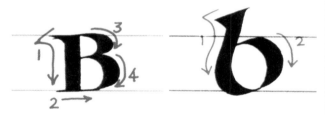

Serifs occur as natural extensions of the pen strokes; on a vertical stem, for example, the serif is formed by pulling the pen from a leftward direction to form a line flowing easily into the broad stem. It can be squared off at the right-hand edge by drawing the pen down vertically over the original curve. The rounded version of 'W' has a serif extended both ways; this is made by a light stroke coming in from the left, crossed by a similar stroke from the right, which follows into the main curve. Since the edge of the pen is horizontal in forming

these strokes, the evenness across the top of the serif is automatically established. In general, the curved and extended strokes of uncials have a naturally graceful finish owing to the rhythm of the pen's progress; tiny hairline "tails" can be created by a quick twist of the nib before lifting the pen.

1 Uncial is a broad face, the pen being held at a very flat angle of 10°–20° to obtain the broad down-stroke.

2 The pen is lifted from the paper before drawing the broad stroke of the 'G'.

3 The slimmer tail stroke is added. This face is characterized by full, rounded letters with very short ascenders and descenders.

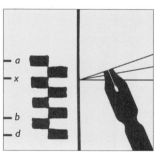

A regular, even-height script such as uncials can be used to good effect in a repetitive pattern.
Here, basic uncials give a textured, woven look in a design for florist's wrapping paper.

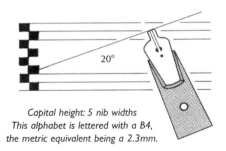

20°

Capital height: 5 nib widths
This alphabet is lettered with a B4,
the metric equivalent being a 2.3mm.

Arrows denote direction of stroke.
Numerals indicate order of
character construction.

Uncials with half uncial 'I', showing
relative positions on guidelines.

Lining numerals

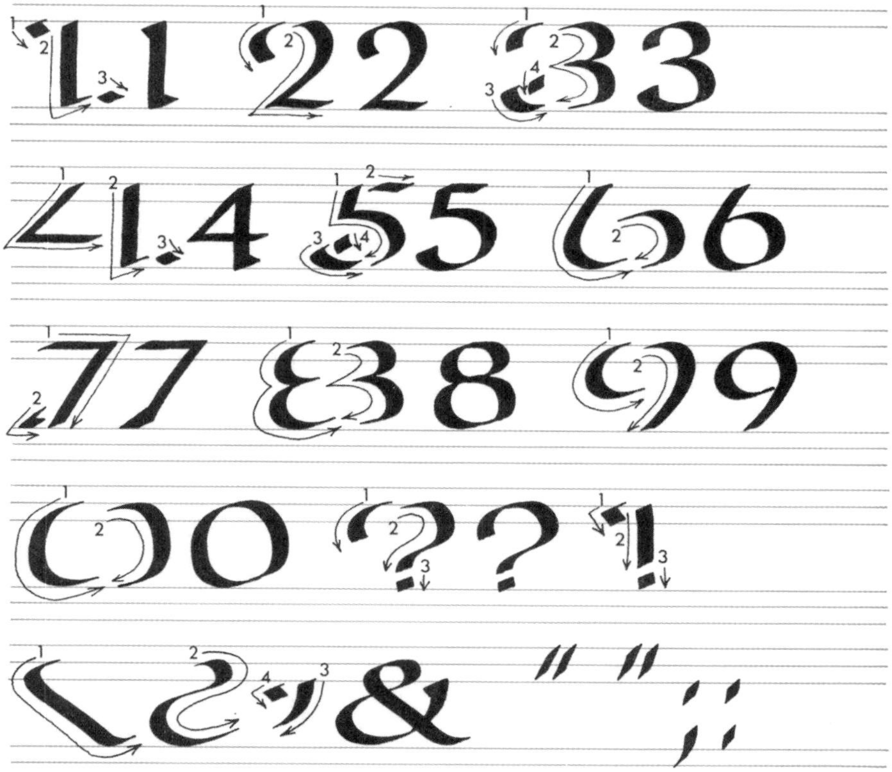

Alternative capitals

Ascenders: 2 nib widths

x-height: 4 nib widths

Descenders: 2 nib widths

Alternative lower case

ABCDEFGHIKLMN
OPQRSTUVWXY
abcdefghijklmn
opqrstuvwxyz

English Uncials and Half-Uncials

This alphabet shows another modern transcription of the early uncial form, followed by a half-uncial alphabet, the book hand which followed on from uncials. In this case the half-uncials are based on early English lettering from the beautifully decorated Lindisfarne Gospels, written in the seventh century AD. In the half-uncials, the characteristics leading to minuscule, or lower-case, forms are readily apparent. This is a systematic and formal script, with deliberate ascenders and descenders breaking out of the body height of the letters. Despite the lingering reference to the capital form of 'N', this is otherwise the precursor of lower-case forms and it is particularly noticeable that the semi-capitalized 'A' still in use in the uncial alphabet has been completely modified into the more rounded, compact character.

VERSALS

These elegant capital letters appear deliberately throughout early manuscripts, but were seldom used to compose an entire block of text. Their main purpose was to serve as chapter openings, to draw the attention of the reader to an important section of the text, or to begin a paragraph, or verse. Standing in any of these commanding positions on the page, these extraordinary letters were at times emblazoned almost beyond recognition. There were no minuscule forms, so the accompanying body of text would be executed in Uncial, Half-Uncial, or Carolingian letters.

In Medieval times, Versal letters used as initials were simply colored green, red or blue. Richly burnished gold versions were limited to use in manuscripts deemed of particular importance.

The usual feature of Versals in calligraphic terms is that they are built-up, not written letters. The construction appears straightforward but it is curiously difficult to master. Most of the strokes are formed in the same way, whether they are curved or straight. As a guide to height, base the letter on eight to ten times the width of the letter's stem.

It is advisable to begin by drawing a light pencil outline so that the correct angles and counter shapes are established. Then you can work the letter stroke by stroke using a medium-fine pen, starting with the uprights. These are slightly "wasted", tapering inward to the center and broadening a little at the ends. The diagonal strokes are similarly constructed. Unless you are adding color, a single stroke should fill in the letter once the outlines have been drawn. The slightly extended hairline serifs are formed with the pen held flat.

Letters with rounded counters should fall slightly above and below the actual letter height. When making these letters, complete the inner line of the counter first, so that you achieve the inner line of the correct proportions. The outer curves of the letters are slightly sharper than the inner ones. In letters that have crossbars, these are placed slightly above the middle.

The spaciousness of these graceful letterforms provides much scope for decoration. You can add a contrasting color simply by using a pen or brush to make the filling-in stroke. A heading, or the first word of a text, catches attention when it is richly embellished with color, has hairlines added, and elaborate flourishes swirled into intricate patterns. Beginning a piece of work with a single Versal also offers an excellent opportunity for gilding.

Contemporary design trends have provided new perceptions of works composed entirely of upper case letters. The elegant versal works well in many contexts. A rhythmic texture can be created if careful consideration is given to the spaces the letters occupy. To achieve movement in the design, some of the letters may vary in size, but maintaining a constant letter size can result in a work of great credibility and elegance.

1 In this Versal capital, the inner stroke is drawn first to establish the shape of the counter. Then the outer stroke is drawn.

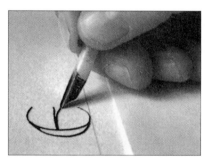

2 The two middle cross strokes start at the width of the nib, and are splayed in two flaring strokes at the end to produce a wedge shape.

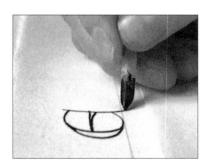

3 The enclosing downstroke is not drawn. These hairline strokes should be lightly drawn with the pen held at 90° to the paper.

4 The skeleton lettering is filled with a single stroke. Filling-in can also be done with a fine sable brush.

Versal Alphabet

These built-up capital letters are excellent forms for headings and decorating and work well with many calligraphic hands. The inner strokes are drawn first to ensure the counter shape is the correct proportion. The waisted vertical strokes are constructed with great care; the waisting is a subtle curve and must not be exaggerated. A metal nib, fine pointed brush or quill can be used to construct these letters. The instrument is manipulated at various angles to achieve a balance of thin and thick strokes.

The slightly waisted vertical strokes of the letter are drawn first. Turn the pen to 0° to the horizontal writing line and draw the serifs. The inner stroke of the counter shape is drawn first to establish the shape, then the outer shapes are added.

Versals—Roman Form

These simple Versals are in a style based on Roman capitals, as commonly used in early manuscripts. The important characteristics of Versals, compared to other calligraphic lettering, is that the letterforms are built up gradually rather than written fluidly. The pen is narrower and more flexible than that used to write the text. In this sample, fine hairline serifs complete the forms; these are in lieu of the proper Roman serif.

Versals are essentially pen-made with a flexible quill or metal pen. Each Versal letter is actually formed with three strokes: a vertical stem, for example, is outlined on each side and the third stroke is quickly applied to fill the space between.

Versals—Lombardic Form

The curving shapes of this Versal alphabet are influenced by both Lombardic scripts and Uncial letters, as demonstrated particularly in the forms of 'D', 'H' and 'M'. The cross-strokes and curves are terminated with a flaring of the width cut across by a hairline, and these lines are rather more bold and flourished than in the Roman-style Versals, creating a lively textural rhythm. The fine, flexible quill or pen used to draw the Versals can be charged with ink or thinned watercolor paint. Two-color Versal can be attractively made by drawing the outer strokes in a dark ink, and flooding the inner area with color. Red, green and blue are traditional colors for Versals: they are strong hues which balance with black writing ink.

These are richer forms, largely based on Uncial letters, producing free and lively expression and used continuously throughout the ages.

Elaborated Versals

The design of this alphabet takes the rhythmic and flourished quality of the Lombardic style a little further. The construction of the letterforms is very fluid and decorative, from the exaggerated tails of 'K', 'Q', 'R' and 'X' to the individual details enlivening the counter spaces of 'B', 'O' and 'Q'. The elaboration is of a consistent style and quality, but intriguingly varied in detail to make the form of each letter not only clearly distinguishable, but also individually ornamental.

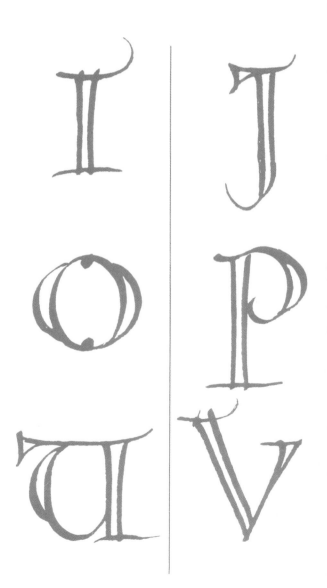

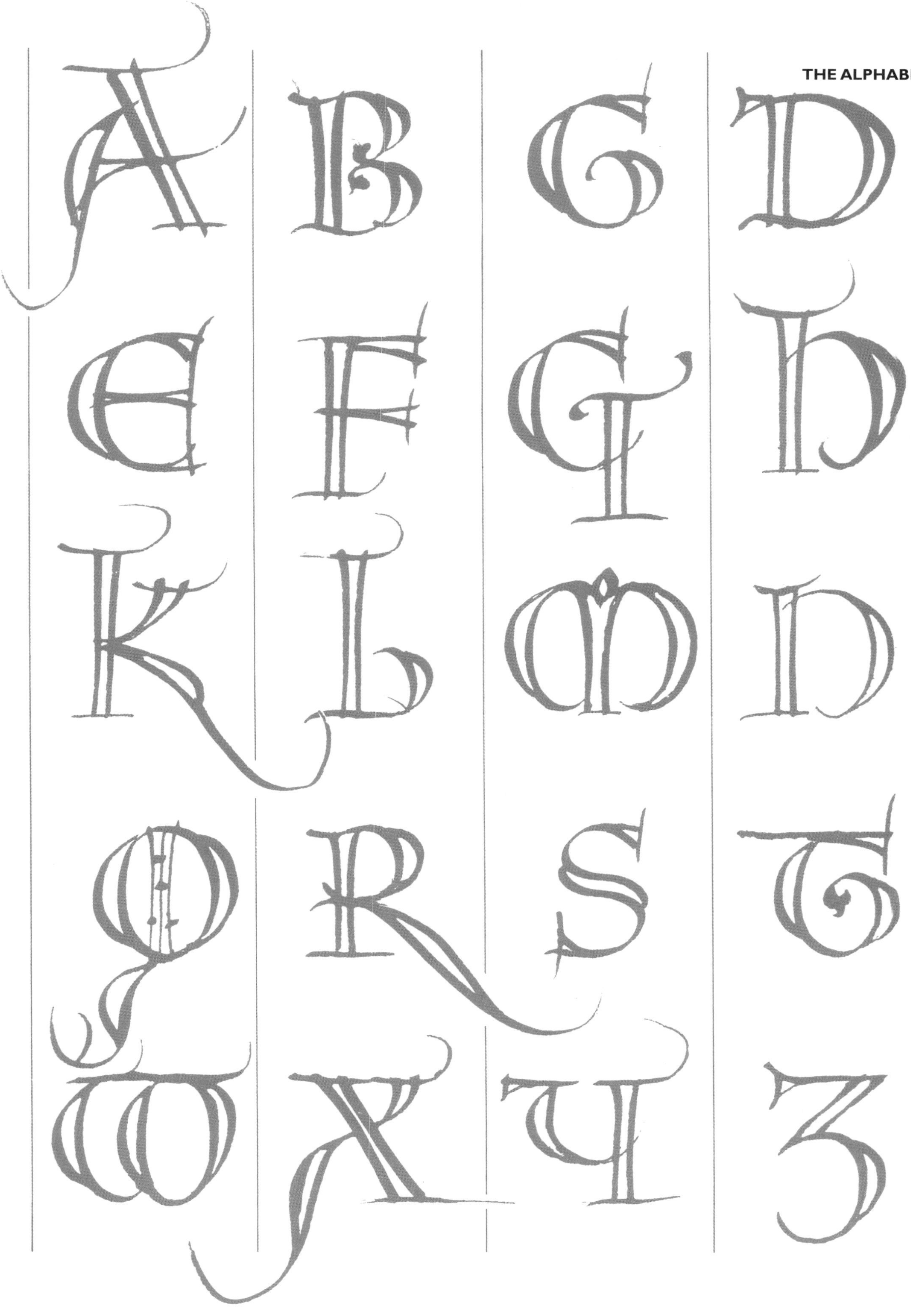

A B G D
E F G H
K L M N
R S T
W X Y Z

Ornamental Versals

The weighty shapes of these Lombardic-style Versals are sufficiently broad to allow a decorative piercing of the curves and stems, in addition to flourished, and ornamental detail. The drawn Versal letter can be the basis of a heavily ornamental or illuminated capital letter, decorated with abstract motifs or, as in the original miniatures of medieval manuscripts, with tiny pictures of figurative images. Colors can be introduced to add variety to the design, and Versals are also traditionally the subjects of gilding, with burnished gold leaf or painted powder gold.

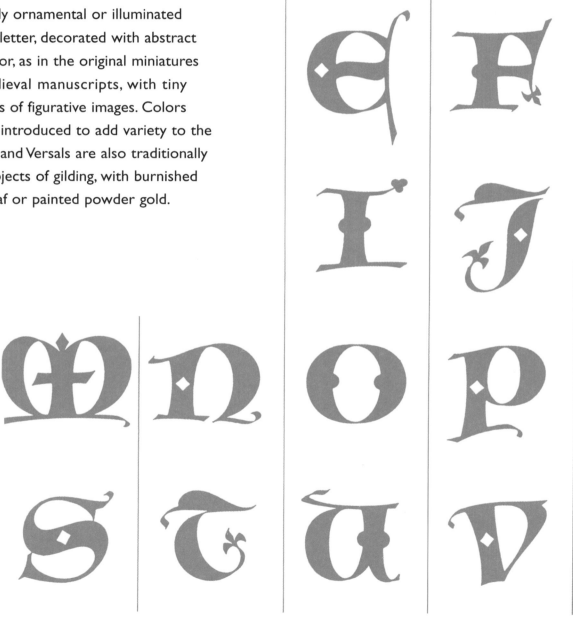

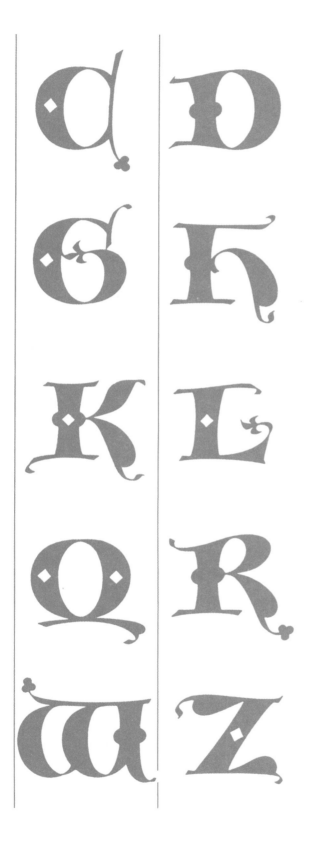

Modified 10th-Century

The modification of tenth-century minuscule script produces a rounded, vigorous letter-form, naturally adapted to the movements of hand and pen in calligraphy. There is both invention and adaptation in this alphabet, as in the curving forms of 'V' and 'W', and in the regular vertical emphasis of 'a' and 'g' in the minuscule form, which are sloping and more freely written in the earlier versions. In addition the tenth-century manuscripts often show use of the long 's', which to modern eyes appears to be 'f'; in the modified hand the 's' conforms to the expected shape in relation to other letterforms. The alphabet of capital letters has been systematically constructed to accompany the modified script and is not typical of tenth-century capitals.

Like the Roman capitals, this hand has a regular system of proportion and a subtle graduation of thick and thin strokes, but it is open, broad and less severe than the square capitals. The pen angle used is 30°, as with the Roman capitals, which gives the tilted, circular 'O'. The lettering is quite sturdy and compact. The vertical, and rounded forms are dominant, so in letters that have a vertical stem this is usually the first stroke written.

Serifs at the top of vertical strokes are simply formed by a slight curve starting the stroke from the left, and then overlaid with a vertical stroke to sharpen the right-hand edge.

Less formally, in oblique strokes the fluid motion of the pen is allowed to begin and end the stroke in a logical manner—tails curve naturally with a tiny flourish as in the minuscule 'g', 'k' and 'y' and the capitals 'K', 'R', and 'X'. This script almost has the freedom of a cursive hand, and the letters should be closely spaced so there is a lively horizontal linking between the forms, occurring easily through the characteristic rhythm and direction of the strokes.

This example by Edward Johnston, demonstrates his Foundational hand, a modification of an English tenth-century hand that was a standard script for scribes. Johnston updated the old minuscule forms, and the result is more upright letters accompanied by similarly modified capitals.
The lower-case and capital letter alphabets of the modified tenth-century hand are written with a pen angle of 30°; the weight is four nib widths to height. The order of strokes is shown for each letter in the lower-case alphabet. A rounded, almost cursive hand, the letterforms should be written fairly close together.

Showing characteristics of both uncials and the modified tenth-century hand, this example was written holding the pen at a slight angle. The overall effect, however, is that of an uncial script. The variation in tone of the pen strokes on the textured paper and the ragged line lengths are evenly balanced in the composition.

GOTHIC

Numerous styles of lettering evolved during the Gothic era, the period broadly straddling the twelfth to sixteenth centuries. The developments in writing reflected changes of style in the built environment, where lancet arches replaced the rounded Roman arches, and ribbed vaults and thrusting flying buttresses appeared. A variety of Gothic hands emerged sharing many common elements, including a heavy, dense black form, angular letters, rigid verticals and, often, short ascenders and descenders in relation to the height. Sometimes the emphasis on angularity renders the work almost illegible to modern readers.

The many variations, both formal and informal, are attributable to the numbers of people who adapted the forms to suit their own requirements. Often small changes in structure occurred simply through the need for speed and economy in writing. Some rounded versions of Gothic lettering did persist and develop, such as Rotunda. Other Gothic forms practiced today are, Blackletter, and Textura.

A Gothic hand can be produced using a broad pen held at an angle of 45° and a height of five nib widths. A height of six nib widths achieves a slender letter with more clarity.

A neat, tidy, and textured work results from making the white spaces within, and between the letters, the same thickness as the upright strokes. With due consideration, Gothic lettering can be very effective. To use it successfully, plan the piece carefully and do plenty of rough workings, developing your ability to space the letters consistently. When working on the final piece, execute the strokes with determination.

Originally, there were no specific capital letters in the Gothic forms. Usually, a decorated letter was dropped in, and this worked surprisingly well. The Gothic upper case now used is distinctly open, even rounded, compared with the lower-case lettering. The height is seven nib widths. Gothic capitals work best on their own as individual letters. Seldom are they used successfully for an entire word.

In the lower-case letters, a square serif is used which sits atop the strokes. In the upper-case forms, the same square serif is seen, but more usually sited on the left-hand outside edge of the upright strokes.

The splendid Gothic 'S' is easier to execute than it appears on first viewing. Breaking it down into constituent parts to work out how it is made, it transpires that it is constructed of similar strokes travelling in the same direction, as the stroke diagram illustrates.

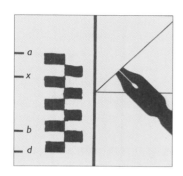

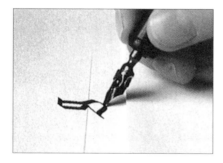

1   The first stroke of this Blackletter is formed by holding the pen at an angle of 35° and making a fine line diagonally to the left. Almost immediately the pen is pulled down into the strong vertical line. Before this stroke reaches the base line, it is stopped, and a strong diagonal stroke is pulled down to the right and onto the base line.

2   The pen returns to the top of the letter and rests at the pen angle where the first stroke began. The pen is pulled to the right, beyond where the next vertical line will begin. The vertical stroke that becomes the descender curves out to the right before it reaches the baseline. At about two nib widths below the baseline, the stroke is pulled back to the left, and to the thinnest part of the stroke, where it stops.

3   The final stroke begins with a hairline drawn from the end of the diagonal stroke resting on the baseline. It travels down to the left. To complete the descender, a wave stroke is made to the right, where it joins up with the middle of the descender.

Blackletter

Blackletter was born of a need for speed and economy, like so many developments in writing. The style is composed of thrusting, upright strokes that create an overall vertical effect, but the eye can find rest in the horizontals breaking the spaces at the top and bottom of the letters.

To write this hand, you hold a broad pen at an angle of 30°- 40° to the writing line. The weight of the letter can be varied by adjusting the height between three and five nib widths. The counter spaces, the vertical strokes, and the spaces between letters are usually of identical thickness.

Blackletter is exceedingly economical, as constant condensing means more letters per line, and more words per page. The spaces between lines can be reduced, and the ascenders and descenders shortened to a minimum to create a very dense texture. This occurs in the version of Gothic lettering known as Textura, which can be seen as pure pattern.

The upper-case letters, seven nib widths in height, are not conducive to use in whole words, as legibility becomes a problem.

This Gothic hand works surprisingly well with decorative capitals, and there are many fine historical examples. Contemporary uses for Blackletter occur in various contexts, including presentation documents.

Gothic Blackletter Alphabet

The upper-case letters of seven nib widths in height have a roundness which contrasts well with the angularity of the lower-case letters of five nib widths height. The distinctive, angular 'o' is a good guide for the lower-case letters. The short ascenders and descenders permit tight interlinear spacing.

Gothic Cursive Alphabet

This elegant hand is perhaps less well-known and therefore not widely used. A single upper-case letter used with lower-case letters can be used for a heading with eye-catching effect. The lower-case letters are written four-and-a-half to five nib widths high.

The letters have a distinctive almond (mandorla) shape, thought to have been a Middle Eastern influence. The letters are pointed where they touch the baseline, and some have fine line extensions from this point. Some of the descenders end in sharp fine line extended strokes. The upper-case letters are written six-and-a-half to seven nib widths high. Many of these capital letters are more recognizable as lower-case forms. It is evident when looking at the lower-case letters, that this hand evolved to be written at speed.

The Gothic cursive upper-case 'A' is presented in a shape more recognizable as a lower-case letter. The cross stroke, which begins the letter at the top, holds and balances the rest of the letter. The fine lines must contrast with the bold strokes to give this hand its own particular identity.

Rotunda (Rotonda)

Variously referred to as Italian Gothic, Half-Gothic or Round Gothic, this crisp hand was used as a bookhand in medieval and Renaissance Italy. While in northern Europe, the hard, dense, Blackletter style, flourished in the southern countries. There was a distinctly softer form, especially by comparison with the compact and angular Textura, a style never seriously pursued in Italy. However, a further comparison with the Gothic hand practiced in the north reveals that in the spaciousness of Rotunda, there is a slight angularity, particularly pronounced on letters with enclosed counter spaces.

Medieval Italian manuscripts show the form exquisitely. The ascenders and descenders are often minimal, which creates a very even linear texture. The space between both letters and words is often pronounced, but there still exists a balanced letter structure of bold upright strokes and fine, thin strokes.

The serif style varies according to the preference of the scribe. Fine hairline extensions are often applied, and many strokes simply terminate with the pen angle. There are a few examples that show the use of the truly Gothic-style lozenge-shaped serif.

The simple, clean letters need to be carefully formed in order to display their pleasing proportions. The letters are written with a pen at an angle of 30°.

This rounded, open hand, was skilfully combined with splendidly illuminated Versals. Some early manuscripts include pen-drawn capitals constructed in a similar manner to letters in the body of the text, but they are more rounded.

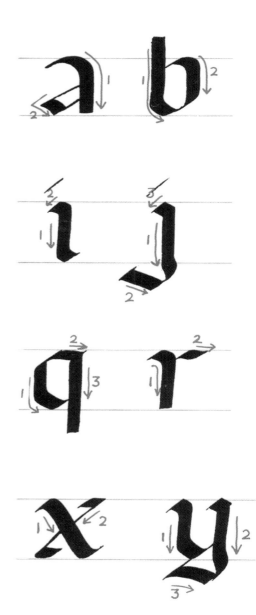

Rotunda Minuscule Alphabet

The Rotunda minuscule is a more open, and rounded, Gothic hand. The letters are written four-and-a-half to five nib widths high, and with a pen angle of 30° to the horizontal. The letters maintain some of the obvious Gothic characteristics. There is a distinct softening of stroke compared to the more familiar angularity of some Gothic hands.

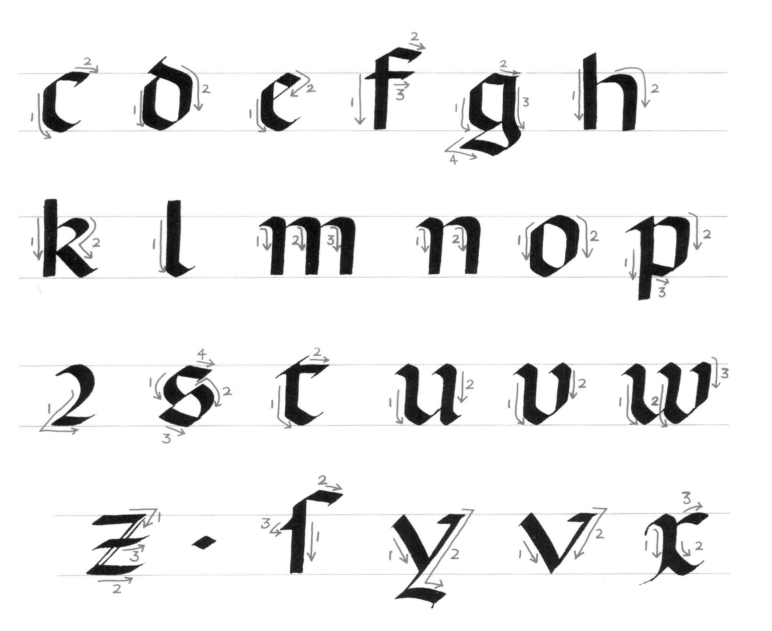

Textura

This Gothic script, which was mostly practiced in northern Europe, takes its name from the Latin *textum*, meaning 'woven fabric' or 'texture'. Used as a bookhand and widely found in early psalters and prayer books, this lower-case alphabet developed in many formal and informal styles. Two of the formal hands were *textus precissus* and *textus quadratus*. The former was characterized by strong upright strokes standing flat on the baseline, the latter by distinctive diamond-shaped serifs, and forking at the tops of the ascenders.

The Textura hand, as its name suggests, is built of condensed, bold black verticals. These are identical in thickness to the counter spaces and the spaces between the letters. The spacing between lines is minimal, which is ideal for accommodating the typically Gothic short ascenders and descenders.

To execute this hand, you hold the broad nib at 40°. The letter height is six nib widths. Variations in height create further interest in the texture of the overall design.

The letters have a distinct angular stress. Extra hairlines can be added by lifting one corner of the pen at the end of a stroke and dragging a little wet ink outward to become the hairline extension.

A recognizable feature of manuscripts written in Textura is the line filling. Where a line finished short of the right-hand margin, the scribe would complete the line with exquisite patterning. If the line was short by only one or two letters, a simple flourish or pen pattern would serve the purpose. This is a solution that can be utilized for many design problems. The patterning must pay respect to the lettering style: thus, for Textura, it must be quite solid.

*Renate Fuhrmann—a fine example of Textura—
a dense Gothic hand which at its most extreme displays no
difference in thickness between vertical strokes, counter strokes,
and letter spaces. Delicate tonal changes occur throughout the
text, which has been written using watercolor. Distemper and
wood tar are the other materials used.*

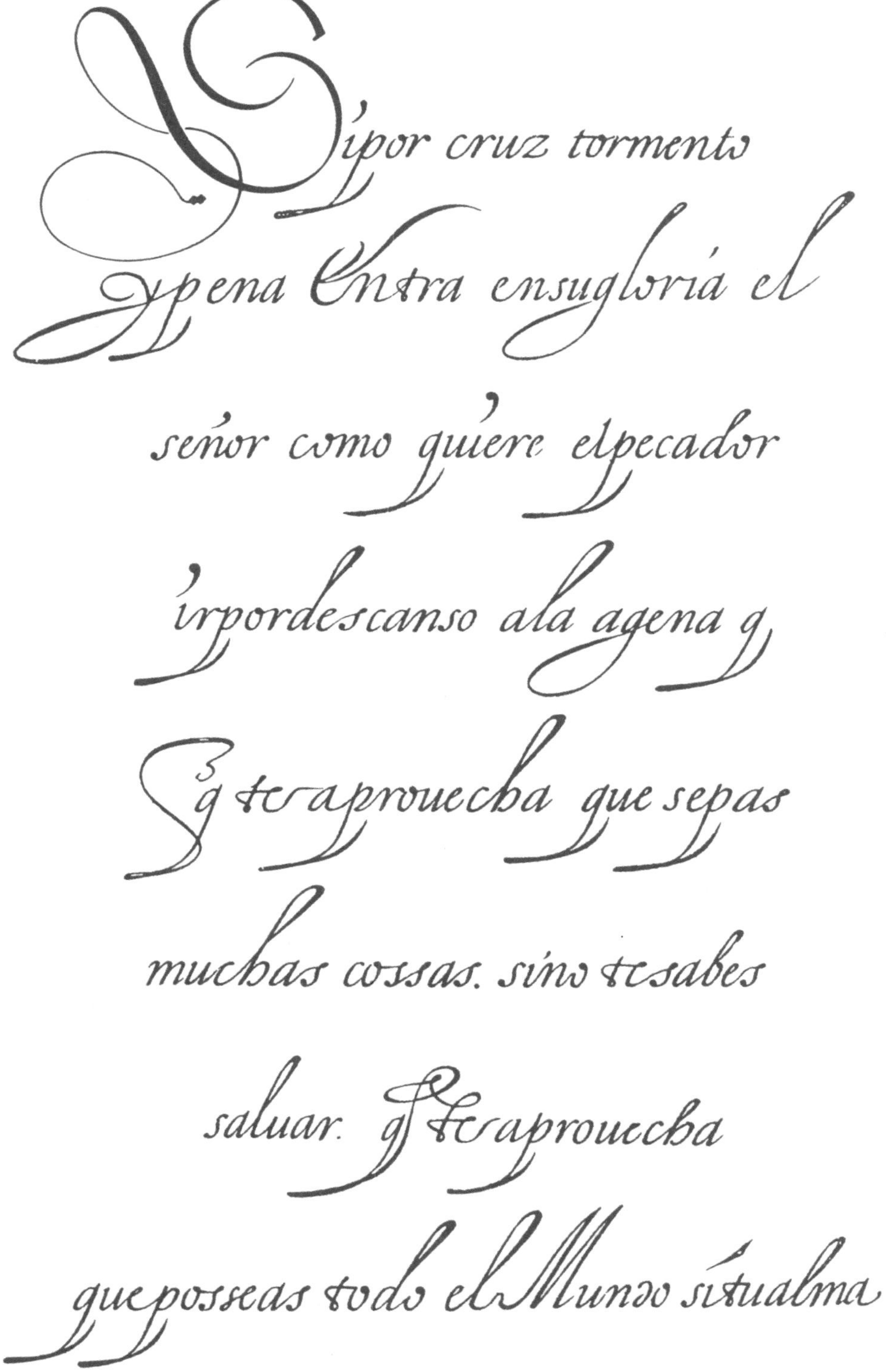

Sí por cruz tormento

y pena Entra en su gloria el

señor como quiere el pecador

'irpor descanso ala agena q,

g te aprouecha que sepas

muchas cossas. síno te sabes

saluar. g te aprouecha

que posseas todo el Mundo si tu alma

A sample combining the elaborate, Gothic-influenced Neudorffer capital, with an early Copperplate script as Spanish calligrapher, Morante, demonstrates the influence of Copperplate technique on the forms of the letters— the tendency is toward fine, and fluidly, swiveling strokes, compared to the emphatic thick/thin contrasts of edged-pen lettering. Even more than those early writing masters, modern calligraphers and graphic artists can draw upon a vast range of styles and techniques as the basis for the new designs, and combinations of letters.

Textura Alphabet

The forms of Gothic script, known as Blackletter, are instantly recognizable from the compressed, angular and vertically stressed letters. The original proportions of Textura were based on three strokes of the pen, so that the counters, or interior spaces, were the same width as the pen strokes. This regularity can make the combined letterforms very difficult to read as a script.

This version shows a slightly more open form with serifs which are naturally contrived in the pen angle at the top of the stroke. The bases of the letters are finished with the characteristic lozenge-shaped feet corresponding to the width, and consistent 40° angle of the edged pen. These feet are set slightly off-center on the vertical stems. The form is ornamental and evocative of its period. Development of Blackletter scripts continued through the introduction of printers' types in Europe, and they became the models for the first mechanical letters.

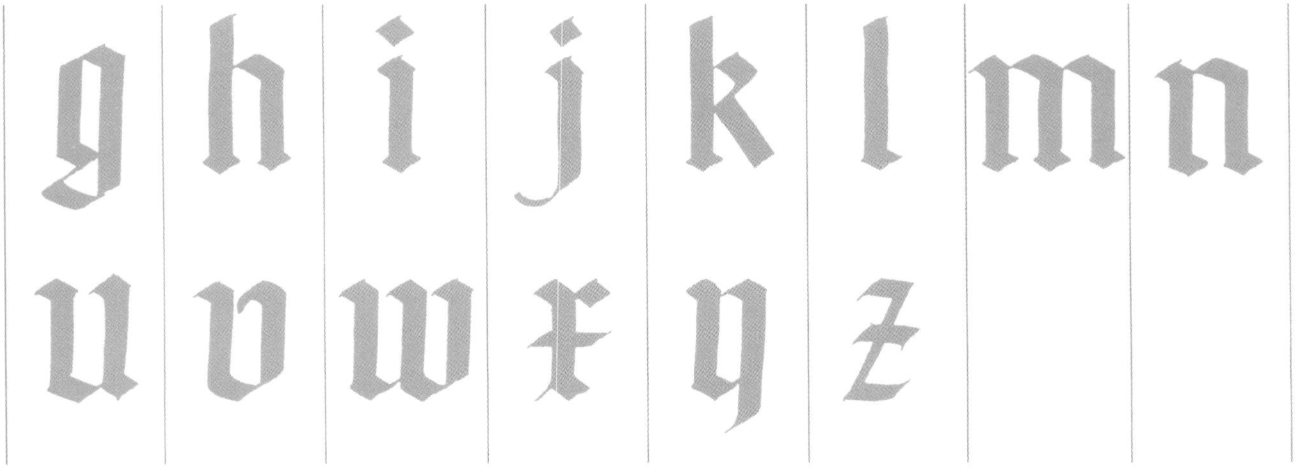

g h i j k l m n
u v w x y z

g h i j k l m n
u v w x y z

mit figur und pildnus

Gothic Majuscule

These majuscule letters are noticeably rounded and open in form, texturally far less dense and heavy than other styles corresponding to the Blackletter script. This suggests that the alphabet derives from capital letters used as decorative initials, since the strokes are of medium weight by reference to the body size of the letterforms, providing interior spaces sufficiently open, to allow for ornamentation of the form. They include pen-drawn decoration in the features extending from the structural outlines—small flicked protrusions and double hairlines

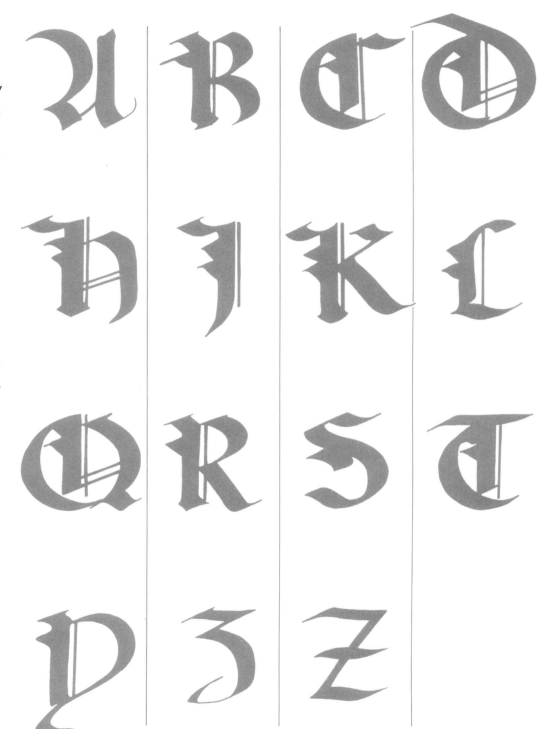

attached to the counters and vertical stems. The curving strokes show the influence of Lombardic and Uncial lettering.

An unusually light alphabet, the capitals have a filigree detail. The Uncial influence is clearly seen in 'U' and 'M'.

MODERN LETTERS

Fine Capitals

Modern calligraphy, while repeatedly based on traditional lettering styles, at its best, offers a reworking of such forms with a distinctive flavour of its own time. These elegantly refined capitals, based on the classical roman model, are written with a fine pen that creates a very subtle modulation of width in the strokes. The basic proportions of the letters are seen almost as they appear in the skeleton form, but the fineness of the line is more appreciable for the deliberate contrasts and fluid variation along the width. The alphabet has a deceptive simplicity: accuracy in the relationships between letterforms is carefully preserved, yet there is a vitality to the design which does not overwhelm the sensitivity of the rendering.

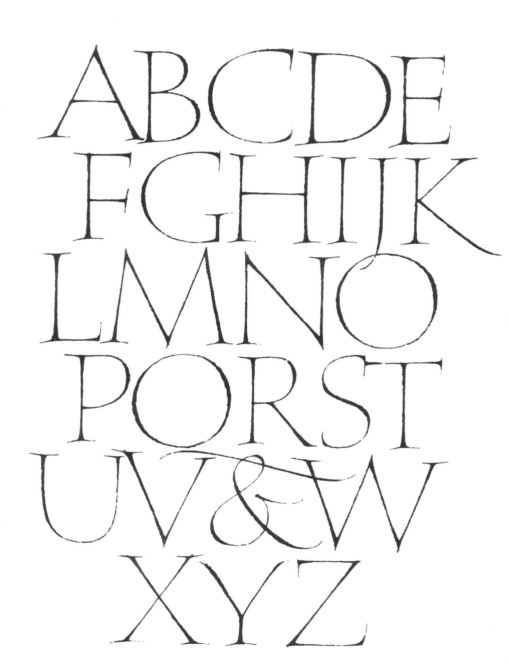

Modern Gothic

The vertical stresses and richly angular patterning of Gothic letterforms have a continuing fascination to the calligrapher in formal terms. This modern reworking emphasizes the narrowed structures and textural density of the letters, written with heavy, vigorous strokes. The overall design has a symmetrical balance but the lively execution of the letters ensures there is no rigidity in the format. The spidery, light-colored script written through these dense and ordered forms creates an emphatic and effective contrast, enabling the successful combination of form and function; which is the essence of calligraphic skills.

EMANUEL GEIBEL

Triple-Stroke Alphabet

The aesthetic qualities of a well-crafted work are always reliant, not only on the skill of execution, but also on the inherent capabilities of the materials and equipment used in the making. The modern calligrapher has a wide range of traditional and recently developed materials to choose from; any of which may suite particular intentions, or suggest alternative elements in the design. Multiple-stroke pens naturally endow lettering with a heavily patterned and even character. The ribbon-like quality of this triple-stroke writing is effectively applied to a simple lower-case alphabet form. Neatly executed turns of the pen create a flowing, scrolled effect of rich texture.

Few serious attempts have been made to create new alphabets with modern nibs.

These triple- or five-pronged pens can produce interesting 3 dimensional effects.

Cursive Lettering

In some cases the specific character of an alphabet demands absolute consistency in the weight and texture of the strokes, but in this case, the textural variations actually caused by the flow of ink lend additional vitality to the travelling lines. There are elements of italic script in the slanted, branching arches of the lower-case letters, but this is an informal interpretation which also exploits the contrast between rounded and compressed forms. The basically horizontal emphasis draws the eye across the writing line. However, there is movement in all directions suggesting rapid and spontaneous execution. The alphabet combines the calligrapher's appreciation of lettering construction with the functional fluidity of ordinary handwriting.

    These alphabets have the lively informality of most cursive alphabets with less contrast in weight of line. Written at speed, the judgement has to be almost intuitive.

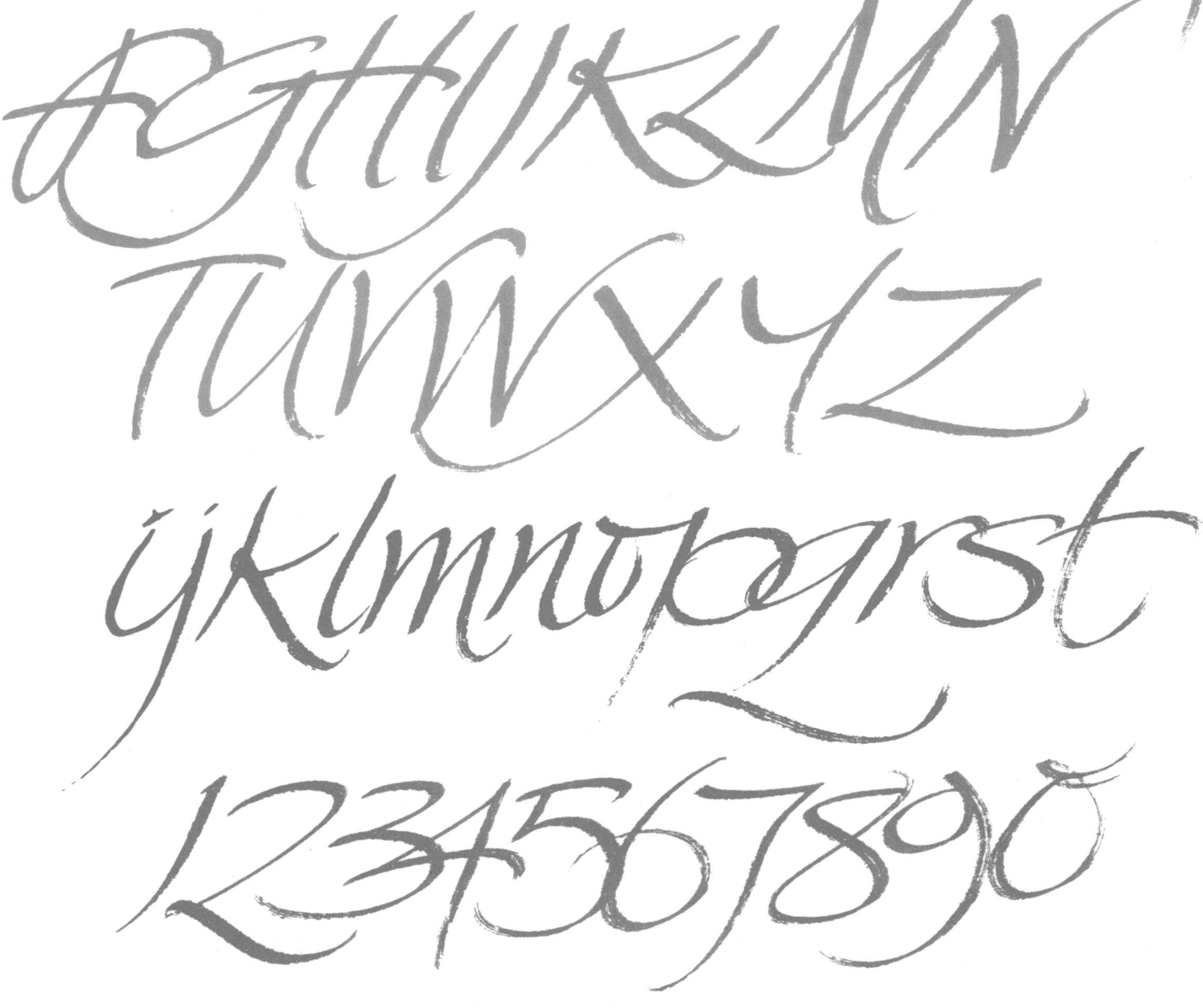

A F G H I J K L M N

T U V W X Y Z

i j k l m n o p q r s t

1 2 3 4 5 6 7 8 9 0

Script Alphabet

The continuing function of calligraphy in modern design work is demonstrated by this script alphabet. Designer Richard Bird, constructed it specifically for use in lettering on wine labels. His requirements were for a traditional letterform with the quality of a script, but closely set and joined, and with heavy emphasis on the body of the letters. Existing examples of Copperplate scripts, and the typefaces based on them, appeared too widely spread and spidery in character, so he designed this full alphabet—capitals, lower case, and numerals—to his own specifications. The capitals are weighted in the body of the letter by broad, but fluid, strokes. The finer flourishes provide appropriate and unexaggerated ornament. The joined lower-case letters are somewhat compressed and have a cursive quality.

Numerals and punctuation marks are carefully worked out, in line with the distinctive features of the script.

Flourished Capitals

The rolling rhythms of Copperplate writing are here updated in a spiky, but fluid, capital letter alphabet in which the letters are elegantly interwoven. The forms are not strictly consistent – 'E' and 'S', for example, are enlarged and the 'Y' is present almost as a lower-case form, to terminate the design with an extravagantly looped flourish. However, modifications to the letters are logically contrived to fit the pattern of the overall construction. The flowing movement of the pen is particularly seen in the way the outer stroke of 'N' rolls over into the curve of 'O'. Lettering design of this type is a well-judged balance between spontaneity and control, and the pattern of the alphabet, though finely textured, is compactly displayed.

Fine Pen-Drawn Letters

This alphabet form presented in upper and lower case has an elegance similar to that of classical Roman models. However, there are a number of refinements in the design which provide a distinctive quality of modernity.

Unlike Roman square capitals taking their proportions from the circular 'O', the rounded letters here are constructed of very shallow curves which compact the outline shapes. Another notable difference lies in the serifs, which cut across the main stroke in classical

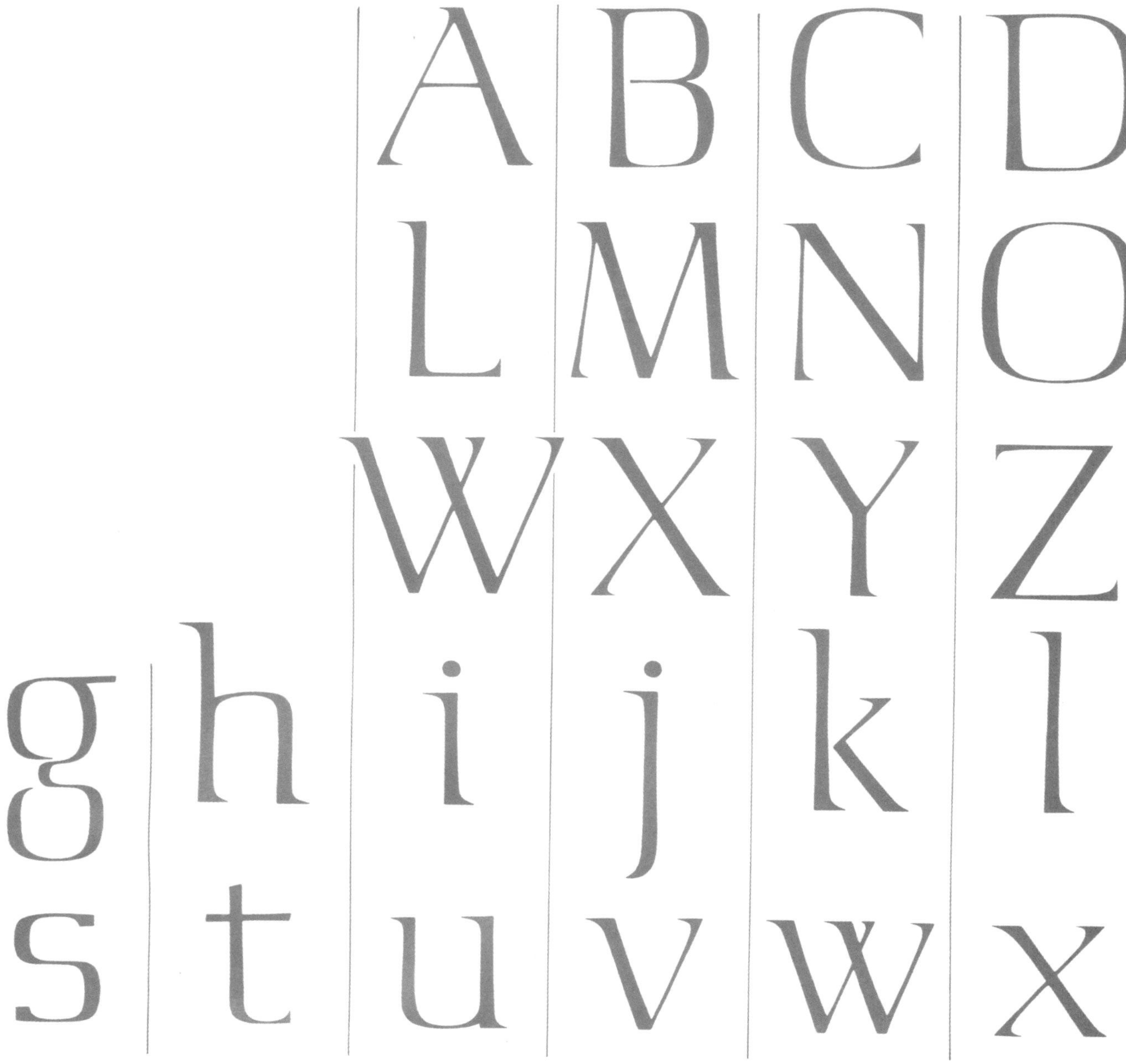

ABCD
LMNO
WXYZ
ghijkl
stuvwx

forms, but here lead in only from the left, adding a subtly minimal horizontal stress to the upright lettering. Not only is there the natural variation between thick and thin pen strokes travelling in different directions; the width of line is delicately graduated within a single

stroke, creating a slight flaring of the vertical stems and slanted strokes, as well as the fluid swelling on the curves. The capitals and lower-case letters are perfectly matched in style and proportion.

E F G H J K
P R S T U V
a b c d e f
m n o p q r
y z å ä ö

ITALIC

Italic was the typical pen form of Renaissance Italy. It came into being in the interest of developing a greater writing speed while maintaining an elegant, finely proportioned form in pen script. The characteristics of italic are the elliptical 'O', on which model all the curved letters are constructed, the lateral compression and slight rightward slope of the writing, and the branching of arched strokes flowing rapidly out of the letter stems.

Italic is by nature a lightweight form and is usually written with a nib width narrower than those used from the rounded forms of medieval book hands. There is less variation in the widths of italic letters, but they are elongated, with extended ascenders and descenders. For this reason, the height should be carefully controlled to keep the pen strokes firm and cleanly curved. In keeping with the flowing elegance of italic, the tails, ascenders and descenders are often elaborately flourished or looped. For practical purposes, a simple, basic form is easier for the beginner.

It has an inclined angle to the right, which can vary from a few degrees to 13° from the vertical. After 13° the pen forms produced are not balanced, with straight and curved strokes differing greatly in weight.

Serifs in the capitals are formed either by a change of direction of stroke, or by an upward movement before and after the main strokes. Additionally, serifs are made by overlapping curved strokes over main strokes, such as in the 'B', where the beginning of the curved stroke which forms the upper bowl overlaps the left-hand edge of the main stem.

Lower-case serifs are produced in a similar fashion to those of the capitals. Ascenders and descenders can be finished with an extra flourished stroke, either straight-ish lines curving upward or rounded strokes ending in a slight hook, or merely sheared straight terminals. They extend one nib width above the capital and

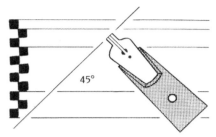

Capital height: 7 nib widths
This alphabet is lettered with a B4,
the metric equivalent being a 2.3mm.

Nib Angle approximately 45˚

Arrows denote direction of stroke.
Numerals indicate order of
character construction.

Flourishing should not be at the
expense of legibility.

three nib widths below the x-line. They can be extended beyond these areas and flourishes, but with discretion.

Loops and tails are finished on the natural curve of the pen stroke. It is common to see ascending strokes carried over on a curve to the right, following the general emphasis of the lettering. This is a convenient way of tailing off the ascenders, but it is a matter of preference whether this style or a simple, pen-made serif is used.

Compression of the letterforms lessens the width differentiation between characters: the capital and lower-case 'M' are proportionally much narrower than their Roman counterparts when compared to, for example, the letter 'P'.

There are two kinds of numerals which accompany the style: lining numerals and hanging numerals. The former line up with the capitals, whereas the latter vary. The '1', '2', and '0', are contained within the x-height; the '3', '4', '5', '7', and 9', enter the descender area to the value of two nib widths; the '6' and '8' are lettered to the height of the capitals.

Lining numerals

Hanging numerals

Ascenders: 3 nib widths	
x-height: 5 nib widths	
Descenders: 3 nib widths	

Broken Letters

This unique and engaging alphabet is constructed form the simplest vertical and slanted strokes made by a square-tipped pen held at an almost constant writing angle. It is an intriguing study of the most basic elements allowing recognition of the individual letterform: for example, 'c' is reduced to two slanted marks, and 's' to three parallel strokes. The complete elimination of curves and joining strokes means that almost every form is broken into separate components, yet the familiarity and sequence of the letter-forms allows the viewer to read the shapes correctly. However elaborate or elementary

an alphabet design, a basic condition of legibility rests in each letter retaining certain essential characteristics, and relating logically to the other forms.

Although the components of these letters are of the simplest form, they are easily recognizable used either singly, or in a group, and are modern in character.

Solid Squared Capitals

Although similar in form to the capitals in a previous sample, this alphabet has a solid construction and dense textural weight derived from clothing: the skeleton shapes of the letters with much heavier strokes varied in thickness but lacking any highly contrasting modulations of width. The clarity of the letter-forms in both examples suggests an equally keen appreciation of both calligraphic writing and typographic lettering. The patterning of straight lines and flattened curves is even and balanced. Individual letters are absolutely distinct in form and consistently proportioned, factors which make an important contribution to legibility.

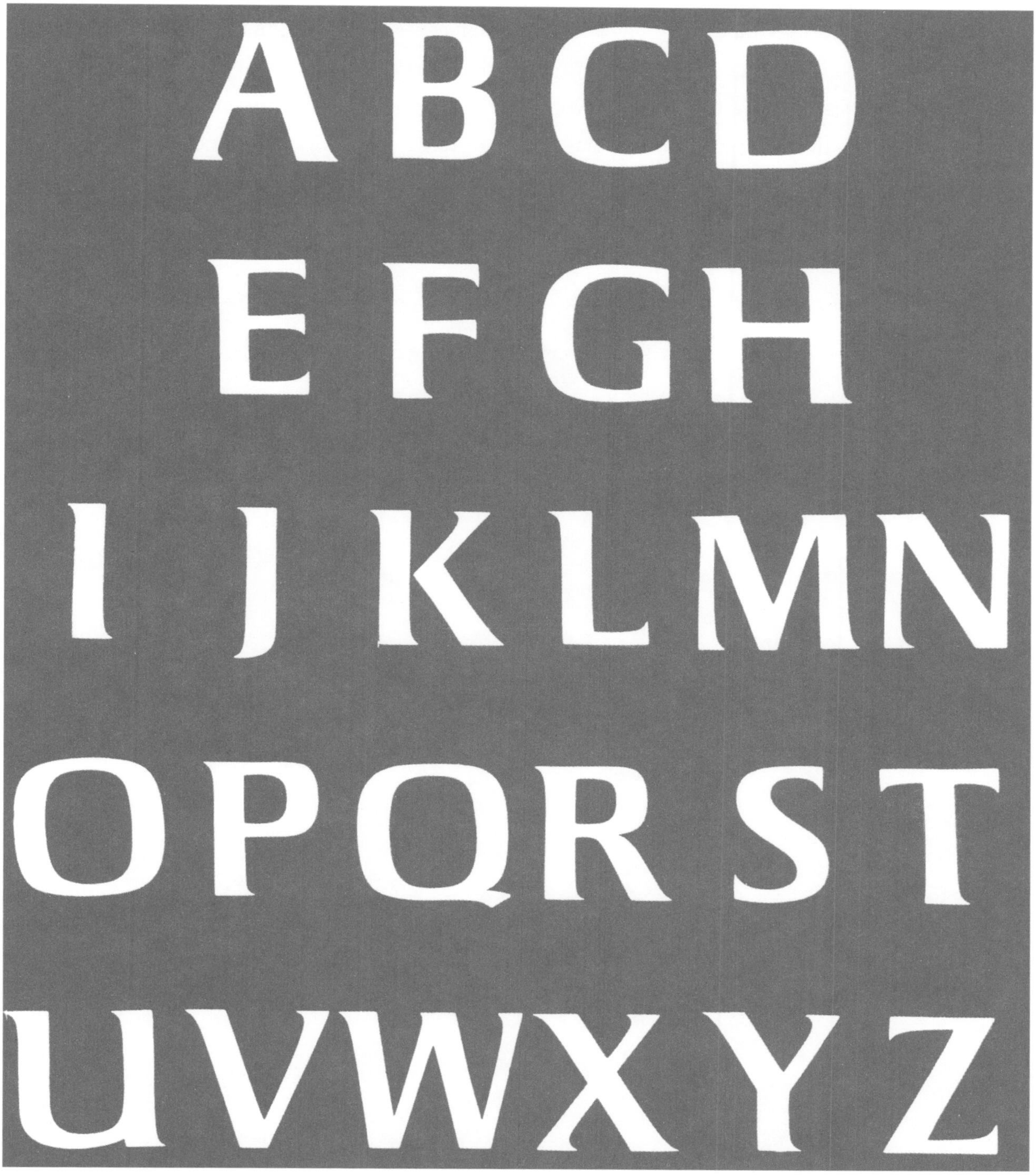

ABCD
EFGH
IJKLMN
OPQRST
UVWXYZ

Modulated Capitals

An extremely broad felt-tipped pen gives a natural exaggerated variation of strokes and a lively texture created by the contrast between solid black and partially broken marks. Felt-tipped pens specifically created for calligraphy offer great freedom and vivacity in the construction of the letters: the loops, angles and slanted strokes are direct and uninhibited. Twists of the pen at the end of the strokes,

as in the cross-strokes of 'E', 'F' and 'H', add to the ragged, pointed quality. Unlike the well-regulated construction of more traditional alphabet styles, these letters owe their shapes to the speed and looseness of the pen's movement, and any repeated rendering of these forms must accommodate the fact that the textural changes are of a more or less random nature.

Fine Italic

The delicate weight and texture of this italic sample derives not only from the finer pen line, but also from the more generous width and openness in the letters by comparison with the previous compressed, cursive example. The oblique angle of italic is very subtly expressed here, mainly visible in the tall, curving ascenders. The fineness of the line where the bowls and arches branch from the main stems contributes to the restrained elegance of the form. The flow of the lettering is emphasized by hairline hooked serifs leading into and out of the stems, and slanted strokes. The alphabet is a good illustration of how the writing tool imposes a distinctive style on the lettering, and by comparison with the heavier italics, shows the different moods given to similar basic structures by the density of the written texture.

Flourished Italic

A decorative italic alphabet by Spanish calligrapher Pedro Diaz Morante (b. 1565) shows the coming influence of Copperplate style, its controlled loops and arabesques anticipating the more excessive linear ornamentation that in later samples almost overwhelmed the written forms. Two alphabets are woven together here to create the overall design. The most readily legible consists of a broadened italic form still influenced by the thick/thin variation of the edged pen, though the natural pen stroke is modified, and the letter stems vary in width. This is framed and embellished by freely written alternative forms of the letters with flourishes flowing back and forth to create a curvilinear framework in which the italic letters are squarely presented. Diaz Morante was a highly influential writing master.

An interesting contrast between the simple, slanted Roman, and the flowing, near Copperplate capitals, both artfully intertwined in this design.

Decorative Humanistic Italic

In the lower case sample, this alphabet follows the features of a classic italic style, but it is in the capital alphabet that the particular characteristics of the designed form come together on their own. The crossed strokes and evenly looped flourishes create a delightful pattern quality, though the letterforms remain distinct and fully functional within this decorative embroidery of the basic shapes. A discreet undulation travels through the assembled forms due to the dropped and extended strokes varying the

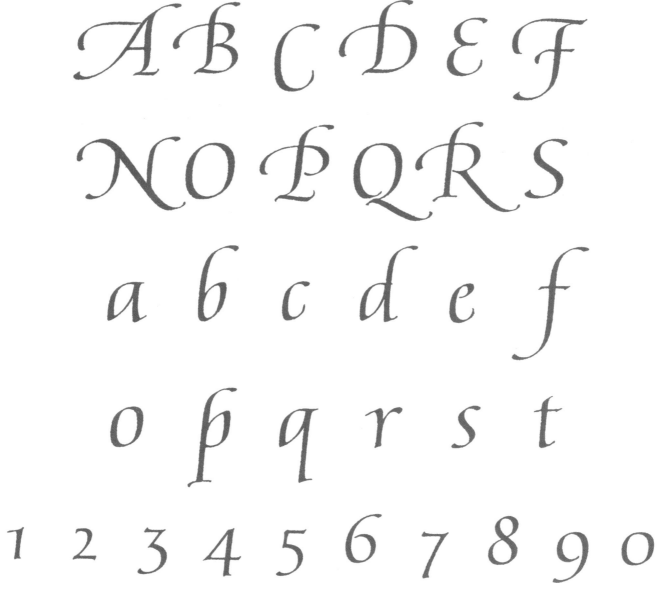

height and depth of the letters. The movement of the pen through the thick and thin modulations in stroke endows the basically lightweight forms with a subtle solidity, emphasized in the capitals because the rounded letters are broad and open. However, a sentence written in capitals might be difficult to read.

These capital and lower-case letters are based on a humanistic script of the sixteenth century. They have a delicate flow.

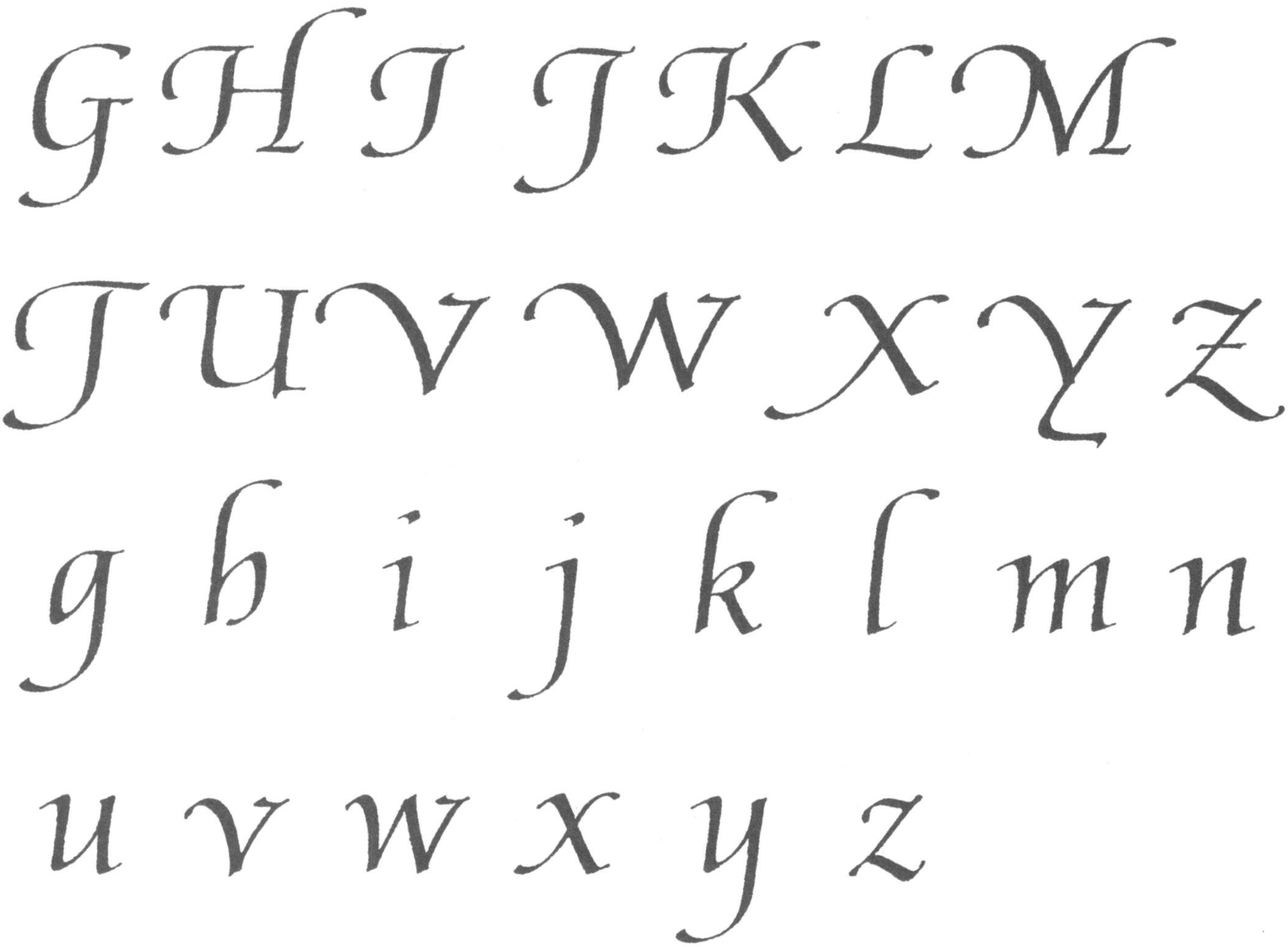

G H I J K L M

T U V W X Y Z

g h i j k l m n

u v w x y z

Modern Italic Alphabet

Based on sixteenth-century italic forms, such modern revisions make the most of the sharply branched and tightly compressed patterning of a cursive italic.

In this example, the sharpening of the letters suggests that edges and angles have been modified after the initial stroke to describe the particular texture of the finely slanted serifs and filled angles. This is apparent in the width variations in the bowls of 'd', 'g' and 'q', where the slight inner curve into the hairline is balanced by a sharp point pushing outward at the base.

The angle at which the pen is held is sharper, too, than in many examples of italic alphabet shown in this book.

Formal Italic

This is controlled and stately lettering, but not well adapted to a rapid or cursive writing method. Even between the different versions of the letters, it is the fluid control of the pen movement that supplies the consistency of texture, the elegance of the line variations, and the aptness of the terminals. The letters with upright, serifed stems have a more static quality than those with finely tipped curving ascenders. Unusually, this device is applied also to the alternative versions of the letter 'P', so that while one of the forms is conventional in style, the other is extended and flowing, equally balanced above and below the body height of the letter. The sharply angled oval in the bowls of the certain letters gives them an upward pull countering the relatively extended width.

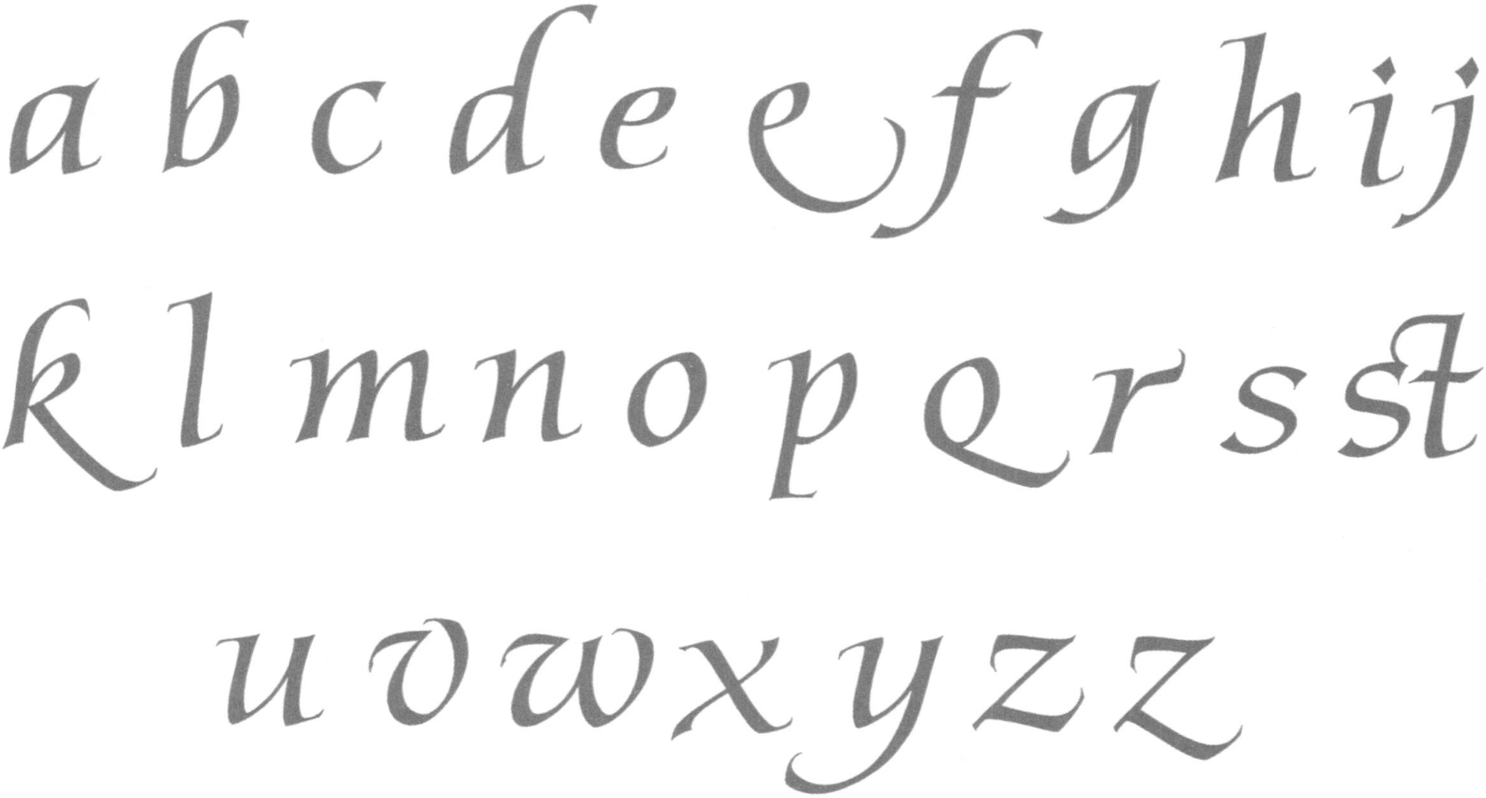

a b c d e e f g h i j

k l m n o p q r s s t

u v w x y z z

COPPERPLATES

In the sixteenth century, the quality of rolled copper sheeting supplied to engravers improved dramatically. Lettering engravers were finally able to work with their burins on a surface comparable to the paper or parchment used by scribes. Inspired by, or envious of the new found freedom expressed by the engravers, scribes abandoned their broad square-cut quills for flexible, pointed nibs. A fine cursive writing emerged; it could be rapidly written, dispensing with the need to lift the pen off the paper except for punctuation and word, and line breaks. The result was elegant lettering that flowed across the page.

A pointed flexible nib responds to the pressure placed on it by the writer. A major feature of Copperplate is the slight swelling of the downward strokes. This is acquired by applying a modicum of pressure to the pen as the stroke is made, thus forcing a little extra ink to flow through the now slightly separated point of the nib. Similarly, by releasing almost all the pressure on the upward stroke between letters, an extraordinarily fine line is achieved.

Other readily identifiable characteristics of this hand are the occasional looped ascenders and descenders and graceful, flowing forms written at a slant of 54° It is extremely awkward to write beautiful Copperplate without the correct equipment - either a pen with an elbow-angled nib, or an angled nib holder. The angle of the nib or holder provides the slant.

The improvement in engraving techniques coincided with increased levels of literacy that had developed after the advent of printing from movable type. People wanted to write and in response to this interest, scribes prepared instructional copybooks. These were printed from metal plates, incised by engravers who executed exquisite, fine lines that flowed and flourished, with an unlimited measure of decorative ornamentation.

Copperplate lends itself to ornamentation, particularly energetic flourishing. If you look at old manuscripts written in any of the numerous cursive scripts, you will find grand pieces of penmanship rendered almost illegible. Here are beautifully executed letters disappearing in a subterfuge of ornament.

Copperplate became associated with more than handwritten lettering and printing. The lettering engravers exercised their art on items made of, for example, precious metal. Other craftspeople followed suit. Glass engravers, clockmakers, and metalsmiths acquired the elegant hand for their own purposes.

1 *The letter shown here is being written with a fine straight nib. The letter begins with a hairline stroke, made with virtually no pressure on the nib so that it glides gracefully over the page. Gentle pressure is applied to the first vertical stroke, which finishes with the square end.*

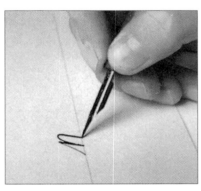

2 *The second vertical stroke is preceded by another fine hairline stroke. Observe where the hairline leaves the first vertical stroke. Notice also the shape of the white space formed by these two strokes.*

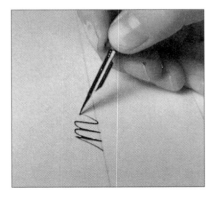

3 *Unlike the first two vertical strokes, which finished with a square end, the final stroke curves around into a hairline. This hairline is usually extended and becomes the first stroke of the next letter.*

Copperplate Alphabet

This elegant script is composed of four basic strokes. The first is the hairline which begins most of the letters. This is a further hairline which serves as a ligature to join the letters. There are some strokes which have square ends. The final stroke to consider begins and ends with a hairline, but swells in the middle as pressure is applied to force more ink through the nib.

The letters can be written with an elbow-angled holder or nib, or with practice, a fine pointed nib. The slant of the writing is 54°, giving fine and flowing lines. The looped or flourished ascenders and descenders are generally of a greater length than those which finish straight.

Copperplate Script

This rather weighty Copperplate form, although rolling and cursive in style, is derived from an attempt to subject script lettering to a geometric system of construction. The letters are remarkably even and regular in proportion. The very straight and clean-cut ascenders and descenders are offered as an appropriate contrast to the elegantly curving tails. The relatively emphatic thick/thin modulation of the strokes refers back to the characteristic texture of edged pen writing, but in this case it is artificially constructed by drawing with a pointed pen, outline and then filling the broader width of stems and curves, as may be seen in the samples of letter construction developed in a skeleton form within a carefully constructed grid format.

Pointed Pen Letters

The lightweight, flowing texture of pointed pen writing has a gracefulness seen at its best when the alphabet form is designed, like this sample, as a series of well-proportioned, unelaborated shapes. The loops and curls are restrained and naturally in harmony with the basic structure of each letter. The cursive nature of the script is demonstrated in the finely slanted joining strokes forming discreet

This alphabet combines round and pointed capitals with some alternative letters in both styles.

links between the letters. The relationship between the script, capitals and numerals are completely consistent and appropriate, including the alternative rounded and angular forms shown for the capital letters 'M', 'N', 'V' and 'W'.

Fine Gothic-Style Script

The fashion for copybooks in the eighteenth century encouraged the most versatile displays of calligraphic skill, and the technique of Copperplate engraving was not employed solely to reproduce the style of current pointed pen lettering. Whereas the Gothic-influenced script, which the original publication terms 'German text', refers to the earlier style of edged-pen letters, the tools of engraving require that a heavy black line be built up from several finely cut lines.

This sample shows a modification to the letterforms with regard to the influence of that technique. The lower-case letters are made light in texture and slightly flourished. The tails and ascenders, though complementary, do not extend naturally from the angular, pointed structures but seem to be an addition, based on contemporary fashion. The capitals are more heavily defined but decorated with finely looped ornamentation.

Round Text

This balance of texture ensures that the letters emerge as distinct and legible despite the elaboration. The round hand is, like the earlier forms of Italic writing, an elegant but extremely practical hand, well adapted to the natural movement of hand and pen. This cursive sample shows the linking of letters through the flowing motion of the pen along the writing line, facilitated by the slanting of the letters. The body height of the letters is equal to the length of the ascenders, and a subtle balance is created by the extended drop of the descenders looping below the baseline.

The forms are compressed but the rounded bowls and arches maintain the even texture of the script in the relationship between height and width of the letters. This evenness is also due to the consistency of the pen strokes, in which the minimal variation of pressure and density is fluidly, and restrainedly applied.

Square Text

Square text is the name given in the original copybook publication to this eighteenth-century calligraphy based on Gothic forms. It is an appropriate designation: although the letters are angularized by the pointed terminals and lozenge-shaped serifs borrowed from Blackletter styles, these are grafted onto an adaptation of rounded letters which gives the script a broad, squared quality and medium-weight texture identifiably of its own period, though influenced by the historical source. In the capital letters, the extended, looping hairlines enhance the lively character of the text. Certain authentic medieval letter-forms show this type of hairline embellishment, but in this case again, the manner of execution seems to owe more to contemporary fashion than to the origin of the device. But the overall structure of the capital letters, and the divided counters of 'C', 'G', 'O', 'Q', and 'T', have a convincing period flavour.

abbcddefoghhijkkllmnnoppqrsfstuvwxyz.

ABCDEFGHIJKLMMM
NNOPQRSTUVWXYYZ.

Round Hand

This round hand sample has all the marks of the standard form in its evenly spaced and weighted letters, deliberate proportions, and controlled execution. The purpose of copybooks was to distribute widely both the forms of letters considered of particular excellence and functional value, and styles of decorative lettering designed to demonstrate the writing master's skills, and tax the discipline of the pupil. Round hand was a ubiquitous style of the eighteenth century, used as a model script until the early twentieth century, and taught in schools as the standard of elegant writing. It is indisputably a formal, attractive hand, though recent fashion in calligraphy has tended to reject the finer Copperplate styles in favor of edge-pen letters derived from earlier sources.

Aa. Bb. Ct. Dd. Ee. Ff. Gg. Hh. Ii. Jij. kk. Ll. Mm. Nn. Oo
Pp. Qq. Rr. Sfs. Tt. Uu. Vv. Ww. Xx. Yy. Zz .

Aambuuudncewfuguuhiuijukuuluuonpuuqurfsmtuuvwxuuyzz
ABCDEFGHIJKLMNOPQRSTUVWXYZ.

Revised Humanistic Scripts

These two samples draw upon the characteristics of Renaissance hands to develop script letters of sharp angularity matched by more generous, flowing capitals. The first is an inventive, eclectic script; the pairing of capital and small letters suggests that it is developed within its own terms of reference rather than being strictly based on a known traditional style. The cursive script originally designated the "secretary" hand, which forms the second sample, is a very tightly constructed, logical and balanced form which, as the name suggests, was intended to be highly functional in day-to-day tasks requiring writing that was rapid but defined, consistent and legible.

The alphabets on this page were engraved by George Bickham, and show a variety of hands current in the 18th century, some still retaining Gothic influences. Sometimes the two styles were combined.

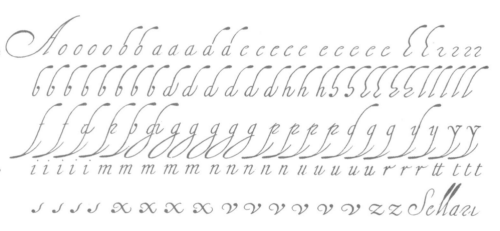

The curved tops of these single characters are reminiscent of the looped tops used by Cresci in the sixteenth century.

THIRTEENTH CENTURY BORDER

This example considers bordering which can have a big influence on the look of letterforms. Their variety is as diverse as the different styles of lettering and ranges from a simple colored line drawn down the margin or between the columns of text, to almost a whole page of the most brilliant and complicated miniature and decorative work, with space allowed for only a word or two. How far you go on this path is up to your artistic inclination and ability, the time that you have to devote to the project and probably the depth of your purse. The borders that I have used in this work are relatively simple, but also complicated enough to add great decorative effect to your work, and to give you great personal satisfaction when you have successfully completed them.

This example is from a thirteenth-century Book of Hours and includes a frame for a miniature picture. The original had the capital letter 'D', which has been included so that you can have some idea of the scale of such a letter, used in this way. You will see that there is very little room left for text and that this would have been confined to a few opening words or titles, and that the bulk would have appeared on the following pages.

The design is of the well-known ivy leaf pattern and the leaves can be colored green or any other color of your choosing, or they can be gilded. You can mix them up, or you can use a different color for the leaves on each of the branches.

YOU WILL NEED

- **Sharp 2H pencil**
- **Ruler**
- **T square/parallel motion**
- **Right-angled set square**
- **Project paper**
- **Tracing or greaseproof paper**
- **Gesso or PVA gilding medium**
- **Paper tube**
- **Gold leaf**
- **Gouache: gold and selected colors**
- **Brushes**
- **Burnisher**

In this project, only colors, red, blue and green have been used, producing a solid, and robust, effect. You will see that white lines have been applied to the leaves and to the frame on the right hand side of the design. By comparing the two sides, you can see what a difference this makes and how that side looks much lighter and more sophisticated than the left hand. Both treatments have their place.

The one that you use, depends on the effect that you wish to obtain.

Whether you paint a miniature in the frame, or use it to contain some significant text is up to you and the use to which the project will eventually be put.

It is worth remembering, that the original page was probably only 6in (150cm) high and would have required the utmost patience and diligence to complete.

1 Draw the framework with a ruler and set square onto a piece of tracing or greaseproof paper. It is worth drawing it up in ink when you are satisfied, as it can be used at a later date, either as it is, or modified, for some other project. Draw it in a size that suits you and then use a photocopier to either enlarge or reduce it to the size needed for your project. (Remember that it is always worth drawing things bigger, if possible, and then reducing them down on a photocopier. This makes them look much neater and tighter.) When you are satisfied, trace your guide-lines down onto your paper, marking the center and the diagonals with dotted lines. Clip the tracing to your project paper with paper clips, so that it does not slide about, and use a ruler to guide you, as you trace down. Once you have finished tracing down, do not use the ruler again. Do the rest of the work freehand. The little irregularities that will inevitably occur, despite your best efforts, help to give the project a natural spontaneity that is the mark of hand-done work.

2 Now within the guide-lines that you have traced onto your project paper, carefully draw up your scheme of decoration. You want to do this on a second piece of tracing paper, so that you can make any necessary corrections without messy erasures on your beautiful paper. If you do this, trace your finished design down onto your page. You should not need to draw over this, the traced outline should be sufficient.

3 Carefully stir up your PVA gilding medium. (If you roll it on the desk, you will mix it well without causing any air bubbles.) Paint all the areas you wish to have gold. One coat will be enough, but it does soak into the paper, and so if you wish the gold to appear slightly raised, you will need two coats. Each of these will take about thirty-five minutes to dry.

4 *Take your paper tube and huff a warm breath onto a section to be gilded. It is important to do this before you apply any gouache paint, or you will find that your hot breath will also soften the gum in the gouache paint and the gold will stick to that as well. While the PVA is moistened and sticky, take a sheet of gold leaf and carefully lay it over the spot. Take your burnisher and rub the leaf, especially round the edges, so that it sticks to the form and peels off the backing paper. You can see through this, and so can tell when the gold has stuck down. You may need to apply another coat if your cover is less than satisfactory. The gold will stick to itself, as well as any uncovered patches of the gilding medium. With a little practice you will be able to place your gold leaf down on the page so that you waste hardly any of it.*

Start at the top of the page and work your way down, so that you do not lean on any of the parts just gilded. When all is completed, take a piece of greaseproof paper, lay it on the work and burnish all the gold to raise a deep, lustrous shine. Finish off with a light burnishing directly onto the gold. Take particular care to work with the point of your burnisher round the edges of each form. From now on you make sure that you have a piece of scrap paper between your hand and the work, so that you do not cause any damage to your completed work.

5 *Take gold gouache and paint the four corners of the frame. When this is dry, you can burnish this to improve the shine, but the contrast between the paint and the gold is quite effective. You may find that you need two coats to obtain a satisfactory cover.*

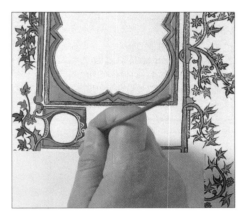

6 *Carefully paint the border and the capital 'D' with your choice of colors. I used two tones of blue. I mixed some ultramarine with some permanent white to make the pale blue and straight ultramarine to provide the darker tone.*

7 *With great care, do the outlining. The paint must be the right thickness. Too thin and it spreads and does not cover. Too thick and it blobs and will not spread and cover evenly. Usually, outlining is done with a mixture of black and burnt sienna, which makes a very dark brown. Too black and it looks severe. Too brown and it looks pale and anaemic. You could try a dark tone of each of the colors used. Green leaves outlined with dark green, and so on, reserving your black-brown outline for the gold areas. This is not as daunting as it may seem as you can do all the green bits, then all the red bits and so on.*

8 *You will need to decide how much you intend to highlight with white. This will depend on the effect that you seek and so some areas have been deliberately left unhighlighted so that you can make up your own mind. You will also see that the leaves have been highlighted in different ways, some more, some less. This, too, will help you to decide what effects please you best.*

Fifteenth Century W

This 'W' was copied from a fifteenth-century manuscript and was originally an 'M'. After tracing the letter, the tracing paper was then turned upside down and the decoration traced, adapting it as necessary. This kind of adaptation will help you enormously if you cannot find the exact letter or style of decoration needed.

The letter was painted using light and dark tones on all the colors, which adds greatly to the richness.

It is highlighted in white and outlined in a mixture of black and dark umber.

Notice that the bottom right-hand point of the gold square has been drawn outward a little to give it more style and take the plainness out of the straight line.

Fifteenth Century W

This impressive capital 'W' was developed from a fifteenth century capital 'M'. It was drawn free-hand from the example, the different elements being reversed as necessary. The muted colors give it a subdued dignity, which is extremely attractive.

2 *The green areas were painted first, as this seemed to be the predominant color: Mix up some yellow ochre and ultramarine. Carefully paint the green. Mix in a little white and paint the light tones.*

3 *Mix a little ultramarine with a little white, and dull it down with a little of the green mixture. Paint the blue elements. Add a little more white and paint the lighter parts.*

4 *Similarly paint the red with madder carmine and then mix in a little white to paint the lighter parts.*

5 *Paint the black with a 0000 brush. Take care to work neatly, using it to tidy up and delineate the green leaves and the gold elements in the center.*

6 *Take some of your green mix, add a very little black and use this to paint the inside of the letter.*

7 *Highlight with white lines and dots.*

8 *Enliven the dark green background color in the middle of the letter with gold dots. Notice that they are placed in threes.*

9 *Paint the rest of the gold areas.*

10 *Outline with a mix of black and burnt umber.*

1 *Take a careful tracing. Note that the black center is not symmetrical. You can leave it as it is or you can correct it in the tracing. The tail has a tendency to drift to the right and would look stronger if it were straighter. Correct this as you trace it.*

Rule a grid on your tracing paper to contain the stem and the shape of the capital. Also rule a cross through the middle of the letter, on your tracing paper. You will quickly see which parts you need to alter. As you trace it off, move the tracing paper about, so that the part you are tracing is correctly located in the grid that you have drawn. Thus, when you have finished the whole will be correctly located on your tracing paper and you will be able to trace it down onto your project paper with every part located in the right place.

Sixteenth Century Italian R

This massive capital 'R' comes from a sixteenth-century book of Italian music. It contains two miniatures: one at the top and the second under the arch of the leg. At first sight this is a daunting project, but take it calmly, step by step, and it will gradually organize itself.

YOU WILL NEED

- **Tracing paper**
- **Project paper**
- **2H pencil**
- **Gouache paints: ultramarine, red, brilliant yellow, green, permanent white, Prussian blue, gold, burnt umber, black**
- **Brushes**

1 *Make a tracing of the main elements of the design and transfer it to your project page using a very sharp pencil.*

2 *Block in the colors one by one: first the blue, then the red and then the green, mixing each color with a little white.*

3 *Paint the darker tones, taking each color in turn. (Prussian blue made the very dark tone).*

4 *Blend a little more white with each color and paint the lighter tones. Where necessary, use a wet brush to blend the tones together.*

5 *Highlight the green areas with brilliant yellow.*

6 *Highlight the blue and red areas with white.*

7 *Paint the small gold areas.*

8 *Highlight the top of the ribbon with white and use a little burnt umber to shade the underside.*

9 *Outline the design with a mixture of black and burnt umber.*

Fifteenth Century P

This project introduces the idea of writing the entire first word of the text within the capital, a concept that could have all kinds of applications. This example is based on a fifteenth-century model.

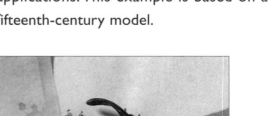

1 *Make a tracing of the design and transfer it to your project paper. (If you want to modify the design, alter the tracing first.)*

2 *Mix the gesso with a little yellow ochre so that you can see it and apply it to the strapwork of the capital 'P', the doves on the finials, and the letters that make up the word. You may want to lay on a second coat to raise it a little more.*

3 *When the gesso is dry, paint a thin coat of PVA gilding medium over it and leave it to dry.*

4 *Blow on the gilding medium through the paper tube and then apply the gold leaf using your burnisher. Start in the corner furthest from you and do a small bit at a time, making sure that you cover the medium well as you proceed.*

5 *Paint the blue areas using neat ultramarine.*

6 *Paint the red areas using neat red.*

8 *Paint the gold area in the center of the letter.*

7 *Paint the green areas with a mixture of brilliant yellow, ultramarine and white.*

9   *Outline the design in a mixture of black and burnt umber.*

10   *Outline the red and blue areas in white.*

11   *Apply a powdering of white dots to the red areas.*

12   *Highlight the green leaves in white and paint white dots along the green stems. Paint gold dots onto the blue areas.*

ADVANCED CALLIGRAPHY

Eus in adiutoriu meu intende Dne ad adiuuandu me festina Gloria
an Dum esset rex.

Dixit dns dno meo: sede a dextris meis Donec ponam inimicos tuos: scabellu pedu tuoz Virgam virtutis tue emittet dns ex syon: dnare i medio inimicoru tuoru Tecu pricipiu in die virtutis tue in splendoribz sanctoz ex vtero ante luciferu genui te Iuraui dns & non penitebit eu: tu es sacerdos ieternu secudu ordinem melchisedech Dns a dextris tuis: confregit in die ire sue reges Iudicabit in nationibus iplebit ruinas: conquassabit capita in terra multoz De torrente i via bibit: propterea exaltabit caput Glia an Dum esset rex in accubitu suo nardus mea dedit odore suauitatis
Ana. Leua eius. Psalmus
Audate pueri dnz: laudate

ADVANCED TECHNIQUES

DECIDING ON A TEXT AREA

There are traditional margin proportions which have been used for many years in the laying out of single sheets and double-page spreads. The unit values of head, foredge, foot and inner (or spine) margins were based on proportions of the quarto and octavo folds of given sheet sizes.

In the UK, a full-size sheet of any size is called a Broadside; a Broadside folded in half is called a Folio; a Folio folded in half, making four sheets, is called Quarto and a Quarto folded in half, making eight leaves, is called an Octavo. Sheets of approximately the same sizes are available internationally.

When deciding on the size of sheet to use for a specific project and the layout and margins to be used, the amount of text and the nature of the work must be taken into account. This section is devoted to continuous text and the margin proportions, and width of measure which relate to this particular aspect of layout.

The proportions given here will be adequate for most works and are given as a point from which to start laying out text. They can be changed to suit a particular requirement, but remember, when changing the unit values, to allow more space at the foot so that the column of text does not look as if it is slipping off the sheet area.

Take a sheet 8¼in (210mm) by 5⅞in (149mm), known as A5, taken from the paper size A system. A5 is used for leaflets and brochures. The A system is unique, as the sheet proportion remains in the same ratio even when folded in half or doubled up in size.

To decide on a text area, the width of the A5 sheet, 5⅞in (149mm), must be divided

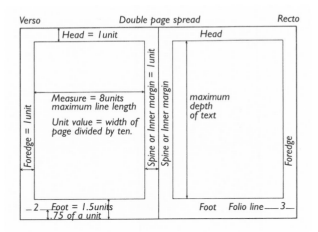

by 10 to obtain a unit width, that is 0.525 in (14.9mm. Clearly, in this example it is easier to use the metric measure.)Round this to the nearest whole millimetre to 15mm. This will be the basic unit and it will be used to create the margins, and text area of the sheet. One unit should be left at the head of the sheet, one unit for both the foredge and the spine and 1 V2 units at the foot. This leaves a text measure of 119mm in width and 172mm in depth.

The size of text can be dependent on the amount of copy to be contained within the format, but emphasis here will be put on continuous text, as in a manuscript or booklet of several pages. The golden rule in continuous text lettering is that the optimum in readability is a line-length of ten words. In the English language this is equivalent to 60 characters, as the average word is six characters long, including word spaces. Therefore the line length can be between eight and twelve words, or 48 and 72 characters. Given this information a nib size can be chosen to give approximately 60 characters to the line in the letter style decided upon. A typewritten manuscript can be easily fitted by counting the characters in one line, multiplying this by the number of lines and dividing the result by the number of characters contained within one line of the layout.

Roman Serif has been used for the example given here and various nib sizes were tested out - B2, Italic broad, Italic medium, and Italic fine - before Italic fine was finally settled upon. Some interlinear space must be allowed to ensure that the ascenders and descenders do not clash. So, letter a few lines with half a nib width, and a nib width space before deciding on the latter. The depth of text will be 25 lines per page. The text in this example has been ranged left. This in itself produces an inherent

problem in that the right-hand margin will appear larger than the left, because of the ragged optical white space being produced. When producing the finished manuscript a minor adjustment for this will be made, by leaving more white space in the left-

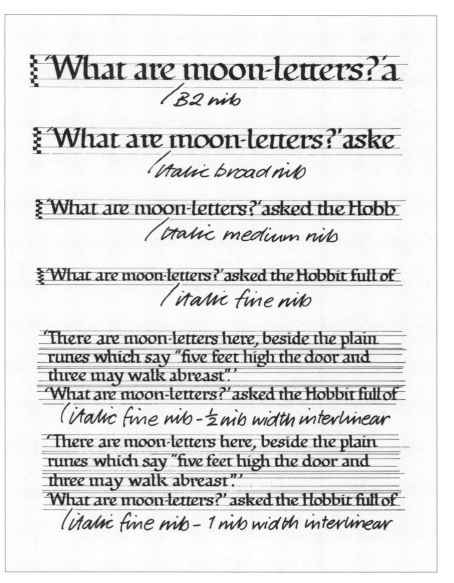

Testing nib sizes for line length.

USING ROUGH SKETCHES AND THUMBNAILS

If the work is for an invitation card, consider its distribution. If it is to be posted, then there will be a limitation on convenient size. Unless you make the envelope yourself, you will need to know the availability of envelopes and matching paper or card. Check with a stationer which envelopes are available in small quantities to avoid having to use the same envelope and paper again, and again. The card used here measures $4^{1}/_{4}$ in (105mm) by $5^{7}/_{8}$ in (149mm) (or A6), which fits into a C6 envelope.

Is the invitation formal or informal? This will determine the type of layout chosen. Centered layouts are generally used for formal occasions but a ranged-left layout can be equally elegant. The use of a ranged-right layout in this instance would be unsuitable, because the work entailed in producing such a layout is too great for lettering a large number of cards. A justified layout can also be disregarded as this is used only for continuous text. An asymmetrical layout could be used for an informal card, if desired. For this project, the copy has been treated in an informal manner using a ranged-left layout.

Before a rough layout can be made, decide which elements should be prominent. The words underlined here are those which will have the most impact for this design, with remaining copy being coded '1', '2' and '3' in order

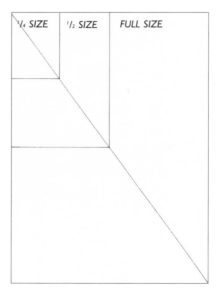

Deciding on the priorities to be given to the lines of text (above).

Preparing scaled-down boxes (below).

*Some initial small roughs
to decide on layout.*

of importance.

Large-sized lettering, which makes up display headings, attracts the attention of the reader. Secondary information should be smaller than the display, but in a size that can be read easily. Subsidiary details can be lettered smaller. The aim of the calligrapher is not only to produce a tasteful letterform, but also to lead the reader through the information in a sequence that relates to the

order of importance of the text.

In the same copy, the words 'Birthday Party' have been underlined, as they are the key words. The person's name has been given code '1', the invitation text, time, and place have code '2' and finally 'RSVP' receives code '3', as it is the least important.

Roughing Out

The next step is to rough out some basic

ideas in pencil before using pen and ink. This initial work is done on layout paper at a size scaled down from the finished invitation. In this instance half the size is adequate to become familiar with the words, and to create an interesting layout by committing any initial thoughts to paper. Rough layouts should be both landscape and portrait formats to discover which shape accepts the text more readily, and uses the area to its best advantage.

Begin by drawing some vertical and horizontal boxes in pencil, scaled down to represent the card. To achieve this, draw the

card on a piece of layout paper and divide the rectangular box diagonally from the top left-hand corner to the bottom right-hand corner. Then divide the top line of the box into two; on my card this measures $2\frac{1}{8}$in (52.5mm) to the center line. Draw a vertical line down from this center point to where the vertical line meets the diagonal. This is the depth of the card at half-scale. Then draw a horizontal line from the diagonal to the left-hand vertical. The area just defined is a half-size of the original card area. Naturally at a half-size, the measurements could just be divided in half

1 *Drawing up the card area.*

2 *Lettering 'Birthday Party' using guidelines.*

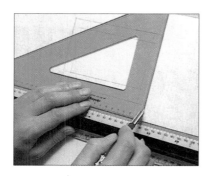

3 *The words being checked against the text area for line length.*

4 *Closing up the letter spacing.*

5 *Checking that the words fit the text area.*

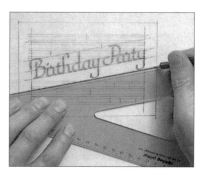

6 *Positioning 'Birthday Party' and marking out guidelines.*

and a rectangle drawn, but on a larger format, where it may be necessary to work on roughs a sixth or an eighth of the original size, this method saves time and calculations. It is also useful when scaling illustrations or drawings up or down.

This is discussed in more detail in the illustrations.

Begin by using the margins discussed in 'Deciding on a text area', that is, one unit at the head and side margins and 1 1/2 units at the foot. However, it is important to remember that for the roughs these margins must be half-size to keep the same proportion. It may be advisable to reduce the foot margin as the format is quite small and, provided there is more space at the foot than at the head, this is quite in order. The text should be placed optically in the depth of the card. Then, using an HB pencil sharpened to a chisel edge, begin to describe the text on the rough layouts (also known as thumbnails owing to their small size.)

From the rough layouts the landscape format works the best with 'Birthday Party' lettered diagonally across the card. The angle has been fixed at the point at which the italicized letters coincide with the vertical

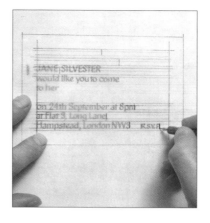

7 *Using a second sheet of tracing paper over the lettered text to mark off line lengths.*

8 *Beginning to letter the text.*

edges of the text area. This gives stability to the layout, and a reference point for the eye.

Working Up the Design

The rough now requires 'working up'. This is a term which refers to lettering out sample lines which one hopes will fit the working layout. The rough needs to work at actual size before the finished card can be lettered. From the small rough, an intelligent guess can be made as to the nib sizes to use by multiplying the stroke width by two, remembering the roughs were half-size. Here a B4 nib has been used for the display lettering, and an Italic medium for the main text.

The layout is divided into three main parts, starting with the person's name and the words of the invitation itself, then the event, and finally the venue. The main display line holds the text together and determines how large the main copy can be.

It is first necessary to draw up the card area and borders on a sheet of layout paper, but full-size at this time. Start by lettering the display heading in an informal script with the B4 on a separate piece of layout paper, having first marked out the guidelines by stepping off nib-widths, then drawing in the lines with a sharp 2H pencil. Once this has been lettered it should be measured against the layout, to check that the line length is correct. If it is overrunning the

The finished working layout.

measure, an adjustment to letter, and word spacing may avoid changing to a smaller nib.

Once the heading fits satisfactorily, the main text is then tackled. Step off the nib widths and draw in the guidelines. Allow a half nib-width interlinear space in the event of descenders and ascenders clashing, and also leave space between the first three lines and the second three lines. After lettering the text, compare it to the layout and mark off the guidelines from the top margin for the first batch of text, and from the foot margin for the second. A vertical pencil mark at the end of each line will help to gauge if lines and letters clash when the Italic line is checked against the layout.

Position the heading between the two sections of text. If it is found that there is insufficient room, use some of the extra space from the foot margin by lowering the second batch of copy. Once the position of the Italic has been established, the guidelines should be transferred to the layout sheet.

A working layout now exists, although admittedly it consists of guidelines only. It is prudent to letter in the text by tracing over the existing lines of copy before turning to the production of the finished card. There may still be some modifications to make; after all the preliminary work it is satisfying to see the completed working layout.

On viewing the finished layout, you may decide to range the 'RSVP' to the right so

1   *Taking measurements from the working layout.*

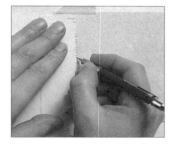

2   *Transferring guidelines to the workpiece using a master gauge.*

3   *Drawing guidelines on to the workpiece.*

4   *Testing various inks for color compatibility.*

5   *Lettering out the text using a guard sheet to keep the work surface clean.*

that it aligns with the 'y' in 'party'. This could be visually more pleasing.

Transferring the Design

The designed layout is then ready to be transferred to the chosen card, which must be slightly larger than the finished size, with a minimum of ½ in (12mm) selvedge all round, to allow for taping the card to the drawing board. It will be trimmed off when the work is completed. The card size, margin lines and guidelines should be drawn using an HB or H pencil, being careful not to gauge tramlines into the surface—a light line is all that is required. First draw the format area, then after stepping off the margins and guidelines on a strip of cartridge paper, transfer them to the card. The diagonal lines will have to be marked from both left- and right-hand margins.

Before beginning to letter, it is necessary to consider the color in which the text will be written—black is hardly party-like. Here, a peach-colored card has been chosen, with red ink for the words 'Birthday Party' and blue ink for the remaining text. A small piece of card was put to one side for trial lettering and color checking. It is always useful to have an extra piece of the chosen material, because the action of the pen, and ink may differ from surface to surface.

Position the card on the writing line, that is, the lettering position at which you feel

The main text completed.

comfortable on the board. Tape it into position and cover with a guard sheet, leaving only the first line visible. Taking the working layout, make a fold just above the x-line, and position it so that the first line is just below the descender line of the first guidelines on the card. Letter the line and repeat the

procedure until all the lines have worked.

It may help to reposition the work after lettering the first three lines. For a small piece of work, where only a small deviation from the writing line is required, you may find it easier to move the guard downwards. However, when lettering a deep column of text it is better to leave the guard in the writing position, and move the work piece, which need not be taped to the drawing-board surface.

1   *Lettering in 'Birthday Party'.*

2   *Erasing the guidelines once the ink has thoroughly dried.*

3   *Trimming the card to size, with a blade, on the waste side of the ruler.*

To letter the Italic line, the card should be turned until the text is horizontal to the writing line. The finished card should be put to one side to give the ink time to dry before removing the guidelines. This is done with a

THE FINISHED WORKING LAYOUT

FLOWERS

Flowers and foliage are the most commonly used decorative subjects in humanity's attempts to render the utilitarian, decorative. Their diverse forms have been depicted both realistically and in formal stylisation.

When you consider the amazing abundance and variety of flowers, as well as their beauty, color and construction, it is small wonder that they have been used in this way. The amazing variety of leaf shapes, too, in their cool shades of green, have such elegance and symmetry that it is not surprising that they represent some of the oldest decorative forms known.

Flowers and foliage are thus a very common element in the decoration of capital letters and page borders. In earlier works it was common to find them represented in stylized form, but by the end of the fourteenth century they were being rendered with greater realism. By the sixteenth century botanical illustrations were appearing, complete with dew drops and realistically drawn fruits, berries and insects.

Choice of Flowers

What influenced earlier artists in their choice of flowers is not known, but there are many possibilities. The most obvious is simple preference. Another is symbolism: it may be that the flower was a badge of the household or even featured on the heraldic achievement of the recipient. It could also have been the emblem of a patron saint or have had some other personal meaning.

The Meanings of Flowers

EMOTIONS

- Agrimony—thankfulness.
- Aloe—grief.
- Anemone—forsaken.
- Balm—sympathy.
- Basil—hatred.
- Bird's foot trefoil - revenge.
- Carnation, pink – a woman's love.
- Carnation, striped – refusal.
- Carnation, white – disdain.
- Campanula—gratitude.
- Chrysanthemum, red – I love.

CARNATION

- • Chrysanthemum, yellow
  – slighted love.
  - • Elderflower—compassion.
- • Forget-me-not—true love.
- • Gorse—love in all seasons.
- • Lavender—mistrust.
- • Lime blossom
  – conjugal love.
- • Myrtle—wedded love.
- • Orange blossom
  – marital love.
- • Lobelia—malevolence.
- • Love lies bleeding
  – hopelessness.
- • Marigold—pain and grief.
- • Mint—suspicion.
- • Pear blossom—lasting friendship.
- • Periwinkle—remembrance
  and lasting happiness.
- • Moss rose—confession of love.
- • Rose, red—love.
- • Rose, yellow—jealousy.
- • Rosemary—remembrance.
- • Rue—regret.
- • Snowdrop—hope.
- • Tulip, red—declaration of love.
- • Tulip, yellow—hopeless love.

Over the centuries individual flowers have come to symbolize specific meanings. To the medieval mind the message conveyed by the flower would have been as real as a written one and, to the illiterate, more intelligible. But note that even if we think we can discern a message symbolized by the floral decoration of a manuscript we may be making an enormous assumption in believing that this

PIETY

- • Acacia—immortality of the soul.
- • Almond—divine approval, favour and also hope. (The Virgin Mary is sometimes shown with an almond.)
- • Bull rush—hope, by the faith of salvation.
- • Carnation, red—pure love. (Ancient varieties had long yellow stamens which were said to look like nails, so red carnations with these stamens were used to represent the passion and crucifixion of Christ.)
- • Christmas rose—the nativity.
- • Clover leaf or trefoil—the Trinity. (St. Patrick is said to have used the shamrock's trifoliate leaf to explain the doctrine of the Trinity in the fifth century.)
- • Columbine—the Holy Spirit. (The flower looks like a group of doves drinking at a fountain, and its name is derived from columba, the Latin for dove. It also represents God's seven great gifts and the works of the Holy Spirit.) Conversely, the columbine also represents folly and anxiety.
- • Cowslip—divine beauty.
- • Dandelion—the passion of Christ (because the leaf resembles a thorn).
- • Glastonbury thorn—the nativity when shown as a single rose with bud and leaves. (Joseph of Aramathea was said to have made a visit to England and to have stuck his staff into the ground at Glastonbury. This apparently took root and grew into a wild rose bush.)

FORGET-ME-NOT

STYLIZED ROSE

TREFOIL

- Grapes—an emblem of Christ, who said: 'I am the true vine. My father is the vine dresser'. Grapes shown with wheat symbolize the Eucharist, the body and blood of Christ.
  - Holly—the passion of Christ. (The prickly leaves are reminiscent of the crown of thorns, and the red berries represent Christ's blood.)
- Iris (the sword lily) – sorrow and suffering. (Particularly associated with the Virgin Mary. When Joseph and Mary took the infant Jesus to be presented in the temple, Simeon took the child in his arms and said 'now your servant can depart in peace, for my eyes have seen the salvation that is promised'. He turned to Mary and said 'a sword will pierce your soul, too'. The sufferings of Mary were said to be as swords that pierced her soul.)
- Lily—purity, the Virgin Mary. (The angel Gabriel is depicted handing a lily to Mary in paintings of the annunciation.)
- Lily, Madonna—Easter and purity.
- Narcissus—triumph of divine love.
- Palm spiritual victory. (Often shown in association with martyrs.)
- Pomegranate—the Church in unity; fertility. (Also the heraldic emblem of the Church of Granada.)
  - Rose, red—emblem of the sorrowful mysteries of the Rosary.
  - Rose, yellow—Emblem of the glorious mysteries of the Rosary.
  - Rose, white—emblem of the joyful mysteries of the Rosary.
  - Strawberry—the fruitfulness of God's spirit.

BROOM

PERSONAL QUALITIES

- Alyssum—worth beyond beauty.
- Azalea—temperance.
- Bachelor's button—celibacy.
- Bee orchid—industry.
- Bluebell—constancy.
- Broom—neatness, humility. (A sprig of broom was also the badge of the Plantagenet dynasty of English kinds.)
- Canterbury bell—constancy.
  - Carnation, cover—dignity.
  - Cherry—good works.
  - Daisy—innocence.
  - Dock—patience.
  - Fennel – praiseworthy strength.
- Fuchsia, scarlet—taste and gracefulness.
  - Geranium, red—comforting.
- Hyacinth, blue—constancy.
- Jasmine, white—amiability.
- Iris, rainbow colored—the bearer of good tidings.
- Ivy—eternal life (because it is evergreen.) Fidelity (because of the way it clings) and also lasting friendship.
- Laurel—victory and triumph.
- Larkspur, pink—fickleness.
- Lemon blossom—fidelity in love.
- Lilac, white—purity, modesty.
- Lily of the valley – humility, happiness.
  - Marshmallow—mildness.
  - Mullein—good nature.
  - Oak—faith and endurance.
  - Olive branch—peace.
- Peach—unequalled.

LAUREL

GRAPES

POPPY HEAD

OLIVE BRANCH

- Pink, variegated—refusal.
- Poppy—consolation. Head showing all its seeds: fertility in our times, remembrance.
- Rose, full open with two buds—secrecy.
- Rose, red and white together—together in unity.
- Sage—long life and esteem; wisdom.
- Salvia, red—energy.
- Speedwell—feminine fidelity.
- Star of Bethlehem—purity.
- Strawberry—righteousness.
- Sweet William—gallantry.
- Thistle—earthly sorrow and sin.
- Valerian, pink—unity.
- Veronica—fidelity.
- Violet—faithfulness, innocence; modesty.
- Wallflower—fidelity in misfortune.
- Waterlily—purity of heart.
- Wheat, a sheaf—riches, thanksgiving.
- Wheat, a single straw—agreement broken, quarrel. Also bountifulness.

DIRECT MESSAGES

- Burr – ' you weary me'.
- Burdock 'touch me not'.
- Pansy – 'I think of you always'.
- Pansy, blue and brown – 'think of me'.
- Salvia, blue – 'you are wise'.
- Tansy – 'I am your enemy'.

PERSONAL AND NATIONAL EMBLEMS

- Iris (sword lily), yellow—the emblem of St Denis, the patron saint of France and, as the heraldic fleur-de-lys, the French national emblem.

HERALDIC FLOWERS

I   Fleur-de-lys
II   Red rose
III   White rose
IV   Tudor Rose
V   Lilies
VI   Quatre Foil
VII   Trefoils
VIII   Conquefoil
IX   Pomegranate

INANIMATE OBJECTS

- Hawthorn—bread and cheese (staple foods).

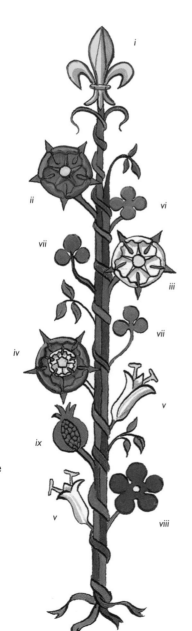

was intended. However, it is worth noting some of the better-known flowers, and their symbolic meanings for future use when planning your own projects.

USING A CENTERED LAYOUT

The centered layout has an air of authority; it makes the work look official and precise. In order to illustrate the processes involved in producing such a layout, the subject chosen here is invariably displayed in a symmetrical format—the certificate.

Calligraphers are often asked to produce certificates for various organisations. Such requests can be of a one-off nature—a long-service certificate for example—or more commonly a series, when the awards for one major event are divided into sections and then sub-divided into first, second, and third placings, etc. This type of certificate can be extremely complicated to lay out: because of the many copy changes, it can be difficult to obtain an overall style which is echoed in each certificate. The copy is made up from both static and variable information.

Again, ask that all important question: what is the function of the piece of work? It is, in this example, as an accolade for achievement, for winning first place in a wine-tasting competition, and the certificate will probably be framed and displayed on a living room wall.

The size of the certificate is 9$\frac{1}{2}$in (240mm) by 7$\frac{1}{8}$in (183mm) and the text area should allow generous margins all round it.

For this example, allow 1$\frac{1}{2}$ units for the head and sides with 2 units at the foot. This gives 1$\frac{1}{16}$in (27mm) and 1$\frac{1}{17}$in (36mm) respectively (one unit being based on one tenth of the width), with a text area of 6$\frac{7}{8}$in (176mm) deep and a measure width of 5$\frac{1}{8}$in (129mm).

Deciding on the priorities to be given to the lines of text (left). An initial thumbnail rough is produced to get a feel of the line length and copy (below).

Planning the Layout

The copy must then be analysed, coded '1', '2', '3' and so on in order of importance with any line breaks marked. The various code numbers will relate to different-sized nibs. Some pencil roughs based on the line breaks and order of importance are then sketched out. As with the invitation card, the roughs will be at either half- or third-size, just to get the feel of the words and line lengths. They need to be fairly accurate as the lettering will be used to help decide on the nib sizes required.

In a series of certificates, it is necessary to use the largest amount of copy for each of the changeable areas to ensure that they will all fit into the same format. For instance, one of the other sections is just 'Aperitif Section'. It would be pointless producing a layout which allows for this one-line heading; 'The Medium Red Table Wine Section' could not fit within the same area. Likewise, the longest name, Dorothy Lawrence, must be selected and the longest placing, which is 'second'.

Although the original copy supplied may have been typed out in a mixture of capitalized words and words in upper and lower case, as it was in this examples, it is the function of the calligrapher to decide upon the visual balance. Those words that should be in capitals have been underlined and superfluous words have been dropped.

From roughs it is necessary to decide which one will form the basis of the working layout. The lettered stroke widths for each size need scaling up to full size and allocating accordingly. When using a fountain-type pen, it helps to have enough barrels to eliminate the changing of the nib.

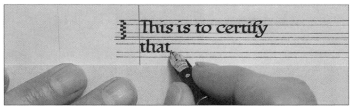

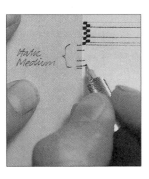

A decision must be made as to which nib size to use (top).

Lettering (above) and marking out the first two lines of lettering (right).

The Working Layout

The working layout should initially be ranged left so that you can see if the nib sizes chosen will fit the measure. Draw up the text area, $6^{7}/_{8}$in (176mm) by $5^{1}/_{8}$in (129mm), on a layout sheet. Take the tightest line of the chosen rough as a starting point. Some lines will fall short of the measure and are of little concern from a fitting point. Here, the longest line is 'Tasting Competition' and, as the test line, it must be lettered first.

On the same layout sheet as the text area, but above it, the measure requires marking, together with the guidelines for the Italic broad nib. The test line must be lettered to check on the width it will make. It appears just to fit, but it will be safer to drop a nib

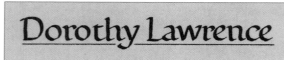

Above: deciding on a space value.

Below: underscoring using the edge of the nib against an inverted rule.

size for the whole of the section from 'The Old Harlow' to '1987'. The layout could be overpowered by this medium if it is left in its present size, but it would be best to leave 'THE MEDIUM RED TABLE WINE SECTION' in the Italic broad.

It is then possible to commence with the working layout. At this point, the depth that the text will have is unknown; so, by returning to the rough, it can be seen that it is unlikely to overrun, provided the space allocated is adhered to. Start by lettering the first two lines, allowing a nib-width of interlinear space. As the layout progresses, you will be shown how to arrive at line spaces between sections of text. Note down the size of the nib for each line of text as a reminder when lettering the finished certificate.

On completing the first two lines, a decision has to be made as to how much space to leave between the base line of 'that' and the cap line of the name. All three lines are related phrases and, as such, should be treated similarly with interlinear space but

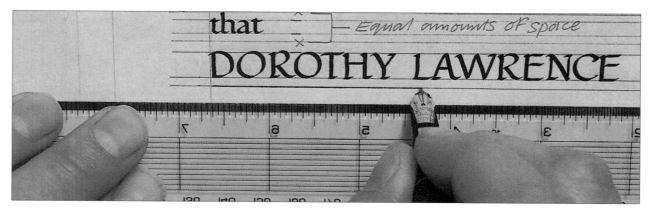

as 'Dorothy Lawrence' is in a larger letter-form and in capitals, the space must be optically changed to compensate for the extra area that capital letters occupy. It should be at least equivalent to the space between the base line of 'This is to certify' and the x-line of 'that'.

Once lettered, the name requires underscoring with a line. It may be that the name will be filled in after the certificates are lettered, in which case don't limit the length of line to the extent of name, and settle for the line being contained by the measure. As to the position of the line, there is nothing worse than underscored words which have a line so far beneath them as not to belong to the word. Here, the rule (line) is positioned two nib widths below the

base line. What if the name were in upper and lower case? No problem - split the rule either side of the descender and place it closer to the base line.

Between the rule and 'has been awarded', repeat the unit of space used before, although this may need changing slightly because there are four ascending letters in the line. The spacing of the lines throughout the remaining copy will be based

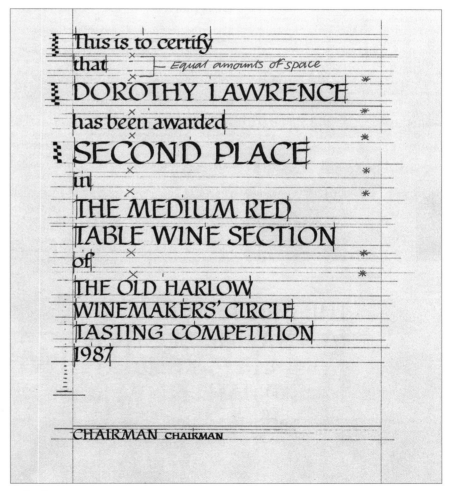

The finished working layout shows that extra space will be added where marked with an asterisk. The pencil lines at both ends of each line of text indicate the optical length necessary when centring the text.

on this unit of space. Where there is more than one line of capitals, insert one nib width of interlinear space, using the nib being employed to letter those particular lines. Once the whole copy has been lettered and a depth arrived at, further alterations can be made, if necessary.

Having reached the signature line, you may prefer to write the word in small capitals as opposed to the Italic fine capitals. They are drawn with the same nib but the heights limited to the x-line. Small capitals can often be seen following a person's name when Honours or Degree letters are present.

The space that is left between '1987' and the rule for the signature can be halved, and ample space will still be left for the signature. Take half of the present space and divide it by eight with one-eighth of the space being inserted as extra interlinear space in the seven asterisk positions marked.

Centring by the folding and creasing method (right).

Marking the center crease (far right).

Finding the center by measuring with a ruler (below).

Centering

The working layout is almost complete. In order to center the lines on the finished certificate, it is necessary to ascertain the center of each line of lettering, or to be more precise, the optical center. The end of each line should be marked as if the work were to be ranged left and right, that is, the part of the first and last letter of each line which would rest on the margin line to give vertical alignment. Show these lines in pencil on the working layout.

Once the lines are marked, the length can either be measured and then halved and marked in pencil or the lines of the layout can be cut up, and each line held up to the light, loosely folded until both ends of the line

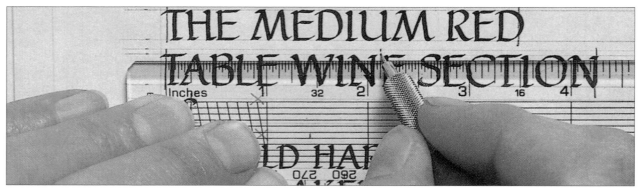

Transferring the guidelines to the finished surface.

and a width gauge showing the side margins, measure and center line (C/L) and any other items that are felt necessary. Each time a certificate requires marking out, the process is simplified considerably by using gauges. Naturally, the system can be used for any type of work which needs the same information to be transferred repeatedly to a finished workpiece. The gauges are taped on to the drawing board in a position above and to the left of the workpiece.

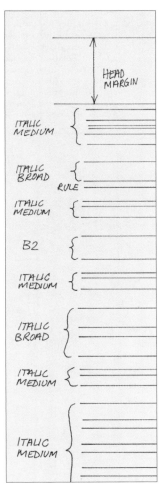

A portion of the depth guage used.

All the lines are transferred to the finished working surface in H or HB pencil. The sheet to be lettered must have a paper guard to prevent it from getting dirty.

The Final Stage

Before commencing final lettering, consider the question of color. Here a sandy-colored paper with black and red lettering has been chosen after

meet, then pinched in the center to give a firm crease. This method is better employed where one-off pieces of work are concerned. For repeated lettering, such as certificates, it is best to keep the original layout intact as pieces of paper have an odd way of disappearing just when they are needed most. If you do decide to use the cutting method, make sure that you have made a depth gauge for the work before slicing your finished working layout into strips.

From the working layout, two gauges must be prepared: a depth gauge showing the full depth of the work, head and foot margins and each line of lettering in its correct position, together with the nib sizes and any additional information that may be required;

producing a small rough just to confirm which lines will appear in red. This rough has been produced with fine-tipped, water-soluble fiber pens which do not bleed (spread) on the paper. Only the name and placing is in red, because to include the section as well makes the layout bottom-heavy.

To use the working layout guide, fold it over so that the ascenders of the first line of text are on the creased edge. Then slip it behind the guard sheet with the center line of the first line of text registered (position) with the center line of the sheet to be lettered so that the guidelines are visible. Begin lettering with the appropriate pen at the start line shown on the working layout.

This process is repeated until the finished certificate is lettered; the layout sheet is folded each time, and the finished work surface raised for each line to the lettered.

Once the certificate is completed, allow a little time to elapse attempting to erase the guidelines. Many a fine piece of lettering has been ruined by students who are too anxious to see the finished product.

Lettering the finished certificate (below) and the finished certificate (right).

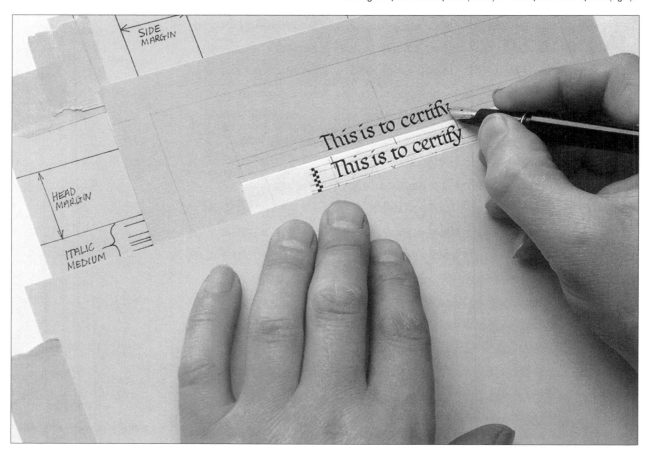

This is to certify
that

JULIAN RENSHAW

has been awarded

FIRST PLACE

in

THE MEDIUM RED TABLE WINE SECTION

of

THE OLD HARLOW WINEMAKERS' CIRCLE TASTING COMPETITION 1987

CHAIRMAN

A CALENDAR

A few months before beginning this piece I had been to the British Museum, London and made drawings of several artifacts, not knowing when or how I would use them. One object was an Anglo-Saxon brooch consisting of several smaller circles set around a central one. The design seemed eminently suitable as a basis for this particular project.

The text I chose was from Thomas Hardy, whose work includes pieces on woodlands and seasonal occupations such as cider-making and tree-planting. Having decided upon the design and text, I began to work on a black and white sketch of the calligraphy. The next step was a pencil rough which established the exact position of each element. Seeing the design in black and white rather than color helps you to look at it as an abstract pattern, and thus to decide whether all the various elements are working together.

The first color rough was executed on cream-colored paper. It is very important when using subtly graded watercolor to work on a white background, otherwise the colors tend to appear muddy.

The outer rim of the wheel was designed in red. The main color of the piece

Basic design questions are best resolved in an initial, rough, black and white sketch.

The next step is a detailed pencil rough. The initial design has been modified; the large capitals in the center unify the design.

A color rough was only begun when every detail of the overall design had been decided.

was green and the eye cries out for the complementary color of red to relieve it. The red band is broken with the little green zodiac signs, which relate it to the green center of the composition.

The design at the center of the piece was taken from a book of signs by Rudolph Koch and is thought to represent the eight points of the heavens. I thought that this emphasized the intention of the calendar while providing an interesting centerpiece to the design.

The finished piece was very carefully ruled up. When each line was in position, the lettering was pencilled in. This is the only way to ensure that no mistakes work their way into such large, and complex pieces of work. The pencil should be used very lightly to prevent the lines from showing under the watercolor paint. When the lettering is complete and the paint is dry, the writing lines can be removed carefully with an eraser.

Text and calligraphy by Diana Hoare

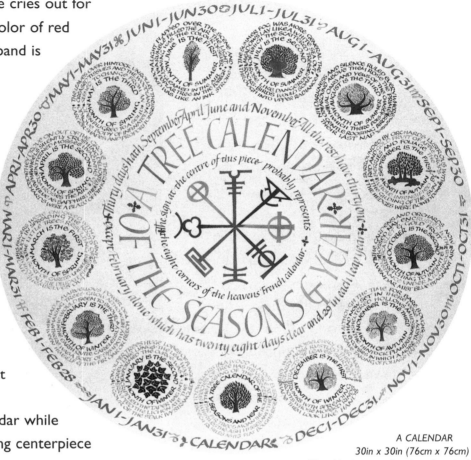

A CALENDAR
30in x 30in (76cm x 76cm)
The white paper makes the colors sparkle.
Greens are light and yellow-based; darker, blue-greens
tended to deaden the overall effect (above).

Detail showing how the leaves have been painted with thick watercolor to give an opaque effect. Adding a little white to the paint increases the opaqueness.

HEDGEROWS

The possibilities for using calligraphy as a propaganda weapon or as a medium for conveying facts are very exciting. With this piece I was initially captivated by the startling fact that every year nearly 8,000km (5,000 miles) of hedgerow in Britain are lost through changes in farming practices. I began to work on ideas for a design in which such a dramatic statement about the destruction of the country landscape could feature prominently. I collected further information about the history of hedges, their function as a habitat for fauna and flora, and the methods of cutting and laying or pleaching hedges. I also used two John Clare poems and a passage from Thomas Hardy. Lettering is about the creation of textures. For this piece I was inspired by the textures of the landscape outside my workshop window. There are sweeping views across fields and hedges to a distant range of hills. The different fields—corn, stubble, red ploughed earth, grass, root crops, hops—and orchards provide numerous different colors and textures, which change constantly as sunlight and cloud play across them.

Inspiration was drawn from the nature around me, such as the strong architectural shapes of the tree trunks and branches silhouetted against the sky.

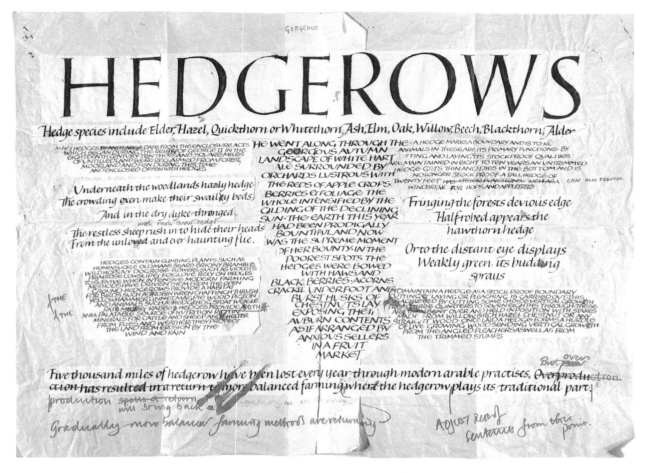

Tree textures also played an important part in my mind: bare branches against a gray sky, trees in full summer foliage, autumn leaves against a bright-blue sky, or the architectural strength of a tree trunk; even the texture of bark, fallen leaves on the grass, apple trees smothered with blossom or encrusted with golden and red fruit.

The arrangement of the lettering follows the lines of a fairly traditional layout, although there is variety and movement within the design itself. The title is echoed by the

The rough version allowed for checking the wording and adjusting the design (above).

The texture and color of bark and stones contributed to the overall effect of the finished piece (left and following page).

The texture of cut and laid hedges—a traditional method of managing hedges in England—inspired the texture of the words.

important quotation across the foot of the broadsheet, which gives it some prominence. The blocks of information about hedges have

a tight, interlinking texture which is reminiscent of the interwoven branches of the cut and laid hedge. The lettering is executed in watercolor which blends and changes throughout, so that no two letters are the same color. This gives a harmonious feel to the coloring of the piece.

Text and calligraphy by Diana Hoare

HEDGEROW

A HEDGE MARKS A BOUNDARY AND IS TO KEEP ANIMALS IN · THESE ARE ITS PRIMARY FUNCTIONS · BY CUTTING AND LAYING ITS STOCKPROOF QUALITIES ARE MAINTAINED · IN EIGHT TO TEN YEARS AN UNTRIMMED HEDGE GETS THIN IN THE BOTTOM AND DIES AND IS NO LONGER STOCKPROOF · A TALL HEDGE OF TEN OR TWENTY FEET CAN ALSO PROVIDE A WINDBREAK FOR HOPS OR APPLES ·

Fringing the forests devious edge
Half robed appears the
hawthorn hedge
Or to the distant eye displays
Weakly green its budding
sprays.

TO MAINTAIN A HEDGE AS A STOCKPROOF BOUNDARY CUTTING AND LAYING IS CARRIED OUT · THIS IS ACHIEVED BY CUTTING SOME CHOICE VERTICAL GROWTH FROM THREE QUARTERS TO SEVEN EIGHTHS THROUGH · THESE ARE THEN BENT OVER AND HELD IN POSITION WITH STAKES MADE OF WILLOW BIRCH HAZEL CHESTNUT OR ANY STRAIGHT WOOD · ONCE LAID A HEDGE FORMS A HURDLE OF LIVE GROWING WOOD SENDING VERTICAL GROWTH FROM THE ANGLED PLEACHERS AS WELL AS FROM THE TRIMMED STUMPS ·

HE WENT ALONG THROUGH THE GORGEOUS AUTUMN LANDSCAPE OF WHITE HART VALE SURROUNDED BY ORCHARDS LUSTROUS WITH THE REDS OF APPLE CROPS BERRIES AND FOLIAGE THE WHOLE INTENSIFIED BY THE GILDING OF THE DECLINING SUN · THE EARTH THIS YEAR HAD BEEN PRODIGALLY BOUNTIFUL & NOW WAS THE SUPREME MOMENT OF HER BOUNTY · IN THE POOREST SPOTS HEDGES WERE BOWED WITH HAWS AND BLACKBERRIES ACORNS CRACKED UNDERFOOT & BURST HUSKS OF CHESTNUTS LAY EXPO- SING THEIR AUBURN CONTENTS AS IF ARRANGED BY ANXIOUS SELLERS IN A FRUIT MARKET

SUCKLE OLD MANS BEARD BRION
OPS IVY DOGROSE · FLOWERS SUC
E COWSLIP AND FOXGLOVE RELY
IVE WHEN MODERN INTENSIVE
S HAVE DRIVEN THEM FROM THE
NS PROVIDE A HABITAT FOR BIRDS
REN CHAFFINCH YELLOW HAMM
GPIE WOODPIGEON AND ANIMA
DG STOAT WEASLE RAT MOUSE A
PROVIDE BOTH SHELTER FROM
AND A PALATABLE SOURCE OF
MINERALS FOR CATTLE AND SH

HEDGEROWS
20½in x 31½in (52cm x 80cm)
The arrangement of the lettering is traditional, but the design conveys the variety and movement of the landscape.

Left: lettering inspired by the texture of the cut and laid hedge.

OAK AND ASH

Where lettering is to be accompanied by illustrations, there obviously has to be a relationship between the lettering and the style of illustration. However, the calligrapher can bring words to life by illustrating their

Woodland scenes which inspired this piece of calligraphy.

meaning with lettering alone. This opens endless avenues for exploration.

Oak and Ash is an attempt to portray a wood through lettering. The piece was inspired by woods in Dorset, England. Instead of illustrating the poems which describe the wooded landscapes, I have used the color and shape of the letters in the tree names to suggest trees, and also used color, and texture in the writing of the poetry to suggest some of the landscapes portrayed in the words.

First, looking into this imaginary wood, the eye can focus on the tree names as if they were trees in the foreground with the poetry as background. When seen as background to the trees, the poetry has many textures. It can resemble undergrowth, leaf canopy and the woodland floor. Alternatively, one can look past the tree names, deeper into the poetry, to explore a variety of different woodland

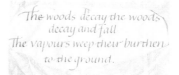
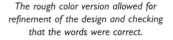

The rough color version allowed for refinement of the design and checking that the words were correct.

landscapes. When seen this way, the lettering of the poetry portrays different landscapes, such as a group of pine trees, a pathway or distant wooded hills seen beyond the wood itself.

In the design, by placing the tree names, and poems evenly around the broadsheet the reader's eye is allowed to wander freely. I am trying to express the feeling of walking at will through a wood.

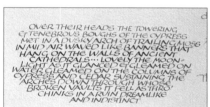

Detail of tree names representing trees in the foreground (top left).

Detail of poetry—the content of the words presents changing vistas and views to the imagination (bottom left).

Detail suggesting undergrowth, leaf canopy and woodland floor textures (left).

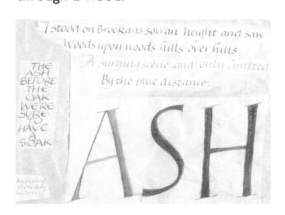

More details of the rough color version (opposite and above).

The viewer is led on from passage to passage to inquire further into the piece.

Rather than leave a white hole inside the letter 'o' of Oak, a small, light-textured piece in italic was chosen to fill the gap. The overall quality of the letter form, which lies in its strength, size and beauty, is kept. The contrast of textures which characterizes the rest of the design is carried into the open texture of the letters.

Although the white space on the broadsheet is filled evenly, the eye is led first to the large letters of 'Oak' and 'Ash' which form the title. The style of the lettering of these words was designed to reflect something of the qualities of the trees themselves. The broad, ancient oaks are like the large, classically strong Roman letters which depict them. Originally, these Roman letters were designed and executed with a chisel-edged brush. However, once you understand how the letter forms originated, they can be drawn with a pencil and then painted, using different colors.

The word 'Ash' was the second element to be designed. This is a less substantial tree, one which always gives a sense of rushing movement when the wind blows through its leaves. These versal letters are based on the Roman letter forms, but they have been adapted to be written more freely. The shape of the letters is slightly reminiscent of ash twigs.

The use of color in the piece is two-fold. Each of the larger letters has been painted in several shades of one color, but within the blocks of lettering as a whole there is considerable movement of color.

Text and calligraphy by Diana Hoare

Details taken from OAK AND ASH
43in X 30in (106cm X 76cm)
The color and shape of the lettering combine with the texture of the design to convey the atmosphere of a wood.

OAK

QUICKBEAM or ROWAN

WE PAUSED AMID THE PINES THAT STOOD
THE GIANTS OF THE WASTE
TORTURED BY STORMS TO SHAPES AS RUDE
WITH STEMS LIKE SERPENTS INTERLACED
A SPIRIT INTERLACED AROUND A THINKING SILENT
LIFE TO MOMENTARY PEACE IT BOUND OUR MORTAL NATURES
STRIFE AND STILL IT SEEMED THE CENTRE OF THE MAGIC CIRCLE
THERE WAS ONE WHOSE BEING FILLED WITH LOVE THE
BREATHLESS ATMOSPHERE

THE LEAVES
OVER
HINTOCK
UNROLLED
THEIR
CREASED
TISSUES
& THE
WOODLANDS
SEEMED TO
CHANGE
FROM
AN OPEN
FILLIGREE
TO A
SOLID
OPAQUE
BODY

MY ASPENS
DEAR WHOSE
AIRY
CAGES
QUELLED
OR IF THEY
DRENCHED
IN LEAVES THE
LEAPING SUN

TO THE
MAN
OF
IMAGIN
ATION
NATURE
IS
IMAGIN
ATION
ITSELF

WYCHELM

The roaring dell o'er wooded narrow deep
And only speckled by the midday sun
Where its slim trunk the ash from rock to rock
·Flings arching like a bridge;
that branchless ash
·Unsunned and damp whose few poor leaves
Ne'er tremble in the gale yet trembles still
·Fanned by the waterfall.

How
Pleasant

NEATH THE
WILLOW BY
THE BROOK
THAT'S KEPT
IT'S ANCIENT
PLACE FOR
MANY A
YEAR
TO SIT AND O'ER
THE CROWDED
FIELDS
TO LOOK & THE
SOFT DROPPING
OF THE SHOWER
TO HEAR
OURSELVES
SO SHELTERED

AND
HERE
WERE
FORESTS
AS
ANCIENT
AS
THE
HILLS
EN
FOLD
ING
SUNNY
SPOTS
OF
GREENERY

Here waving
groves a
chequered scene
display
And part exclude
and part admit
the day
There interspersed
with lawns &
opening glades.

Far left: versals give a sense of movement,
reflecting some of the qualities of the ash tree.

Top: the large
Roman letters reflect the qualities of the oak tree.

I stood on Brockans sovran height and saw
woods over woods, hills over hills
A surging scene only limited
By the blue distance—

THE
ASH
FORE

The woods decay the woods
decay and fall
The vapours weep their burthen
to the ground

FLOURISHES & SWASHES

The embellishment of letters with ornamental flourishes goes back to the Renaissance. The manuals of the Renaissance writing masters contain a wealth of inventive flourishes. Although the term suggests flamboyance, flourishes can range from subtle stroke extensions to elaborate traceries of loops and lines. They can be a wonderful enhancement to calligraphic work, provided they are carefully matched to their context. Sign-writing, commemorative inscriptions, diplomas, greetings cards and personal work are just some of the areas in which they can be used with a restrained or spirited effect.

Flourishes must appear to be an intrinsic part of the letter, not a contrived addition. They need to be written with flowing movement, speed, directness—and good pen control. In the enthusiasm for writing flourishes, it is easy to neglect the letter shapes themselves. These must be accurate if letter, and flourish are to form a harmonious whole.

Some people take rapidly to writing flourishes, but whether you find flourishes easy or not, it helps first to understand the principles of good flourish design. Remember that the choice of flourish depends on the design context and the purpose of the calligraphy. Begin by leaning some basic flourish shapes, but also study the creative ideas of other calligraphers, past and present. Look for inspiration in the imaginative flourishes of such Renaissance calligraphers as Arrighi, Tagliente and Palatino, which you can find in illustrated books, and in the work of accomplished 20th century calligraphers, who have developed innovative lettering for contemporary needs.

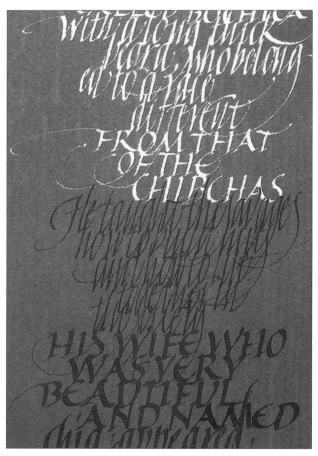

Poetry Panel—Paivi Vesanto
Elegant flourishes form a natural part of these freely written italics and italic capitals.

Flourished Capitals

Because of their role in titles and at text beginnings, capitals are usually the first letterforms to be considered when learning flourish design.

You can add flourishes to the entire capital alphabet with the aid of four basic flourish types. These are shown below.

Lead-in flourishes

Flourishes aligned to slant of script

Extended diagonals to right

Extended diagonals to left

1 *Rule lines ¹/₄in (7mm) apart, the equivalent of 8 nib widths of a Mitchell No 4 nib.*

2 *Use a pencil at first, so that your hand and arm are not restrained by the resistance of the broad nib against the paper. With practice, this resistance should not be a problem.*

3 *Loosen up with some large, sweeping movements, such as the tail on the R. Let the pencil move lightly over the paper.*

4 *Copy flourishes from each group, in the order shown, until you have memorized them well enough to write without hesitation.*

5 *When you feel confident with your pencil, repeat the exercise with a No 4 nib.*

6 *You may need to make several attempts at each flourish to produce flowing lines.*

Each flourish is complete. Each group begins with a simple flourish and progresses to more complex variations. Acquire a basic repertoire of flourishes by practicing the direction groups below.

Swash Capitals

Swash capitals are relatively simple flourished letters that are ideally suited to line beginnings—for instance, in poetry. Swash capitals also make an excellent script for use in posters, and other display work. The alphabet at right provides a good starting point for beginners. To write these letters with both flow and control, copy the alphabet, following the stroke order and direction indicated.

1 Rule lines to a height of 8 nib widths of a Mitchell No 2 nib.

2 Practice the capitals in alphabetical order, writing each letter several times before moving on to the next letter.

3 Take care with letter spacing so that swashes do not overlap.

4 When you have gained confidence, try some swash capitals in a text of your choice.

262

D E F G H

K L L M N N

Q R S T U V

W X Y Y Z

Flourishes for Lowercase Italics

Flourish design for lowercase italic follows the same principles as for capitals. There are two main directions in which the flourish can travel. You will see in examples for 'y' and 'h', movements from a simple flourish to more complex designs.

1 Rule lines ³/₁₆in (5mm) apart, the correct x-height for a Mitchell No 4 nib.

2 Practice each letter several times in pencil until you are familiar with the design.

3 Repeat the exercise using a Mitchell No 4 nib, omitting any flourishes that are too difficult at first.

4 Make sure that the reservoir moves easily up and down the nib, or the ink flow will be restricted and the pen will not move easily over the paper.

Experimenting with Flourish Design

Once you are familiar with some basic flourishes, try making your own design. Planning in pencil or felt-tip pen will enable you to work faster and more freely.

1 *Write spontaneously, letting the ideas flow.*

2 *Follow up with design refinements using the edged pen.*

FLOURISHED PANEL
– Lawrence R. Brady
This panel, produced as part of a corporate-identity programme, uses carefully considered flourishes at the top and bottom. These flowing strokes help to integrate the different elements in the design.

FLOURISH EXPERIMENT
In this decorative piece of work, carefully planned flourishes connect the spaces and carry the eye into the design.

CHECKLIST FOR IMPROVIZED FLOURISHES

- **Spontaneous flourishes depend on knowledge and pen control.**
- **Write flourishes smoothly and rhythmically. Speed develops with practice.**
- **Write flourishes continuously. It is necessary to break them into component strokes only when writing with a very large nib, and not always then.**
- **Where straight lines and curves join, make sure the transition follows through in a fluid movement.**
- **Establish a sense of spaciousness around the letter. Over-close flourishes create a cramped design.**
- **Diagonal strokes are usually parallel. Do not write them too close together, or the flourish will look heavy.**
- **Design and Practice flourishes in pencil for uninhibited movement and speed.**
- **Practice with chisel-edged brushes or large chisel-edged felt-tip markers to loosen arm movement and encourage experimentation.**

Using flourishes

Flourishes should be carefully proportioned and must relate to, and not obscure, other parts of the text. For a certificate, poster, title page or dust jacket such as the one shown here, a decorative flourished heading or other flourished design element may be useful. There is more scope for flourishing if there is adequate surrounding space.

5 *The paper is then trimmed to the dimensions of the book, leaving a flap 1 in (2.5 cm) wide on each end that folds inside the cover.*

Ampersands

Symbols other than standard letterforms may also be flourished or written in unusual ways. An example is the sign for 'and' known as an ampersand. An ampersand must harmonize with the script being written, and a simple design may suit the context better than a flamboyant one. Three examples of ampersands suitable for use with contemporary calligraphy are shown below, together with the stroke sequences for writing them.

1 *Much of the success of flourishing comes from detailed planning of the design. Here preliminary pencil roughs are sketched.*

2 *When first learning to design flourishes, it may help to pencil the flourishes on to the simple letterforms written in ink.*

3 *Several different flourish designs are written using a Mitchell No 2 nib. Each design is then considered within the context.*

4 *The final design is written in gouache, and a decorative border is added in gouache with a brush.*

1 *Rule lines to a height of 8 nib widths of a Mitchell No 2 nib.*

2 *Practice each of the ampersands in turn, first on their own and then in context with appropriate script.*

VELLUM STRETCHING

The traditional method of stretching vellum involves damping the vellum, stretching it over a support and letting it dry. Application of glue then ensures that the vellum is held firmly in position over its support, providing a flat, smooth surface. The problem is that vellum stretched in this way often has a rather dead appearance, and can produce an unpleasantly hard writing surface. As a result, many calligraphers prefer to complete their work first and stretch the vellum afterwards despite the possible hazards involved. The method of stretching vellum described below has been developed as an alternative to the traditional way; it is more sympathetic to the vellum, providing a working surface which retains some flexibility and life.

If you begin by stretching a piece of vellum of average size and thickness, you should have little trouble following the instructions. Experience and confidence will soon be acquired with practice.

YOU WILL NEED

- **Canvas stretcher**
- **8 wedges**
- **Cotton builder's twine or hemp twine for lacing— not nylon or polyester, which is too slippery or stretchy**
- **PVA glue**
- **Conservation card**
- **Silicone-release paper**
- **2 sheets of polythene**
- **Houseplant sprayer**
- **2 drawing boards**
- **Weight**
- **Set square**
- **Hole punch**
- **Metal rule**
- **Scalpel**

(Above) Equipment needed includes (clockwise): vellum, hole punch, wedges, stretcher, builder's twine.

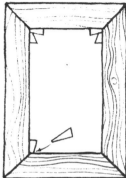

Canvas stretcher with 8 wedges to keep it square.

Although the system described uses a canvas stretcher, a support made of plywood or marine ply could equally well be used if desired. In all cases, the wood should be sealed with polyurethane varnish or diluted PVA medium. The vellum should measure at least 2in (5cm) larger than the stretcher. Check that the latter is absolutely square, using the set square, and if necessary knock in the wedges to hold the corners securely in position. It is an advantage to have a crossbar on stretchers of 20in (51cm) or more.

Ruling up the back of the vellum using a pencil and a metal ruler.

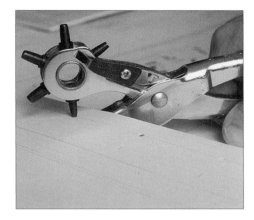

Use a hole punch for making holes in the vellum.

Method

Rule up the vellum on the back. The inner line indicates the size of the stretcher and the outer line marks its depth. Allow an overlap of 1½–2in (4—5cm) beyond this. Damp vellum has a tendency to move; it can shrink or stretch. To allow for this movement and to ensure that the guide lines will still be visible when positioning the stretcher on the back of

Glue the top corners of the card to the stretcher.

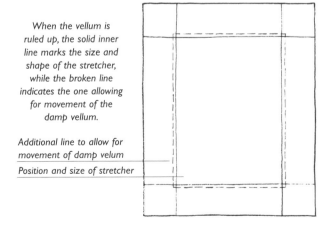

When the vellum is ruled up, the solid inner line marks the size and shape of the stretcher, while the broken line indicates the one allowing for movement of the damp vellum.

Additional line to allow for movement of damp velum

Position and size of stretcher

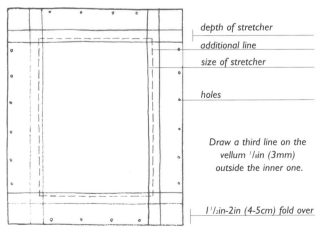

depth of stretcher

additional line

size of stretcher

holes

Draw a third line on the vellum ⅛in (3mm) outside the inner one.

1½in-2in (4-5cm) fold over

the vellum, a third line should be drawn $\frac{1}{8}$ in (3mm) outside the inner one.

Having carefully ruled up the back of the vellum mark an even number of holes along each side $1\frac{1}{2}$–2in (4—5 cm) apart, and about $\frac{1}{4}$–$\frac{1}{3}$in (6—8mm) in, depending upon the size of the vellum. Punch these with the hole punch. To prevent the cord tearing very thin vellum, fold over the outer edge and punch the hole through the double thickness.

Cut a piece of conservation card slightly smaller than the stretcher size. The color of the card will depend on the see-through effect desired. The vellum will look very different over a cream-colored card rather than a stark white one. Colored papers can be used but they may not be acid-free, so you should check this: use as near to a neutral pH as possible.

Lightly sandpaper the edges of the card to obtain a bevel. The card acts as a support, especially when writing after stretching. Using PVA, lightly glue the top corners of the card to the stretcher.

Cut four lengths of cord for the lacing, using the lacing diagrams as a rough guide to calculate the amount of cord required.

Damp the vellum. Make a polythene and blotting paper sandwich. First lay some polythene on a drawing board and then lay some dry blotting paper on top. Place the vellum face down on this, but insert a sheet of

Dampen a piece of blotting paper with a mist sprayer.

Lay the damp blotting paper on the back of the vellum.

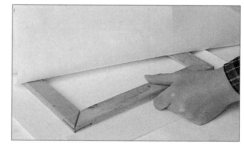

Slide the stretcher with its glued card into position.

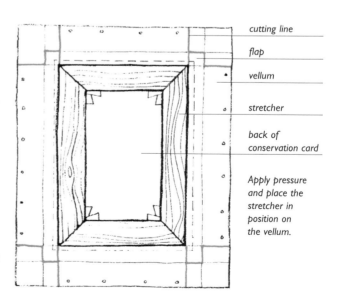

cutting line

flap

vellum

stretcher

back of conservation card

Apply pressure and place the stretcher in position on the vellum.

silicone-release paper if it is already written on. Next, damp a piece of blotting paper with a mist sprayer of the kind used to water plants. The damp blotting paper is laid on the back of the vellum. Two pieces may be necessary for thick vellum or one damp and one dry for thin vellum. Excessive water should be removed before the paper comes in contact with the vellum, by blotting with a dry sheet of blotting paper. A second piece of polythene is put on top of this, and finally another drawing board with a weight to supply some pressure.

Leave the vellum for between 10 and 30 minutes, depending on its thickness. When it is damp enough it should feel rubbery. Keep checking after the first 10 minutes. Particular care should be taken with thin skins as they can easily become over-damp. Err on the side of caution; a skin can always be left a little longer.

Remove the weight, board and top layers of paper. It may be best to unroll these carefully since damp vellum has a tendency to curl. The stretcher with the card glued in position may then be slid into place

If the lacing has gone wrong, or the vellum has not stretched properly, undo the lacings and start again.

Reef knot with extra twist (top) and postman's knot (bottom).

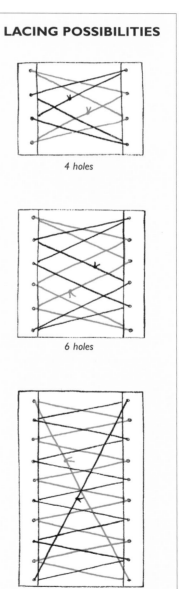

LACING POSSIBILITIES

4 holes

6 holes

10 holes (or any even number)

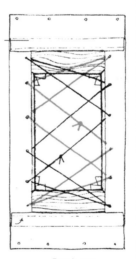

Use the set square against the stretcher, adjust the corners and cut them carefully with a scalpel and metal ruler.

First lacing

Alternative lacing (right) Only one set of lacing is shown for clarity.

simultaneously. The stretcher should be so placed as to align as closely as possible with the lines ruled on the back of the vellum.

Using the set square against the stretcher, adjust the corners if necessary, and cut them carefully with a scalpel and metal rule, leaving a little flap to fold around the shorter side.

The finished piece showing cords and knots.

Lace up the longer sides using two cords. Tension should be lightly firm but not tight. The cords are tied using a locking postman's knot or a reef knot with initial double twist. Tuck in the corner flaps and lace the shorter sides. If a hole tears readjust the tension or punch a new hole. The lacings look complicated but are designed to avoid having a cord running underneath any of the turned-over edges. Note that each cord remains separate, laced and knotted to itself.

Leave to dry. If necessary, adjust the tension in specific areas as the vellum dries; this is particularly useful with larger pieces.

If anything has gone drastically wrong or the vellum has not stretched properly, undo all the lacings and start again.

There are certain disadvantages with this method of stretching, but they should not be difficult to overcome. First, deep mouldings are required to accommodate the stretcher within a frame. Nowadays this tends to limit the choice of moulding, but it is certainly possibly to find suitable frames. Second it can be difficult to keep a stretcher absolutely square. Third, conservation card seems to have a tendency to buckle on larger sizes.

However, these problems are greatly out-weighed by the advantages. As the whole procedure is reversible, it is quite difficult to go drastically wrong. The finished piece is lightweight compared to a solid support, and if the writing is to be completed after stretching, the vellum still has some life and spring to it, offering a much more pleasant writing surface upon which to work.

Ecclesiasticus Project

The well-known quotation from Ecclesiasticus ch.38 V.25-34 beginning, "How shall he become wise that holdeth the plough…" was read at the funeral of my father, who had been a superb craftsman and engineer. This provided the inspiration for a piece of calligraphy to commemorate the occasion.

My first idea was to use a rather special

piece of vellum which had beautiful gray-brown markings. The lettering was to be small square capitals, in pale gray, packed closely together to produce an overall texture. A few important parts were to be in a darker gray and slightly larger. Unfortunately, the rough turned out to be an unsatisfactory shape for the skin and looked too uniform and boring. The close texture would have conflicted with the markings in the vellum and each would have destroyed the other. As a result, the whole idea was shelved for about 18 months.

At this point, I acquired a piece of vellum with interesting markings in warm brown and cream. The first rough was similar to my previous work, and was still uninteresting. A new angle of approach was needed to convey the feeling of the

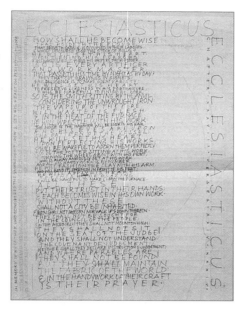

The first rough for the second attempt at the Ecclesiasticus project was still uninte resting visually.

A new angle of approach produced a second rough which conveyed the feeling of the words far more effectively. This shows two possibilities for the title.

The finished piece is 16in x 12in (41cm x 30cm)

'fabric of the world', both a living fabric and at the same time a woven one. Eventually, varied letter spacing, warm-brown ink and vertical bands of letters seemed to solve the problem.

The vellum was stretched around a canvas stretcher using the method described above. All the lettering was made with the same steel nib. The brown was a mixture of black and vermilion stick inks, sometimes quite dilute.

In retrospect, the problem with this piece was balancing uniformity and variety. The long text needed to remain a totality and yet have enough variety to maintain interest. It was also one of those pieces which could not be worked to a fixed timescale, and instead lay dormant until all the right elements coalesced at the right time.

'Story of my heart'

The idea of trying to cover a three-dimensional shape came from studying limp vellum bookbindings. The shape was made first in stiff paper on a trial and error basis, then in card. This had to be forced into position and was covered in Japanese paper, which is both thin and strong. Starch paste was used throughout.

I found this Richard Jefferies quotation about eternity: "Realising that spirit, recognising my own inner consciousness, the psyche, so clearly, I cannot understand time. It is about me in the sunshine; I am in it, as the butterfly floats in the light-laden air. Nothing has to come; it is now. Now is eternity; now is the immortal life. Here this moment, on earth, now; I exist in it. The years, the centuries, the

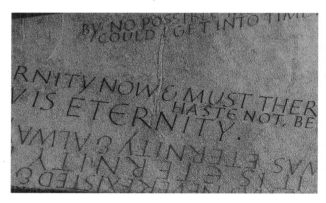

A close-up of the lettering for the "Story of my Heart".

cycles are absolutely nothing. To the soul there is no past and no future; all is and ever will be, in now. For artificial purposes time is agreed on, but there is really no such thing. Time has

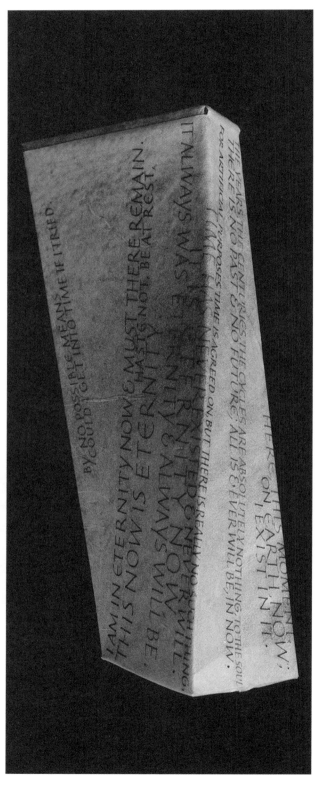

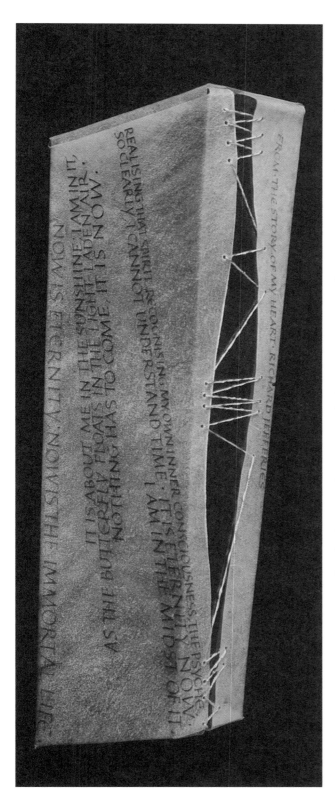

never existed, and never will. It is eternity now, it always was eternity, and always will be. By no possible means could I get into time if I tried. I am in eternity now and must there remain. Haste not, be at rest, this Now is eternity."

The words seemed to suit the monolithic shape I had created, while an off-cut of transparent vellum over black paper produced an appropriately mysterious color. At first, I tried pencil lettering, but it disappeared and became totally illegible, so eventually a gray ink was used. Several paper roughs were made on the shape, experimenting with alternatives, and adjustments of line position and letter height. The lacing pattern was also worked out at this stage. The card shape was then covered in black paper. A paper pattern was made for the vellum and the position of the card shape was lightly marked. The writing was executed with a steel pen and dilute stick ink. Small holes were punched for the lacing and the vellum was dampened, cut and folded around the shape. Finally, the edges were laced together using bookbinder's thread, and some ancient silver embroidery thread twisted together.

Text and calligraphy by Alison Urwick

The edges were laced together with silver embroidery thread twisted with bookbinder's thread (left)

Three-dimensional shape 8½ x 3 x 2½in (20 x 7 x 6cm) covered with transparent vellum over black paper (far left)

INTERPRETING THE TEXT

The mood and meaning of the text you are writing will suggest the choice of color, design and letterform. Aspects to consider include the sense and inflection of the words, associated connotations and the use of contrasts. These have parallels in color terms. Tonal changes and use of the analogous range create color harmony. This is also a good method of invoking mood and warmth or coolness.

Explore color considerations during the layout stage of a design. Paint your color choices on tracing paper, which you can place over the layout and adjust as necessary.

It is wise to keep your colors understated at first and to work from light to dark. Color immediately attracts the eye and bright colors will appear to come

CONTROLLING COLOR
One rough idea for this quote suggests winter colors giving way to warmer tones (top). Another shows the lifting of winter gloom (middle). A third moves from winter to spring in a monochromatic progression (bottom).

forward off the page. This can be helpful in enlivening a design or adding judiciously chosen emphasis. The eye's unconscious tendency to travel around a layout, linking like colors, can also be used to create unity. But color can easily be over-done, and it should therefore be approached with caution.

Visualising color as mass and the lines of text as strands to be linked compatibly with it can help you to assess suitable contrasts. For example, if the text suggests liveliness and activity, contrast this with a calmer background to avoid a muddled effect.

Elements such as verticals and horizontals can also create contrasts and tensions. A design can be strengthened by emphasising these. The text itself, being a linear form, may be written vertically or horizontally, or compressed and angled to intensify tensions. To relax this tension, spread the verticals or horizontals further apart.

 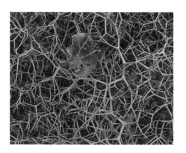

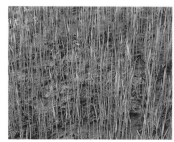 

Sources of Inspiration

Ideas for the dynamics of design—structure, layout, color, pattern, texture rhythm and mood—are most readily found in the environment. Look keenly at the world around you, analysing it in visual terms and training your eye to seek out patterns, harmonies and juxtapositions of texture, line and color. Here a starfish, grass shoots, thorns and woven rushes illustrate contrasting design possibilities. Practice interpreting what you see in terms of color and design. Record your observations in notes, sketches or photographs, putting together a valuable source of stimulation for design ideas.

Color and Design

The design for a piece of colored calligraphy should be started with a number of thumbnail sketches.

1   *The quote mentions leaping, which suggests a vertical design..*

2   *However, trout do not leap in a regular fashion, so an asymmetrical design is tried.*

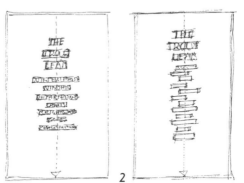

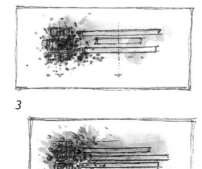

3   *In fact, a combined vertical and horizontal layout for the river works better.*

4   *The design is refined, and the color of the background is developed. The finished work combines the splash of the leaping trout with the peaceful colors of woodland and water.*

Words and Illustration

Whether you use color or not, any image you choose should augment the meaning of the words. Text and image should be visually harmonious. Decisions on how to blend the two take place when you make thumbnail sketches or at the layout stage.

It is important to consider the overall space in which image and text appear, and not to use decorative letters or illustrations merely as space fillers. The 'negative' areas—those which are left free—are as essential to balanced layout as the positive ones. It is the shapes of spaces, and marks together that make up the design. An image or illustration also contains negative areas, and these should be given equal consideration.

Keeping Layout and Illustration Notes

There can be many sources of ideas for calligraphic composition and illustration. Get into the habit of looking at the environment around you and taking notes on interesting colors, textures and objects that could be used in your work. Keep a scrapbook of these notes. Sketch in ideas for layouts, glue in photographs you find interesting and use these for color and letter-form observations.

Choosing a Focal Point

Begin by choosing a focal point: the part of your layout to which the eye will be guided first. You could feature this as a larger, darker, lighter or more colorful letter, word or image. You could establish an 'active' area in which greater numbers of shapes or letters are closely gathered. Or you could draw, write or paint an especially vigorous textural or visual element.

It is usually best to work from the focal point, so that no other text or image competes with it. If you establish two equally active areas, for example, the eye will look from one to the other, separating the design into rival parts. This does not mean that you cannot use another focal point, but that the second one should be more muted and should enhance the strength, and direction of the main focus.

The position of the focal point needs to be carefully chosen. In the exact center of the design, it may look too obvious and therefore uninteresting. Too near the edge of the page, it may seem about to slip off. If it links too powerfully with another part of the design, it may divide the paper. In the same way, the text and the image should not divide the surface equally. If each occupies half the sheet, for example, the design is likely to be monotonous. Using too many colors steals attention from the image and the words. Intense color should not be used on insignificant detail.

Seeing Negative Shapes

Try to see each of your layouts in terms of the negative areas that it creates. These shapes are an essential part of the design. The layouts shown at left are shaded to draw your attention to the negative areas that they create.

If you decide to fill a negative area with an illustration, be sure to check that this does not alter the balance of the design.

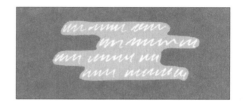

Determining the Focal Point

The focal point is the point of the image to which the eye is first drawn. Here, the left-of-center focal point is determined by the area of darkest color in the background wash.

Focal Point with Words and Image

Always ensure that the words and the image work together to reinforce the focal point. In this rough design, the left-of-center text placement is balanced by the extension of the wash to the right.

This ensures that the focal point in the darkest wash area is maintained.

Focal point links foreground, middle ground and sky.

Passive middle ground balances relative activity of foreground and sky.

Placement of text helps to emphasize foreground detail.

Diagonal sweep of furrows draws eye towards focal point.

A Finished Composition

In this piece of illustrated calligraphy, the composition was carefully planned around the focal point formed by the flock of birds. The furrows of the ploughed field draw the eye across the text in the foreground to this point. This diagonal movement also provides a link across the horizontal divisions of the sky and landscape.

The use of color enhances the unity of the composition, with the purple-brown of the text echoing both the browns of the fields and the indigo of the sky.

IN THE BLEAK MIDWINTER

As a calligrapher, I have an intrinsic interest in words: their content, the sound of their language, the feeling they inspire within me. This interest has given me a passion for collecting poetry and prose from all sources.

Some pieces lie in my collection for years. The initial excitement often wanes until an outside influence gives new impetus. This might be from a variety of origins: a vivid image of nature, a paper of unusual color or texture, a letter shape, or a lettering texture suggested from an unexpected source, such as a magazine advertisement.

spontaneity of working immediately, pen to paper, and of the unfolding of an idea. I was drawn to this verse written by Christina Rossetti, hearing it as the well-loved Christmas hymn. The music by Gustav Holst revealed a softness belying the harsh reality of wintry winds.

The language begins sparse and brittle, and this made me conscious of the need to reflect its sound in the positioning of the lettering. The hard, precise images of earth and water are subdued by the constant layering of snow on snow. I heard the muffled quietness

Detail showing how texture and color combine with the lettering to capture the mood of the verse.

The calligrapher walks a tightrope. A balance has to be struck between clearly expressing the meaning of the words, and the desire to express an emotional response to those words through the lettering. I enjoy the

of past midwinters, and by setting the last line slightly apart, I gave pause for breath. Snow will fall, seasons will pass and winter will come upon us again.

In this piece I chose the light, transparent quality of tissue paper, which possessed within it a sense of wind-torn images. Laying down the paper in a strong diagonal direction created movement, like clouds chasing across the sky. The opening words were set in a white background, representing the blanket whiteness of snow. Cool grays and blues captured the mood of the piece, icy water arrested in the brighter clear blue which "lifted" the design. A creamy white Japanese paper, which had inconsistent thickness of pulp, layered upon the gray tissue paper evoked the drifting snow.

I tore the paper to give a broken edge and by layering the gray and blue tissue paper, I was able to create intensities of color and texture. A spray adhesive proved easiest to handle and it was possible to write upon when completely dry. The letter forms had to be strong enough to avoid competition with the background. By passing a brush of clear water over the word 'water', the paint became more intense, and the background whiteness of the paper receded, unifying the design.

I used water soluble crayons to give a broken, softening effect which intensified some parts. By not using ruled lines, the composition was able to grow and develop freely. In seeking to balance the demands of the poem and my interpretation of it, I have, as with all my work, sought to express the unity of hand with mind.

Text and calligraphy by Christine Oxley

IN THE BLEAK MIDWINTER
12¹⁄₂in x 10in (31.7cm x 25.4cm)
Tissue paper layered over white paper. Written in gouache with metal nibs, softened by crayon.

HALLEY'S COMET

No design is instant. It is hard work developing an idea, but it is always rewarding. The Halley's Comet Christmas Card project required a different approach, and attitude from In the Bleak Midwinter. The need to produce 40 original cards acted as a restraint upon the design. But, because there were differences, each card possessed a feeling of liveliness as opposed to the flatness of a mechanically-reproduced card.

The trial cards illustrated show the ideas developing one from another until the final design was reached. This method is a relatively quick way of creating original designs.

Text and calligraphy by Christine Oxley

(Top) First draft on a dark background. Masking fluid suggests speed and light; silver paper forms the comet's core.

(Left) Paper impressed over a coin forms the embossed center, the tail is suggested by washes paint strokes.

*The tail has been masked
and splattered and the text layout changed (above).*

*The text was too long to write out
40 times; it was replaced and, in the final draft, further reduced (left).*

*The final design—5in x 3¹/₂in (13cm x 9cm)
– stressed 'stars' and 'leap', the comet core was embossed, and streaks of
pink and blue crayon were added to the tail (below).*

283

WRITING SURFACES

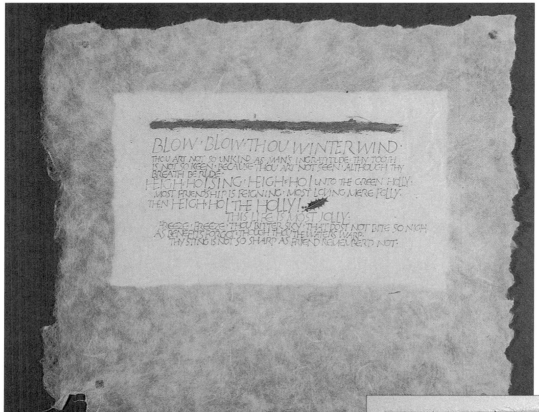

BLOW, BLOW,
THOU
WINTER WIND
– Peter Halliday
14in x 12in
(35cm x 30cm)
Pencil, crayon, gold
and aluminium leaf
on 18th century
Nepalese paper.

IN THE
WARM HEDGE GREW
– Liz Farquharson
6in x 9in (15cm x 23cm)
Embossed letters on
handmade paper (right).

HEAVEN HAVEN
– Liz Farquharson
6in x 9in (15cm x 23cm)
Embossed letters on
handmade paper
(far right).

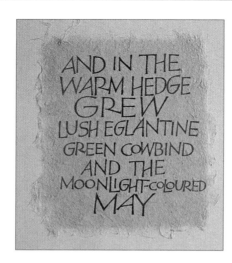

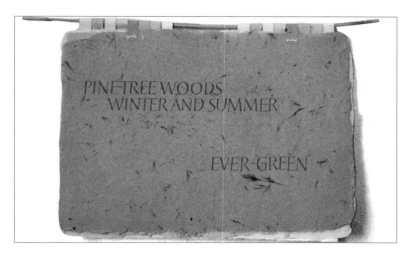

SAILING HOMEWARD
– Sue Hufton
9in x 6in (22.5cm x 16.5cm)
Letters painted in gouache
with a pointed brush on sheets of
handmade paper, some of
which include plant fragments
and dried grasses.

SHALL I COMPARE THEE TO A
SUMMERS DAY?
– Liz Farquharson
6in x 9in (15cm x 23cm)
Brush letters written on a very rough
handmade plant fiber paper.
The letters were built up with a
series of short stroking movements.

USING WORDS AS IMAGES

Words not only convey information but suggest images. Language itself is born of the double need to communicate ideas in both a direct and vivid way, coloring meaning with imagery. Calligraphy, the art of writing, can add an important visual dimension.

English is a particularly rich and potent language, drawing its inheritance from a variety of sources. Through the centuries, many linguistic streams have intermingled, giving us a wonderfully precise, varied and expressive vocabulary. Poetry and prose use all these dimensions of language, capturing the sound, meaning, and association of words so they resonate in the mind.

Calligraphy, with its ability to enhance words by using different styles, forms and colors, is a perfect vehicle for exploring this vocabulary further in a visual way. For instance, 'water' written in a flowing Italic hand is perhaps more evocative than water written in stiff, upright capitals.

The traditional way to become a calligrapher is first to study historical manuscript hands. In understanding the shapes of letterforms, and the influences that tools and materials have had on determining those shapes, and by the actual process of writing, calligraphers gradually evolve their own interpretations of those letters and invent new ones. By acquiring a repertoire of different styles of writing and by understanding the structure of the forms in each style, their significant aspects and inherent potential for development, so the ability to communicate ideas effectively is expanded.

Calligraphy can enhance words. These three versions of water each evoke a difference response. To write it in blue, traditionally the symbolic color of water, goes even further towards capturing the essence of the word—or rather, the perceived essence, as no two people see things in the same way.

Development of letterforms in an attempt to capture the essence of the words.

Exploring the letters and assessing their shapes and sounds enables the calligrapher to choose the elements that are relevant.

Shine can be developed so that the active flavour of the word is visually enhanced by exaggerating the vertical stress of the 'I' (upright lines symbolize the active principle—humans stand vertically on a horizontal plain); the added rays burst forth from a central point, suggesting a shining star of light.

The embellishment of shone reflects the past nature of the event where the emphasis has flowed to the outside circle. If the rays are removed the resonance of the symbolism may still be absorbed subconsciously.

mainly from Latinate and Germanic roots. From the Latin, our intellectual words are derived: for example, consider, circumstance, recognition. Many of these are compound words changing, and expanding their meaning with different components. From the Germanic languages come the emotive, monosyllabic sounds: for example, grind, grieve, groan; slip, slide, sling and slink. Some of these words have obvious onomatopoeic origins.

However, there are also many etymological theories. One of these concerns vowel sound groupings. The more active and present the verb, the sharper and thinner the vowel sound: for example, sink, sank, sunk; drink, drank, drunk. Thus, shine and shone could be developed as illustrated.

Through a process of exploration, assessing the seemingly accidental shapes of letters (remembering that the shapes also indicate sound), choose only those elements that are helpful to you in that instance. Each context is unique, and what is significant in one situation is not necessarily so in another.

But are the shapes of letters accidental? The English language evolved

More important, in the actual process of exploration and experimenting with the letters, and words in order to portray them on the page, we discover more about the words themselves. We bring our own insights, experiences and discoveries to the making of them, and in this way find out more about how and what we think. So, exploring words can also be a way of exploring ourselves.

Be still and know that I am God

As experimenting with the shapes and arrangement of letters can present a way of discovery into the deeper

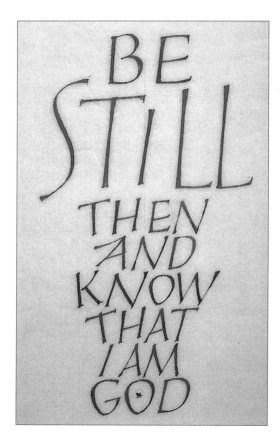

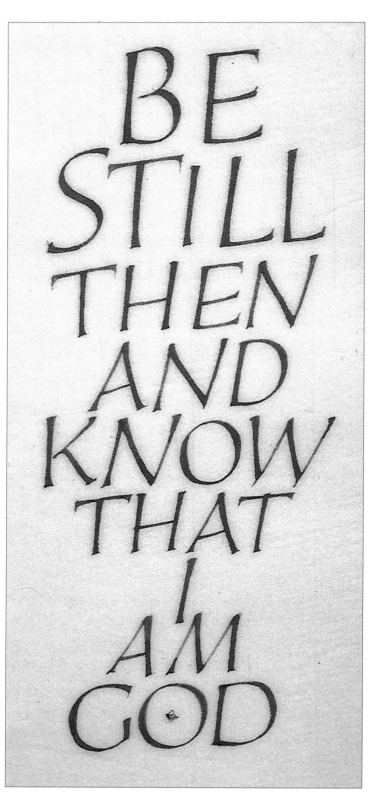

Right: from Psalm 46, verse 10
5in x 2¹/₂in (13cm x 6.5cm)

4¹/₂in x 2¹/₂in (12cm x 6.5cm)
The emphasis is on stillness (above).

meaning of words, the same is true with whole phrases. This verse from Psalm 46 seems to be exceptionally profound, and gives rise to many possibilities, thoughts, questions, associations and meanings. All the pieces are in watercolor with raised and burnished gold, on vellum. In this series the captions are self-explanatory.

Text and calligraphy by Ann Hechle

2¹⁄₂in x 2¹⁄₂in (6.5cm x 6.5cm)
The center of the stillness is the same as the 'i' of God (below).

4¹⁄₂in x 2¹⁄₂in (12.5cm x 6.5cm)
Left: The center of the stillness is echoed by the 'I' of 'I am God' shown by the gold 'I'

2¹/₂in x 4in (6.5cm x 10cm)
Two equally balanced and related phrases. The linking ampersand is emphasized in gold (left).

3¹/₂in x 3¹/₂in (9.5cm x 9.5cm)
Through stillness, there is a spiralling inwards to where the vertical, temporal, moment by moment 'I' meets and fuses with the horizontal and eternal God. Where these two lines meet forms the critical moment of 'now' symbolized by a gold point (below).

BE STILLTHEN AND KNOW THAT AM GOD

3¹/₂in x 4¹/₄in (8.5cm x 11cm)
The moment of 'now' takes place in the center of God. By using capitals, the letters form an image which is very nearly symmetrical— an idea that is reflected throughout the series (above).

2¹/₂in x 4¹/₄in (6.5cm x 11cm)
'Knowing' or intuitive understanding lies between the practice and the outcome. Is this true of other things we do? (right)

BE STILLTHEN ×KNOW· THAT I AM GOD

ILLUSTRATIONS

When combining illustration with calligraphy, it is important to create harmony between both elements. The illustration should reflect the square-edged pen, as do many early manuscripts, with line drawings making full use of the implement, and the varied stroke widths it will produce. Textures can be built up by cross hatching (strokes in opposing directions) or by moving the pen angle from a thin stroke gradually through to a thick stroke position and vice-versa, giving a vignetted (gentle graduation of) line weight.

There is no easy way to learn how to draw with a square nib, and if you do not regard yourself as an illustrator the only way to succeed is by involvement and practice. One of the best things to do is to look at photographic and printed references.

1 *Tracing the image to be used from illustrative reference.*

2 *Shading over the underside of the tracing.*

3 *Tracing the image on to the finished surface.*

4 *Inking in the initial outline.*

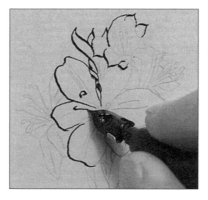

5 *The finished illustration.*

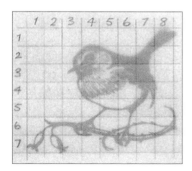

1 Confining the illustration to a gridded square on tracing paper.

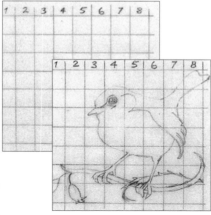

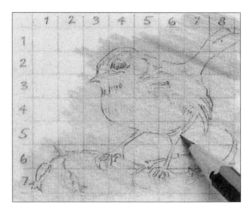

2 Drawing a gridded square to the required enlargement.

3 Plotting the image on the grid.

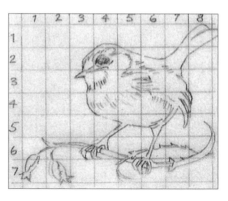

4 Building up the illustration.

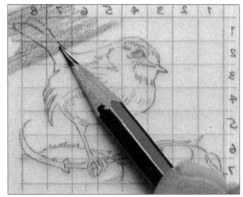

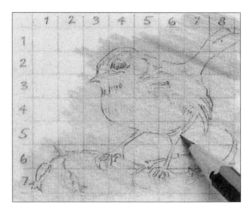

5 Shading over the underside of the tracing.

6 Tracing the image on to the finished surface.

7 Traced image on finished surface.

8 Inking in the initial outline.

9 The finished illustration.

On the first
day of
Christmas
my true love
sent to me.
A partridge
in a pear
tree.

George Evans—Some designs which have been used for bookmarks and Christmas cards.

The Jolly Miller

There was a jolly miller
once,
Lived on the river Dee;
He worked and sang
from morn till night,
No lark more blithe
than he.
And this the burden
of his song
Forever used to be,
I care for nobody, no!
not I,
If nobody cares for me.

Once you have an idea of what image you want to use to accompany a piece of calligraphy, search through your own books, photographs and pamphlets, or through those in your local library for suitable images. Searching for material will heighten your awareness of the images you see every day. A scrapbook of likely subject matter is a wonderful idea and takes very little time to add to each week. References should be as detailed as possible so that new images can readily, and accurately be created from them at any opportunity.

Once the necessary references have been found, you will need to transfer them to tracing paper. If the size of the illustration required is the same as that of the reference material, it can be traced directly on to the tracing paper, using a 2H or H pencil (or lead in a technical pencil). Take care to interpret the image exactly, because what is produced on the tracing sheet will be the image traced down on to the finished piece of work. Once the tracing is completed, the sheet must be

SIGNS OF THE ZODIAC—George Evans. Some have been taken from English and German woodcuts and adapted for the pen. The Crab, Scorpion and Scales are the calligrapher's addition, as the originals were not suitable to be contained within a circle. The shading in the lower portion was necessary to give a uniformity to the twelve symbols.

turned over and the underside of the drawing area shaded over with an HB pencil. Turn the tracing paper over again so that the image side faces upwards, and position it on the finished surface of the work using masking tape at the head to hold it gently in place.

Then trace the drawing down by going over the lines of the image using a hard, sharp pencil, 2H or 4H. When completed, lift the tracing sheet, without unfastening, to make sure that the drawing has been successfully transferred to the finished surface. The faint image must now be inked in with a fine, square-ended nib. Build up the image slowly, referring to the original reference for the finer points.

Should the reference material found not be the correct size for the design, then it will be necessary either to enlarge or reduce the image. First contain the illustration within a square or a rectangle on a sheet of tracing paper, subdividing this by small grid squares. The size required should then be drawn as a square or rectangle on another sheet, and subdivided as before. Number the squares horizontally and vertically on both sheets of paper, and plot your image from the reference material to the correctly-sized grid.

BOOKBINDING

The binding of a book protects the pages and enables them to open. A delicate book, made from Japanese tissue can be protected by a delicate cover. This is because the tissue and the materials are compatible in strength. As a result the reader respects the book's fragility.

Japanese Tissue Binding

This book is adapted from the Fukuro-toji style. The book is made square to accommodate a letter of the alphabet on each page. The letters are painted in watercolor on the Japanese tissue.

One sheet of koju-shi tissue will make the 12 leaves. Each leaf is double thickness with the fold at the foredge. This makes only 24 pages, so that four of the letters, such as 'I' and 'J' or 'T' and 'U' need to be paired up to save using another sheet of tissue.

Japanese tissue is made on a mould constructed from slates of bamboo tied together, which makes laid lines, and chain lines similar to those in Western paper. This tissue is assumed to have a short grain direction, running parallel with the chain lines.

As with all books the paper is cut so that the grain direction is parallel with the spine. When the pages are cut and folded, fit the book neatly inside the cover by knocking up the edges on the work bench. Mark a line $^1/_4$-$^3/_8$in (6-10mm) in from the spine and mark four holes along this line: one at the head, and one at the tail (these should be the same distance from the edge as from the spine; the other two holes spaced evenly between them.)

Use a pair of dividers to set the distance. Pierce the holes with a thin awl. Thread a needle with the mercerized cotton, and knot the thread onto the needle.

1 Fold a sheet of tissue 35in x 25^1/$_2$in (89cm x 65cm) into 12.

2 Trim it to 11in x 5^1/$_2$in (28cm x 14cm). Cut one long edge, mark a line 5^1/$_2$in (14cm) from it and cut.

3 The short edges can be cut square using the lines on a cutting mat or with a set square.

4 Using a page as a template, take some scissors and roughly cut out colored tissue for the cover. It should be double the size of the template.

5 Fold all the pages and the cover in half.

6 Make a second fold in the cover to allow for the thickness of the pages.

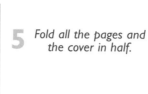

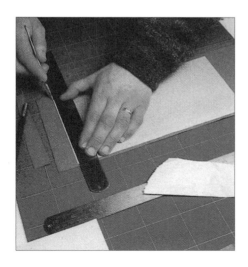

7 Use an open page to cut the cover on long edges and at 11in (28cm) from center folds.

8 Fold the cover in to the central folds.

9 Work the sewing in a figure of eight, tensioning the thread as you go. Finish by tying a reef knot.

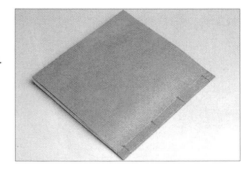

10 The finished book.

11 The stab-stitching restricts the book's opening. Take this into account when spacing letters.

Karlgeorg Hoefer—The title page of this small manuscript book reflects its delicate and tactile nature. A fine lightweight paper has been chosen to make the text block. Through these pages preceding and succeeding alphabets can be glimpsed. The book contains a visual feast of personal and calligraphic alphabets. An alphabet book such as this should grace every calligrapher's bookshelf—a personal exploration and rendering of elegant calligraphy displayed on well laid out pages, all in a beautifully handmade book.

Single-Section Binding

Combining the weak pages of a single-section binding with a tough cover made from millboard, and leather can be a problem. One possible solution is to use thread to act as the only hinge between the two. In this way one can avoid creating a tension between the pages, and the cover when the book opens.

Multi-Section Binding

The purpose of a design binding is to attract the reader. The cover is a vehicle for the binder's self-expression. The binding itself needs to be protected in a box.

The problem of making the soft watercolor paper compatible with heavy boards, and leather is solved by sewing each fold of paper onto strong, flexible supports, linen tapes, which are in turn attached to the boards. The linen tapes act as the hinges for the boards, rather than the leather. The leather has no part in the structure of the binding. The linen tapes also act as a flexible backbone for the pages so that they can open out flat.

1 A strip of thin leather, reinforced by a strip of aerolinen is sewn on to the pages using a figure of eight stitch.

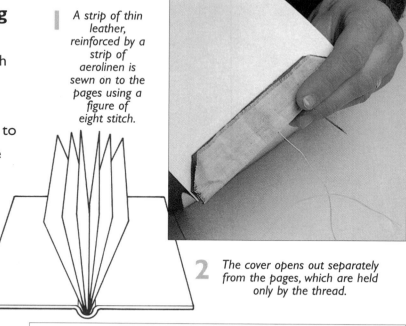

2 The cover opens out separately from the pages, which are held only by the thread.

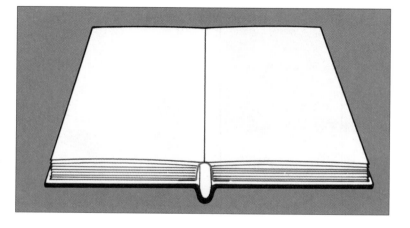

3 With the cover open flat the leather strip is pasted out with starch paste. It forms a 45° mitred joint with the leather turn-ins of the cover.

4 The structure of the book.

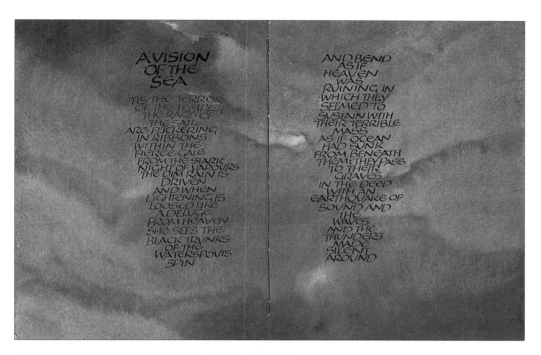

A VISION
OF THE
SEA

TIS THE TERROR
OF THE TEMPEST
THE RAGS OF
THE SAIL
ARE FLICKERING
IN RIBBONS
WITHIN THE
FIERCE GALE
FROM THE STARK
NIGHT OF VAPOURS
THE DIM RAIN IS
DRIVEN
AND WHEN
LIGHTENING IS
LOOSED LIKE
A DELUGE
FROM HEAVEN
SHE SEES THE
BLACK TRUNKS
OF THE
WATERSPOUTS
SPIN

AND BEND
AS IF
HEAVEN
WAS
RUINING IN
WHICH THEY
SEEMED TO
SUSTAIN WITH
THEIR TERRIBLE
MASS
AS IF OCEAN
HAD SUNK
FROM BENEATH
THEM: THEY PASS
TO THEIR
GRAVES
IN THE DEEP
WITH AN
EARTHQUAKE OF
SOUND AND
THE
WAVES
AND THE
THUNDERS
MADE
SILENT
AROUND

William Taunton – The calligraphy is written in dark blue watercolor on 300gsm (140lb) watercolor paper over multicolored washes.

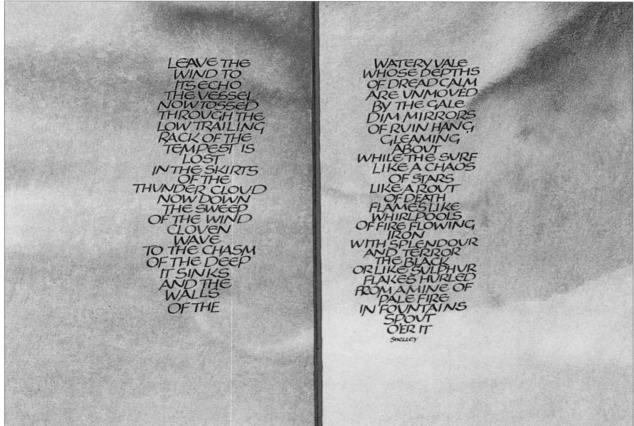

LEAVE THE
WIND TO
ITS ECHO
THE VESSEL
NOW TOSSED
THROUGH THE
LOW TRAILING
RACK OF THE
TEMPEST IS
LOST
IN THE SKIRTS
OF THE
THUNDER CLOUD
NOW DOWN
THE SWEEP
OF THE WIND
CLOVEN
WAVE
TO THE CHASM
OF THE DEEP
IT SINKS
AND THE
WALLS
OF THE

WATERY VALE
WHOSE DEPTHS
OF DREAD CALM
ARE UNMOVED
BY THE GALE
DIM MIRRORS
OF RUIN HANG
GLEAMING
ABOUT
WHILE THE SURF
LIKE A CHAOS
OF STARS
LIKE A ROUT
OF DEATH
FLAMES LIKE
WHIRLPOOLS
OF FIRE FLOWING
IRON
WITH SPLENDOUR
AND TERROR
THE BLACK
OR LIKE SULPHUR
FLAKES HURLED
FROM A MINE OF
PALE FIRE
IN FOUNTAINS
SPOUT
O'ER IT
SHELLEY

LETTERING IN CUT PAPER

The calligrapher learns that the shape of the letter derives directly from the use of the square-cut pen. Cut paper involves the use of a different tool, a sharp pair of scissors or a craft knife, and the character of the letter form changes accordingly.

In this project, the letters are cut freely in paper, without any preliminary drawing. It can be useful to use newsprint, as the printed columns give a rough guide to the size of the letter being cut, and letters cut in thin black paper work well. The basic form is that of a traditional letter, but natural variations arising from the use of the new tool are exploited and allowed to develop.

HOME SWEET HOME
Pat Russell 16¹/₄in x 22¹/₄in (30cm x 56cm)
Cut paper lettering was used as a pattern for a panel in layered and cut net and machine stitching, mounted on fabric (above).

ALPHA AND OMEGA
Pat Russell and Elizabeth Ford
8ft x 2¹/₃ft (68.5cm x 280cm)
Hanging in free appliqué and machine stitching, based on cut paper letters (left).

The family relationship of letters, learned from calligraphy, are respected, but the character of the letter reflects the direct cutting action of a pair of scissors or a craft knife. This can result in a somewhat angular letter form, and the round letters present interesting problems. Alpha and Omega and Home Sweet Home, show some ways in which this problem has been resolved. Letters cut with a knife will be subtly different in form from those cut with scissors.

Method

Work on soft board and stab-pin the cut-out letters into position on their appropriate background. Adjustments are easily made by altering or discarding and recutting the letters. They can be changed and moved around until the right balance between letter shape, and space is achieved and you feel the whole design presents a satisfying unity. This method enables you to keep a careful watch on the background spaces, those important areas inside and between letters, between words and between lines. Considerable patience and much hard work is required at this stage, but it is worth persevering until you are happy with the design. You can then paste down the letters accurately in position.

Alternative Forms

Another form of cut-paper letter can be built up from small strips of paper, each element of the letter being cut separately. This method is extremely flexible and can result in original, lively lettering. Since these letters are not pen-made, the distribution of their thick and thin strokes need not necessarily correspond to that of traditional letter forms; instead their placing is governed solely by the demands of the design. This works well with both

BEVERLEY
Student's work in progress using torn paper (above).
(Metchosin Summer School of Arts, Victoria, B.C., US)
Letters can be changed and moved until correct balance is achieved.

HOME SWEET HOME
Pat Russell 15in x 18in (38cm x 46cm) (below)
Small banner in colored felt. Color emphasis is on spaces between the letters.

capital and lower-case letters. Home Sweet Home was designed in this way, the elision of the letter forms developing spontaneously from the method of design used. Two fabric versions are shown, each based on the original cut-paper master pattern, one in layered and cut net, the other in colored felts. In the second, the color emphasis is on the spaces between the lettering, giving an entirely different aspect of the design.

Cut-paper lettering may also be used in graphic design and the paper collage can stand as an art form in its own right. The use of torn paper provides added dimension, the characteristic rough edges, and uncertain outlines producing letters of a very different nature from the cut variety.

Text and lettering by Pat Russell

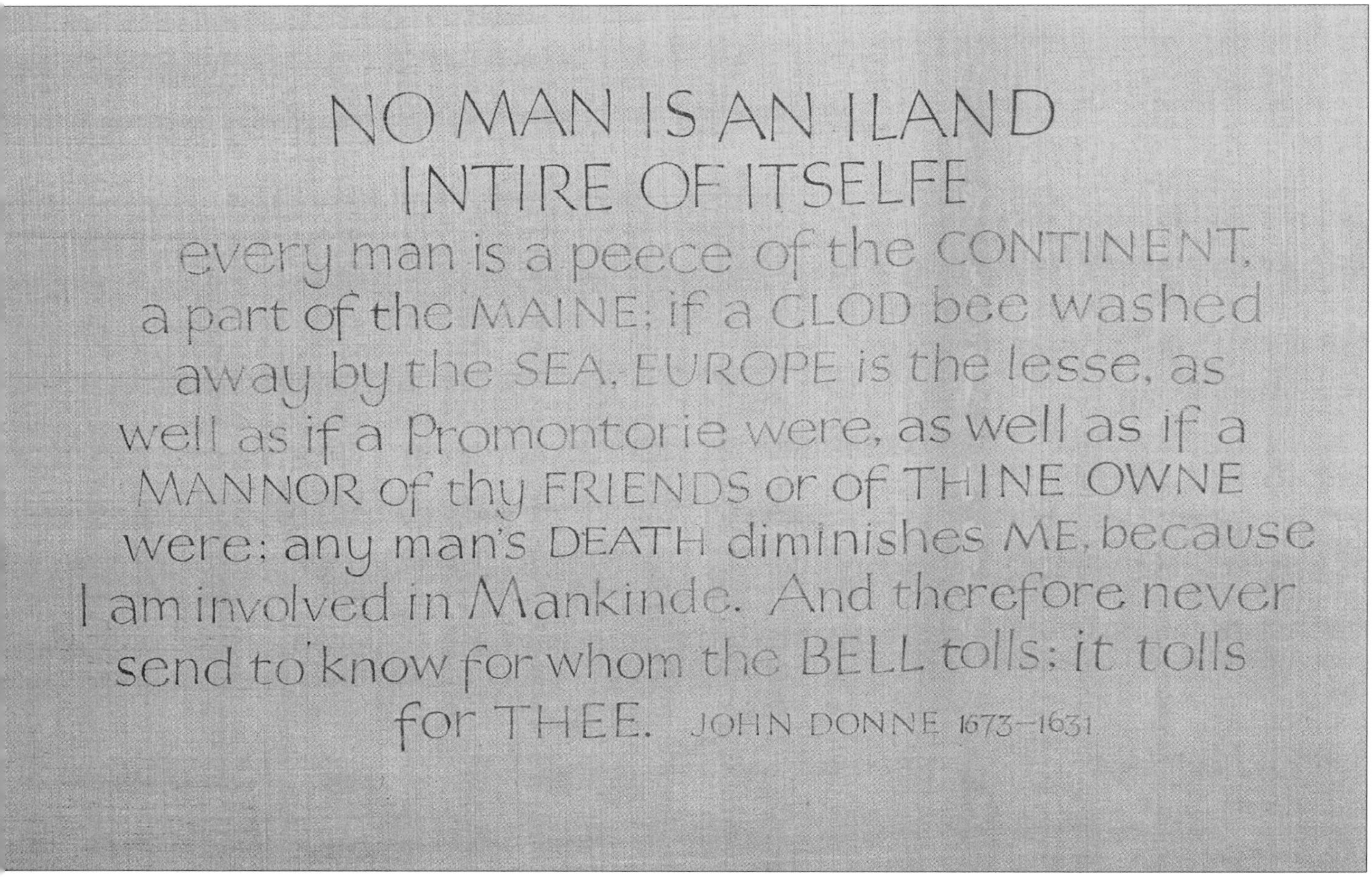

NO MAN IS AN ISLAND
– Brenda Berman
24in x 18in (61cm x 46cm)
Watercolor on Chinese silk.

ARIES
– Denis Brown
8in x 5in (20cm x 13cm)
Brush painted letters in gouache and bronze powder and raised and burnished gold on gesso. Paper was crumpled lightly while wet and dyed. Where the paper was creased more dye was absorbed.

WARM RAIN LADEN EAST WIND
– Susan Hufton
15in x 34in (120cm x 87cm)
Detail from a triptych. The background layer is of raw silk with a leaf pattern made by sponging gouache around leaf-shaped templates and then embroidering the veins. The remaining two layers are of silk organza; the watercolor letters have been painted on the top layer with a pointed brush.

USING A REED PEN

Reed pens, among the earliest forms of nibbed writing instruments, were commonly used by Middle Eastern scribes because of the plentiful supply of sturdy and suitable reeds in their regions. The Egyptians, too, made reed pens and soft reed brushes for writing on papyrus. The Romans, having adopted the use of papyrus, found the reed pen a most suitable instrument with which to write. It was sometimes referred to as a 'calamus', after the particular species of palm that provided the raw material. Cut to shape, the reed pen was used to apply ink to parchment and linen as well as papyrus.

A reed pen can be made quite easily and certainly cheaply. Garden cane is the material most commonly available now that provides an equivalent to the original type of reed. The hollow cane is easily cut to length and shaped, using a sharp knife, to form a writing nib. Inspect the cane carefully to make sure it has no splits or imperfections that could result in any number of disasters when you start using it to write.

The cane, being nothing but a hollow tube, provides an excellent reservoir for ink. You must take care not to let it flood the writing, so work on a flat or only slightly inclined surface. In common with most calligraphic implements, the reed pen resists a

1 *Assemble the materials. Soak the reed and cane for at least 15 minutes, then cut it with a sharp knife while it is still wet. Cut the cane to a comfortable length—about 8in (20cm) is usual. The first cut, shown here, is an oblique slash down toward one end.*

2 *Shape the shoulders of the nib. Then, using the point of the knife, clean out any pith inside the cane which has been exposed by the first cut.*

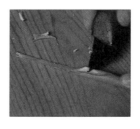

3 *Firmly hold the pen on the cutting surface and trim the end to nearer the eventual nib length. Turn the pen through 90° and make a small slit down the center of the nib, at right angles to the writing edge.*

4 *If the nib seems too thick, very carefully pare it down to make it thinner. Holding the nib underside up, make a vertical cut across the nib end.*

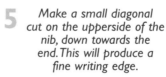

5 *Make a small diagonal cut on the upperside of the nib, down towards the end. This will produce a fine writing edge.*

6 *The reed pen is now ready to use. A brush is used to transfer ink onto the underside of the nib.*

USING A REED PEN

1 *A reed pen has a different 'feel' to a metal-nibbed pen; because it is made all in one piece, it feels almost like an extension of your hand and is very pleasurable to use. The width of the strokes made with a reed pen is dictated by how wide the nib has been cut. This illustration demonstrates the firm and solid strokes which this simple instrument is capable of producing.*

2 *The reed pen has the ability to produce both the extremely fine lines and the thick strokes required for calligraphy. Holding the reed pen at the prescribed pen angle, a fine line is extended from the tail of the letter. To complete the line the right-hand side of the nib is lifted off the paper, and the left-hand side of the nib drags wet ink onto a hairline.*

3 *The lower-case letters are written confidently, and show how a nib made from an inflexible material can produce very well the familiar characteristics of calligraphy. When working with a reed pen, always keep the top side of the nib clean. Take care not to overload with ink, as this could result in blotting or smudging.*

pushing motion and you obtain best results from pulling the stroke.

In comparison with the quill, the reed pen has less flexibility. It cannot sustain such fine and accurate shaping, and the overall effect of work written with this pen may not be as eloquent. It does have excellent qualities, however, which make it a valid implement for many styles of writing. The calligrapher can select canes of different sizes, and prepare a varied range of nib widths accordingly. The resulting bold lettter forms are highly effective in poster work, headings, and titles, and can be matched to specific 'one-off' jobs where a particular nuance is sought.

The Romans used the reed pen in the execution of their square capitals and rustic hands. The method of holding the pen between the index and middle fingers must have influenced the way Rustica letters evolved, with thin uprights and thick cross strokes. Other variations occurred with these letterforms, including a slight pull to the right in curved strokes, and a condensing of the overall shape, especially as compared to the roundness of the Roman capitals.

BRUSH LETTERING

Brushes are an excellent tool for practice and experimentation. The ability to use different brushes and a variety of inks and paints is a great asset, providing a range of instant visualisations.

The best way to learn the possibilities of brush lettering is to work on quite a large scale and freely, in an informal style. A 'hidden agenda' exists when working with brushes; particularly when the ink or paint on the brush diminishes, resulting in interesting textural contrasts. For example, if the ink runs dry in mid-letter, you can make a positive feature of the change of emphasis, rather than dispensing with the work.

Experiment by placing wet, different colors side by side and letting them merge. Planning the color selection can produce exciting, and interesting results. Broad, flat, or square-cut brushes produce bold lettering. Manipulation of the brush angle, particularly when doing a horizontal stroke, creates further interest.

When working with brushes, you will soon realize that, having found a successful solution in rough form, recreating the exact same image in the finished work is not easy. Regard this as an exciting challenge, not as a deterrent. Because of the free movement of the brush, a good understanding of letter shapes is essential to achieve convincing lettering.

Discovering which brush to use, to achieve the required impact, is truly a matter of

ARRANGING LETTERS

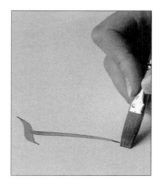

1 *Working with a large square-cut brush permits much freedom of individual expression. The first letter provides an anchor from which the remaining letters can hang or around which they can be grouped. The letters are constructed in the traditional manner of following a stroke sequence. The brush is held at an angle either suitable to the chosen style of lettering or to produce the intended weight of stroke for a particular piece.*

2 *Pleasing arrangements can be arrived at, often unintentionally, when practicing lettering with a brush. An extended stroke to create a swashed letter is easily accomplished with a brush.*

3 *The introduction of a second color and a different weight of letter provides two immediate contrasts. Delicate strokes made with a fine-pointed brush further contrast with the weight of broad strokes made with a flat brush.*

4 *The completed piece illustrates contrasts of color, letter size, and style. Consideration has been made up of the space occupied by the freely written individual letters, and of their collective arrangement.*

EXPLORING SINGLE LETTER SHAPES

1 *Practicing single letter shapes with a large square-cut brush provides an excellent method for learning about letter construction. The sequence of strokes which make up the letters is the same as that used with a pen.*

2 *Using a brush provides a flexibility of physical approach not available with other instruments. The springiness and lightness of touch of the brush hairs on the page, compared with the rigidity of a steel nib, allow much freedom of movement across the page.*

3 *The opportunity to dispense with the confines of guidelines is a chance to experiment with offsetting letters on the page.*

4 *The head of the brush is kept at a consistent angle to enable thick and thin strokes to be formed.*

5 *Even if some of the letters do not 'feel' right, do not abandon the piece: the purpose here is simply to Practice manipulating the brush. Exercises like this one should be approached in a relaxed manner.*

trial and error. Favorite solutions will reveal themselves so get to know the marks of as many brushes as possible. The traditions of Eastern calligraphy are founded in the use of brushes; the hairs of which come to a fine point, making different marks from those of square-cut brushes. Your attempts at lettering with pointed brushes may result in images related to Oriental brush-writing styles. Study of Eastern brush techniques will make an enriching addition to your repertoire.

Brush lettering can be incorporated in a wide range of designs, creating strong visual effects with an enticing air of informality. For example, a brush lettered headline next to the more formal writing of the metal nib is very effective. In this rule, brush lettering played a major part in advertising design of the 1930s and 1940s particularly in the United States of America. If you look at examples of advertising design from that period, you will see the potential of using freely written brush script with formal typeset copy.

USING A POINTED BRUSH

1 *A pointed brush, of the kind used for Chinese calligraphy, is excellent for practicing freely constructed letters. Chinese brushes are designed to hold much more paint or ink than a traditional Western watercolor brush.*

2 *Chinese brushes are also versatile: fine strokes can be produced with the tip, and broad strokes with the body.*

HERALDRY

No work dealing with art up to the advent of printing in the fifteenth, and sixteenth centuries can fail to take note of heraldry.

In an age when the majority of the population was illiterate, easily recognized heraldic devices were used to signify ownership, patronage, possession, authority and corporate identity. Heraldic forms and devices were so important that they appeared on manuscripts and documents, on churches, colleges and buildings, as well as on personal possessions and everyday items. The art form has since developed over the centuries, and although nowadays due regard is paid to historical precedent, it is still evolving and will no doubt continue to do so.

The origins of heraldry lie in the painting of devices on warriors' shields that were intended both to terrify the foe and to invoke the supernatural powers of a protective deity. With the advent of metal weapons, a protective garment of chain mail was adopted, over which was worn a long, loose-fitting surcoat made of stout material.

This 'war coat' or 'coat of arms', would be painted with the same device displayed on the shield. (The heraldic coat of arms is more properly called an 'achievement') With the advent of metal helmets covering the face, heraldic devices were necessary to identify people in the heat of battle, and so they became personal emblems of identification.

At first people would often use different emblems for different occasions, but later these became both personal and hereditary, when personal emblems, in the form of seals bearing the device displayed on the shield, were used to mark possessions and authenticate documents. An absent lord who needed to communicate with his distant, and often illiterate servants would send a messenger wearing a tabard (a garment decorated

with his master's arms) to provide his identity. The messenger would then display the master's seal attached to the message that he was carrying to prove its veracity. When a son inherited his father's estates, he would display the family arms as a sign of his right of possession.

Thus it was that heraldic devices became both hereditary and associated with the titles that were being claimed. Later the achievements became associated with land, and so it became common to see several different devices displayed on one shield as its bearer became more powerful and acquired more land. Each component of such a device is known as a quartering. A shield can have any number of quarterings (sometimes even more than 200).

Sometimes disputes arose over the use of arms, for it was not uncommon for completely unrelated people to adopt the same designs. Eventually the monarch's

messengers, the heralds (from whom the word 'heraldry' is derived), adjudicated in disputes and issued new coats of arms to aspirant 'armigers', as one who has the right to bear a coat of arms is called. They also were charged with keeping records, and making themselves familiar with the devices of armigerous people. When the monarch went to war, the heralds were able to recognize members of the opposition by their heraldic devices, and thus advised the king of the strength of their forces. After a battle, they identified the slain.

Heraldry is still in use today, for many successful individuals continue to be granted the right to bear arms. Modern heraldic devices are devised to contain elements and designs that both reflect our own time, and preserve and uphold the traditions of the last millennia. Corporate bodies, too, can draw on heraldic tradition to proclaim the corporate identity of their institutions.

Heraldic Design

Because heraldry has its roots in military usage, the few rules that govern it were designed to promote visual clarity on the battlefield. The principle rule concerns color. The surface of the shield is known as 'the field', and anything that is placed on it 'a charge'. It is vital that the color of any charge is distinct from that of the field to enable it to be seen clearly. To this end, the colors used in heraldry are split into three groups: 'metals', 'colors' and 'furs'. Metal must never be placed on metal or color on color. (Furs are not bound by these restrictions). In practice, gold and silver are not used because of their tendency to tarnish, and so white and yellow are used instead.

With only this small number of colors available to the designer, it would be impossible to keep arms unique, and so it has become the practice to divide the field into different colors. Each of these divisions has a name that can be described in two words (see Figures 2 and 3).

Charges

Any object that is placed on a field, be it of a whole or divided color, is known as a charge. A charge is usually chosen because it has some significance for the person who is to bear it. It is impossible to list all of them here but a few groups need a special mention: the ordinaries, the subordinaries, geometric shapes, crosses, animals and birds.

The Ordinaries

This group of charges is so commonly used that it is known as 'the ordinaries'. It is

FIGURE 1
1,2: THE METALS:
GOLD (YELLOW) AND
WHITE (SILVER).
3,4: THE FURS:
ERMINE (IN VARIETY),
VAIR (IN VARIETY).
5, 6, 7, 8, 9: THE COLORS:
RED, BLUE, PURPLE,
GREEN AND BLACK.

thought that the designs were derived from the shield's original strengthening bars (see Figure 4).

The Subordinaries

The subordinaries are a group of lesser ordinaries (see Figure 5 overleaf).

Geometric Shapes

A number of geometric shapes are used in heraldry (see figure 6 overleaf).

Crosses

The cross is a very commonly used charge and may appear in over 150 different designs.

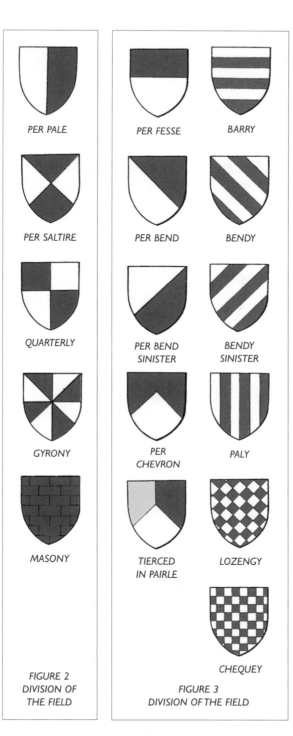

FIGURE 2
DIVISION OF THE FIELD

FIGURE 3
DIVISION OF THE FIELD

As the number of gentlemen bearing arms increased, single-tincture coats of arms were no longer sufficient, despite the variety of changes placed upon them, to distinguish one from another. Two-colored shields were therefore introduced.

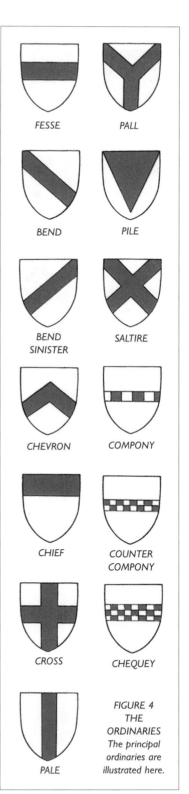

FIGURE 4
THE ORDINARIES
The principal ordinaries are illustrated here.

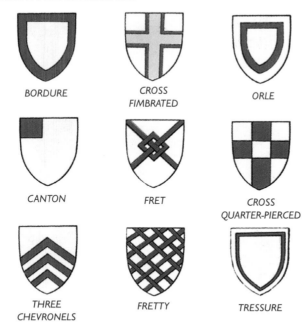

FIGURE 5 THE SUBORDINARIES

BORDURE

CROSS FIMBRATED

ORLE

CANTON

FRET

CROSS QUARTER-PIERCED

THREE CHEVRONELS

FRETTY

TRESSURE

Animals and Birds

Animals are very commonly used and appear in a variety of postures (the more common are shown in Figure 7). Similarly, birds often appear in heraldic art and also have a variety of set postures which enable them to be described verbally (see Figure 8). Special terms are reserved for fish and deer, as well as for parts of the human body. The limbs of creatures and humans are shown either 'couped', as if cut off cleanly, or 'erased', as if torn off. The lion and eagle are traditionally considered the most noble of the animals and birds, and the mythical griffin (part lion and part eagle) is said to combine the best characteristics of both and to be the fiercest creature.

Supporters

Although the shield is the main vehicle for the display of heraldic devices, it is not the only item in a complete heraldic achievement. A pair of supporters—two figures, animal or human—standing on either side of the shield and holding it up are common. (These are derived from the days of knightly tournaments, when the contestants; shields were borne round the arena by two pages.)

Helmets and Crests

Helmets appear in different forms, according to the rank of the person. The crest is displayed on top of the helmet. (In medieval times it secured the mantling that hung down behind the helmet to protect the back of the wearer's neck.) The mantling is secured by either a torse or wreath—usually material of two colors twisted into a band that fits round the helmet, coronet or cap of maintenance to keep everything in place. If the bearer is a member of the nobility, their coronet of rank may be displayed below the helmet.

The whole group may be shown standing on a 'compartment', which may display a motto on a riband draped across it.

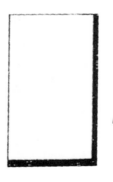

FIGURE 6 GEOMETRIC SHAPES

MOLLET

BILLET

FIGURE 7 ANIMALS

A LION GARDANT HAS ITS
FACE TOWARDS THE VIEWER.

A LION DOUBLE-QUEUED
HAS TWO TAILS.

A FORKED TAIL IS CALLED A
QUEUE FOURCHY.

A LION LOOKING BACKWARDS
IS CALLED REGARDANT.

FIGURE 8
BIRDS

ADDORSED

DISPLAYED

DOUBLE-HEADED

INVERTED

THE ANIMALS

1

5

9

2

6

10

3

7

11

4

8

12

1. Two lions walking in opposite directions are said to be counter passant.

2. Two lions leaping in opposite directions are said to be counter salient.

3. A lion at rest is dormant.

4. Small lions charged on a shield are called lioncells.

5,6,7. A lion walking across a shield is passant; when it is also looking at the observer (passent guardant). It is known as a leopard.

8. A lion rearing up is rampant.

9. Salient describes an animal leaping across a shield.

10. A lion on its haunches is statant.

11. A lion simply standing, motionless, is described as statant.

12. Two lions rampant, back-to-back, are called addorsed.

ILLUMINATED LETTERS

If you have ever looked closely at any medieval illuminated manuscripts, you will probably be struck by the fact that its survival is a miracle. Illuminations are obviously delicate works of art, with intricate designs painted and embellished with gold on parchment and vellum and yet they were often handled daily by generations of owners—monks or priests, academics or courtiers—as they turned the pages to learn or teach from them or merely to look at them. Often such illuminated manuscripts were taken on travels overseas—and yet you can still see them today, with the brilliance of the gold leaf and the rich colors of the painted pigments as fresh as ever.

In this chapter, we glance back over the history of illuminated letters, at the artists who created them as well as patrons who commissioned them. In the second part of the chapter, several illuminated letters are adapted from original masterpieces, and their re-creation is clearly demonstrated in step-by-step stages, starting with an initial from the Lindisfarne Gospels and finishing with a contemporary horoscope letter created in the 1990s.

HISTORY OF ILLUMINATION

Who Were The Artists?

There are medieval drawings and paintings which show monks at work in cloisters, bowed over books, pens in hand. They were busy transcribing or illuminating books for people to learn from, and pray with and books to be used for missionary work. The magical properties which illumination gave to medieval books heightened the standing of their creators: we even know the name of the scribe, and illuminator of the Lindisfarne Gospels, Eadfrith, who became the Bishop of Lindisfarne in May of 698.

When book illumination became more widely desired by the richer merchant classes at the beginning of the thirteenth century, illumination moved out of the cloister. This created the need for secular scribes and illuminators who would travel to the new university towns, and centers of learning to work. The famous Limbourg brothers, who gave life to *Les Tres Riches Heures* for the Duc de Berry, moved form the Low Countries to take up work in Paris.

How Did They Work?

We can learn much about medieval book production by looking closely at the pages of the original manuscripts. Equally miniatures showing monks at work, particularly the Evangelists from books of gospels, reveal a great deal.

First of all, the materials—vellum and parchment, ink, colored pigments, powdered gold, and gold leaf—would be prepared and gathered together. The vellum and parchment,

Example of illumination from LES GRANDES HEURES of the Duc de Berry.

Fourteenth century woodcut, now preserved in the Soissons in France, shows a monk at work in the cloister.

from calf or sheep-skin, was laboriously prepared: soaked in water and lime, then scraped and stretched. Once dried, the vellum was folded into halves, quarters or eighths, depending on the required size of the book. These pages would then be trimmed and stitched together. Ink was made from powdered carbon—soot or lamp-black or irongall—which was kept in a cow horn and materials for the colored pigments came from a variety of animal, vegetable, and mineral sources.

The magical properties which illumination gave to medieval books heightened the standing of their creators

Often, the scribe would be making an exact copy of another text, so he needed to mark guidelines and rules onto the pages. He did this by marking the top sheet, then piercing through a sheaf of leaves with a sharp tool to form holes on all the pages. These would then be joined together when each new page was started.

Once the materials had been gathered and prepared, the paper marked and the illuminator had indicated the space needed for the decorated borders, initial letters and miniatures, the scribe could begin work. A portrait of the monk Eadwine, the "prince of all scribes", from a Psalter and Gloss made in Canterbury, c. 1150, clearly shows the method of working—with a pen in one hand and a curved knife in the other, the latter being used for sharpening the pen and scraping out mistakes. From this, we can also tell that the techniques of illumination used today are very similar to those used in medieval times.

Why Were Books Illuminated?

Religious texts—gospels and psalters—were originally illuminated to honor God, but some of this decoration seems a little lavish simply for devotional purposes. Indeed, it had other uses. From a purely practical point of view, illumination, for example of the gospels, helped a missionary or priest to find his way around the text. There were full pages of decoration between each gospel, and decorated initials gave a visual clue to the contents of the page. For the missionary, certain miniatures were painted with a large audience in mind. In the Lindisfarne Gospels, for example, the full-color, stylized portraits of the Evangelists could have been seen at some distance. Books in medieval times bestowed a certain standing upon their owners. Illuminated books in particular represented wealth and power. Missionaries could take full advantage of this, as well as Carolingian emperors, kings and feudal princes. For example, in early medieval times, medicines made from water in which pages from a holy book had been soaked were taken in the belief that they were cures for certain illnesses. Equally it was believed that the books, if tampered with, coud inflict great pain.

Throughout their history, illuminated books must also have been appreciated as works of art, and certainly in the Renaissance they were commissioned and collected as such. Let us take a brief look at the style of these works as they developed over the centuries.

Development of Styles

The breakup of the Roman empire almost destroyed the art of illumination and the use of friable papyrus means that there are very few surviving examples from this early classical period. But the art slowly re-emerged in France, Spain, Ireland and northern Britain; described as the Insular style and painted on more durable parchment or vellum, it was heavily influenced by invading tribes from the North.

Celtic Extremes in Style

The Celtic style came within the general term in Insular style. Developed in Celtic Ireland, it was taken to Scotland by a group of Irish missionaries led

Examples of illumination from the LINDISFARNE GOSPELS

by St. Columba in 563. They established a monastery on the island of Iona in western Scotland, and in 635 they founded the monastery of Lindsifarne on the Northumbrian coast, where the Lindisfarne Gospels were transcribed and decorated, c. 698.

A page from these Gospels can be

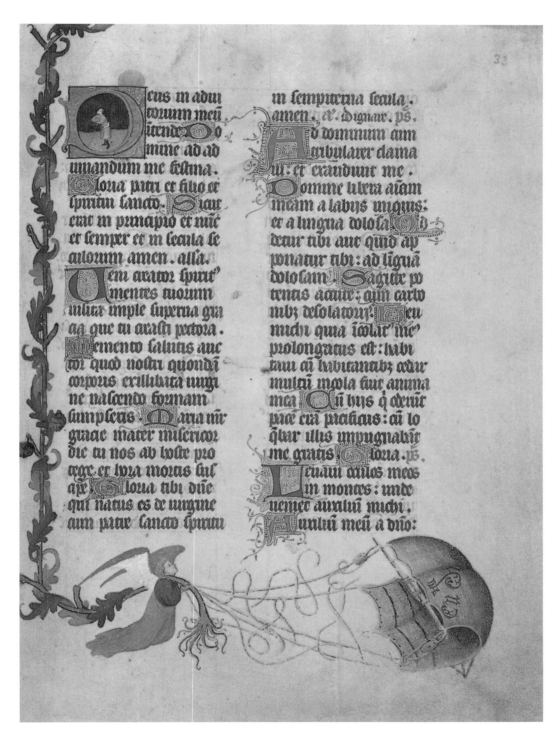

Above: A page from the Egerton manuscript has a refined border on one side which continues to the top of the page. At its base, the foliage border is linked with the illustration, dragged along over the shoulder of an angel. A miniature painting is contained in the counter shape of the first initial letter. Linear and spiral patterns and trailing fine lines decorate the Lombardic Versal letters and the strong influence of Uncial letter shapes is clear.

recognized by the clarity of the linear design—in the spirals, interlaced and intertwined birds and animals—and the purity of color—bright blue, green and red, shades of pinks and purples, as well as yellow used instead of gold. The pages were also given a unique rosy glow by the outlining of the letters with tiny red dots, known as *rubrication*. "Carpet" pages of abstract design - knotwork and interlacing - break up the Gospels, and full-page portraits of the Evangelists are stylized.

The Book of Kells, which shows another face of Celtic art, was first discovered in the twelfth century in Kells, outside Dublin. It, too, may have come from the north of Britain. The principal initial letters are richly decorated in a glorious combination of motifs: circles within circles, intricate knotwork and human heads. The work is highly imaginative and sophisticated and, compared with the Lindisfarne Gospels, there is an unconstrained sense of freedom in the design.

Anglo-Saxon

In 601, the first missionaries came to the south of England from Pope Gregory the Great in Rome. Even with such Roman influence, early examples of Anglo-Saxon illumination, in the eighth and ninth centuries, show much more Celtic influence in the script and decoration. Closer to these roots and a great influence even beyond the shores of England, was the Winchester School, which flowered in the tenth century. The style of this school was characterized by the elongated necks and rippling drapery of its figures, which defy the naturalism of antiquity and capitalize on an early form of expressionism.

Later Anglo-Saxon illumination was influenced by classical Roman and Byzantine sources - the figures were more solid and the

(Above) A detail from a page of the Book of Kells.

(Right) This Anglo-Saxon woodcut shows a group monks with rolls of parchment ready for illumination.

drapery hung in plate-like folds. In general, the illumination was richer and more sophisticated, and the classical curling acanthus-leaf decoration became popular.

A late example of Anglo-Saxon illumination from the Grimbald Gospels,

This spread from an early sixteenth-century French Book of Hours has an uncomplicated layout. A decorative border frames the Humanistic script inscribed text, which has minimally illuminated initial letters. The illustration is surrounded by an architectural device in a style common at the time of the Renaissance.

which were completed in the early eleventh century, shows Celtic influence in the design of the knotwork, but the figures and the border reveal a classical influence.

Revival of Classical Idioms

While missionaries continued to struggle across Europe carrying their illuminated manuscripts, other centers of book production emerged.
One such center
was the court
of
Charlemagne,
who was crowned
Emperor of the West in 800, in Rome. Charlemagne's love of books, and his realisation of the power of the written word helped to establish
illuminated works as essential possessions for the rich and powerful. Popular manuscripts included classical texts, such as the works of Horace and Cicero, as well as standard

religious works, such as gospels and psalters. Design and content at this time were influenced by classical sources, often with gold script on purple-stained vellum, in the manner of the Roman Emperors. A new script, called *Carolingian Minuscule*, was introduced by Charlemagne. It was small and round with vertical ascenders and descenders, and so was easy to read and write. Humanists of the later Renaissance period believed these texts to be classical originals, thus the first script used for printing in the fifteenth century was based on Carolingian Minuscule. This script has since been passed down to us as "Roman".

The Gospels of Otto III

Illumination went into decline after Charlemagne's death in 814, until Otto III, crowned *Holy Roman Emperor* in 983, revived the splendor of Charlemagne's court and with it the importance of illumination. The golden binding from the Gospels of Otto III has survived, complete with studded jewels and pearls, classical carved stones and insets of Byzantine ivory. As you can see from the Ottonian 'V' the illumination of the period was every bit as rich, lavishly decorated with gold, and painted the colors of precious gems.

Below: The adaptation of an Ottonian initial 'V'.

Romanesque

In Britain, a further development of the Insular style in combination with the classical Roman style resulted in the style called Romanesque. At this time, the historical initial—a letter depicting a narrative scene in its center—became more popular, as well as decorations of writhing, snapping beasts.

Early Gothic

Alongside the religious orders, kings, princes and courtiers, a new market for illuminated books developed in the thirteenth century among the rising middle classes. Psalters and bestiaries were popular but very expensive, so

While missionaries continued to struggle across Europe carrying their illuminated manuscripts, other centers of book production emerged.

many households owned just one or two.

Signs of Gothic influence in medieval illumination are easier to identify in the miniatures of the period, where figures are finer and adopt the Gothic sinuous sway. Changes in letter decoration are not so obvious, although the new popularity of books resulted in smaller volumes and illumination on a reduced scale.

High Gothic

The book of hours became very popular in the fifteenth century. It was a devotional book used by laymen for prayer and contained a yearly calendar with the Occupations of the Months and the Hours of the Office of the Virgin, each illustrated with a miniature.

Perhaps the best known of the High Gothic patrons was Jean, Duc de Berry (1340-1416), who commissioned a book of hours for the glory of owning a work painted by the three Limbourg brothers. However, both patron and all three artists died before its completion.

(Above) Detail from LES GRANDES HEURES painted by the Limbourg brothers, c. 1400.

Miniatures from this book are still to be marveled at for their depiction of everyday life, and their use of clear jewel-like colors.

Decoration became increasingly natural too. Illuminated letters from *Les Trés Riches Heures*, as well as the Duc de Berry's Psalter, appear to be intertwined with growing flowers and leaves. Such letters were highly gilded, emphasising the courtly influence of the High Gothic style.

Realism

It was the Italian humanists of the Renaissance who coined the term "Gothic" to define what they saw as the barbaric art that had come before the rebirth of classical learning. What they aspired to was the intellectual knowledge, and realism of the classical artists of Greece and Rome. This required artists to research all sorts of subjects that would not have been necessary in the past and which, in time, gave the artist a new role in society.

This new realism percolated quickly down to the art of the illuminator, particularly in schools in Italy, such as Venice and Florence, that were attached to the city republics. Indeed, illumi-nators were busy all over Europe keeping abreast of the tide of commissions, which came not only from princes and courtiers, but from men made rich by wool, banking or trade. An important school thrived in the Low Countries at this time in Ghent/Bruges. From this came the Hastings Hours, c. 1480, which was made for William, Lord Hastings, in which a height of realism is reached in trompe l'oeil margins, strewn with flowers which cast shadows on a gilded ground.

Whitevine Interlace

Borders and letters intertwined with a flourishing climbing vine, known as Whitevine interlace,

became fashionable in the early fifteenth century. The Italian humanists copied this type of motif from twelfth-century Italian manuscripts, believing they were reviving a classical motif. It thrived and was distributed from the humanist center in Florence.

Whitevine interlace was mainly used to decorate the borders and initials of classical texts such as Thucydides

Above: Painted in Rome in the fifteenth century, this initial "P" has been extracted from a seething mass of whitevine on a page from a classical text (Eutropius' HISTORY OF ROME) with a decorated border and initial.

Classical

The Italian Renaissance generated an even wider interest in collecting books. Some bibliophiles concentrated on obtaining classical Latin texts and, when the originals were not available, they commissioned copies. Vespasiano da Bisticci (1422-98), the great Florentine bookseller, organized thirty-five scribes to complete 200 manuscripts in almost two years for the library of Cosimo de Medici.

Vying for popularity with the Florentine Whitevine style, a more classical style based on early Roman inscriptions emerged in the mid-fifteenth century in northeastern Italy. The initial from Homer's *Iliad* now in the Vatican Library in Rome is in this classical style. The page is framed in an architectural border—a three dimensional illusion supporting the two dimensions of the written page. The initial letter is also three dimensional, gilded and painted to look like Roman inscriptions in stone, then decorated with classical motifs—acanthus leaves and medallions.

Arts and Crafts

The invention of printing in 1471 had no immediate effect on the art of illumination. Books continued to be transcribed and decorated; indeed, some of the first printed books were illuminated with borders and initials. Slowly, though, the art died out, taking with it the skills of the artists and craftsmen. It was not until the birth of the Arts and Crafts Movement in England after the Great Exhibition of 1851 that the techniques of illumination were rediscovered. This movement, spearheaded by William Morris, disliked the poor workmanship that resulted from mass production and tried to re-establish the mastery, and appreciation of manual arts and crafts.

Right: A typical example of a William Morris border with intertwining plant forms from THE KELMSCOTT CHAUCER.

327

Morris himself practiced several of the skills that were re-learned and went on to study medieval illumination. The Kelmscott Press, founded by Morris in 1890, regenerated public interest in fine book production.

Contemporary Illumination

Despite the painstaking and time-consuming character of illumination, this art not only survives today, but thrives in schools and colleges whilst being practiced by individual artists. Rather than schools of artists, there exist individuals who have made a name for themselves. Work is mainly executed to commission, and is nurtured by the late twentieth-century love of calligraphy and genealogy. But a glance at the work shown in this book will show you just how inventive the modern illuminator can be.

Left: This illuminated poem, 'GATHER YE ROSEBUDS', is by contemporary illuminator Margaret Wood and has been painted in Elizabethan style on vellum.

Seventh Century Fish

The two fish depicted in this project are from a seventh-century Italian gospel. Fishes are very adaptable creatures to use in letterforms, as they can be straight or curved.

YOU WILL NEED

- **Tracing paper**
- **Project paper**
- **2H and 6B pencils**
- **Masking tape**
- **Nos 2 and 0000 brushes**
- **Gouache paints: ultramarine, crimson lake, brilliant yellow, flame red, lamp black, purple lake, madder carmine**
- **Crayons in the same colors as the gouache paints (above)**

Design Tips

- Outlining requires practice. However, it is worth mastering the technique because it draws everything together, tidies up the loose edges and adds a crispness to the work. Paint straight from the tube, adding water to the mouth until the paint is the consistency of thin cream. Use the smallest brush that you have. Hold quite close to the tip so that it is almost vertical when you use it. Steadily stroke your way round the outlines, overlapping each stroke as you go. You need to paint the thinnest line that you can manage and keep constant. Do not worry if you end up with a slight irregularity in width, but try to avoid painting an overly heavy line as this spoils the whole effect. You can correct or tidy up the odd wobble, or stray whisker on the outside with permanent white.

329

1 Trace the design from the original using a 2H pencil. Turn over the tracing paper and go over the back of the design with a 6B pencil. Now turn it up the right way.

2 Remove the tracing paper and quickly trace the design again onto a piece of spare paper. Color the design on the spare piece of paper with crayons to test that you are satisfied with the color scheme that you intend to use. (You may feel that this step is unnecessary and be quite happy with the colors as they are. However it is worth doing, because as well as testing the colors for this particular project, you can keep the crayoned roughs for reference and as source material for future projects. Note: I may not specify this step in future projects).

3 Tape down the tracing paper. Draw over the design again with a sharp 2H pencil. An impression of the design will be left on your paper from the 6B lead on the back.

4 Mix a little ultramarine and crimson lake, well diluted with water, to make a violet color and paint these areas. Leave the white of the eye unpainted. Fill in the black of the eye with lamp black or a pen.

5 Paint the red, yellow and green areas using a No. 2 brush and flame red, brilliant yellow and a mixture of ultramarine and yellow. Take the color directly from the tube, introducing just enough water to make the paint a thin, cream-like consistency. Take care not to paint outside the segments of color so that the hues are kept clean and the striking effect of the pattern is not diluted.

6 Outline the design with madder carmine and a No. 0000 brush.

Ninth Century M

This handsome 'M' has been copied from a ninth-century gospel. It is a good project to help you get started because it requires you to be neat and exact, so that all the lines which make up its shape are properly parallel to each other and all the blocks are straight. You should do your best to paint and finish it without the aid of a ruler. In this way you will preserve the essential correctness of the design but retain the individuality of hand-done work, which gives freshness and interest.

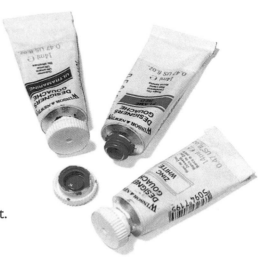

YOU WILL NEED

- **Tracing paper**
- **Project paper**
- **2H and 6B pencils**
- **Gouache paints: yellow ochre, flame red, ultra marine, permanent green (light), madder carmine, crimson lake**
- **Crayons in the same colors as the gouache paints**
- **Nos 2 and 0000 brushes**

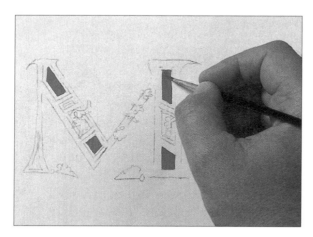

1   Trace the outline with a 2H pencil and go over the
    back with a 6B pencil.

2   Trace the design onto a piece of rough paper and
    color it with a crayon.

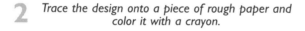

3   Trace the drawing onto your project page, checking
    the image against the original and making
    corrections as necessary.

4   Paint the red, blue and green areas straight from the
    tube, using flame red, ultramarine and permanent
    green (light) and a No. 2 brush. Now mix a lavender
    color from a watery solution of ultramarine and crim-
    son lake and paint the appropriate areas.

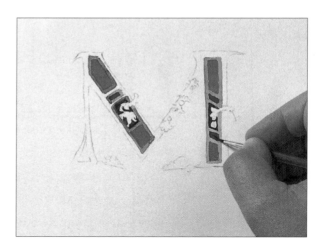

5   Mix a little yellow ochre with some water to make
    creamy consistency and then paint the yellow areas,
    making sure that you preserve the integrity of the
    straight and parallel lines.

6   Mix some madder carmine with a little water to
    make a thin, creamy consistency and, with the great-
    est possible care and using a No 0000 brush, outline
    the design with a slim, slender line.

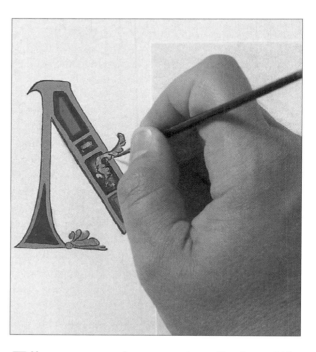

7   You may now need to correct the outline from within,
    using the color that it covers, use permanent white
    on the outside.

Eleventh Century Spanish A

These two fish form an elegantly simple letter 'A' and were taken from a copy of an eleventh-century Spanish Bible. They offer a good opportunity for you to practice your outlining. As the project is quite short, and the design uncluttered you will be able to work on your outlining without having extra visual distraction. With the longer projects that come later on in the book, where maintaining a crisp outline is so important, it is better to leave this task until you are fresh. However this design will not take long to complete, so you can complete it in one go. Furthermore the color scheme is bright and clear, so you will be able to see and correct your outline.

YOU WILL NEED

- **Tracing paper**
- **Project paper**
- **2H and 6B pencils**
- **Nos 2 and 0000 brushes**
- **Gouache paints: yellow ochre, madder carmine**
- **Indian ink**
- **Mapping pen**

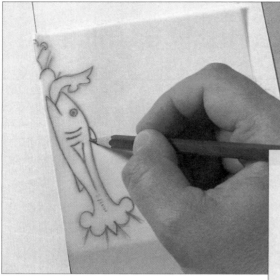

1 Trace the fishes with a 2H pencil. If you want them both to be identical and symmetrical, trace only one on one side of your tracing paper. Fold the tracing paper in half, at the point where the middle would have been ahd you traced the pair. With the first fish on the underside, trace over the outline of the second fish on the top side. You should now find two identical fishes nose to nose when you open up the paper. (This is a very useful method if you have to draw anything that has two symmetrical elements, such as swags, cartouches, shields, hearts and so on.)

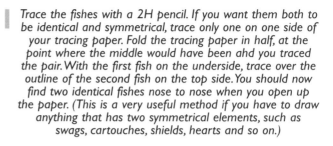

2 Pencil over the back of your first tracing with a 6B pencil. Place the tracing on your project paper and trce down the design.

3 Take some yellow ochre mixed with enough water to make a weak wash and quickly but carefully paint over each fish with a No 2 brush, leaving out the eyes.

4 While the wash is still wet, paint the fishes all over, using a No 2 brush and taking paint directly from the tube of yellow gouache. The damp surface will create an opaque, all-covering coat tat is both dense and even.

6 With a mapping pen and Indian ink, draw in the fish scales. (Take care not to have too much ink on the pen or it will bleed into the paint. Also try to make sure that you do not press too hard when you are drawing on the paint, otherwise you will cut into the surface with the sharp nib.) Finally, draw the fountain.

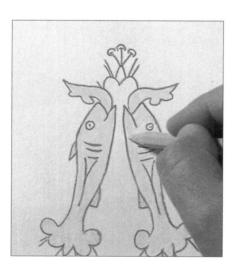

5 Mix some madder carmine with water until its consistency is like soft cream. (It needs to be runny enough to flow onto the work easily without picking up the yellow ochre underneath. It also needs to be thick and opaque enough to cover both the yellow pigment and the white of the paper.) Outline the images using a No 0000 brush. If necessary, tidy up the outline on the inside with yellow ochre and on the outside with permanent white. Paint the pupil of the eye with madder carmine.

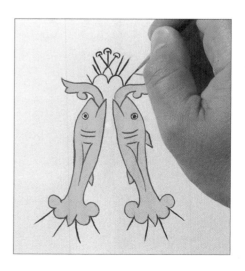

Emperor Henry II's Periscopes

This rich but simple Ottonian 'V' has been taken from Periscopes of Henry II, which date from the early eleventh century, and are now in the *Bayerisches Staatsbibliothek*, Munich, Germany. Pericopes are portions of scriptures written to be read in public worship. The 'V' characterizes the Ottonian style, in almost every way; the letters were very large on the decorated page, with the words of the script fitted around them. The initial has highly burnished gold-foliated branchwork, with intense points of color in the interstices. To complement the richness of the gold, the outlining in red rather than black. This outline also serves to add relief to the main strokes of the initial by indicating the original calligraphic construction, that is, the two strokes of each line of the 'V'. In this project, another type of gold size is used. This size is commercially prepared and overlaid with transfer gold. Color is then added and the outline completes the design. To replicate the full glory of the original, you would need to surround the initial with purple.

YOU WILL NEED

- **Pencil**
- **Tracing paper**
- **Watercolor paper**
- **Size**
- **Fine, old brush**
- **Transfer gold**
- **Dog-tooth burnisher**
- **Glassine**
- **Large soft brush**
- **Brushes—sable 0,00**
- **Gouache paints:
  utramarine blue, light
  purple, zinc white, winsor
  green, winsor blue,
  lemon yellow,
  scarlet lake**

Size painted on in an
even layer.

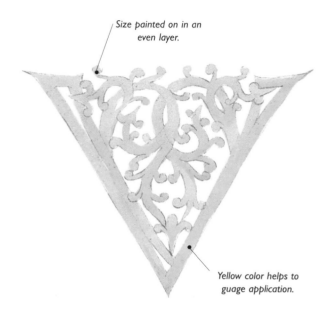

Yellow color helps to
guage application.

1 Transfer the design to a piece of good watercolor paper
and prepare the size (commercial gold size) by diluting
it with equal parts of water. Mix it well and apply with a
fine, old brush. Apply the size thinly to make an even
surface with firm, flowing strokes. Don't work it too
much. Leave it to dry for half an hour. Wash the brush
out quickly with hot water after use.

2 Having breathed on
the size to moisten it
and applied a sheet of
transfer gold, press the
gold firmly into the
size. With a smooth
dog-tooth burnisher,
burnish the gold
through glassine paper
but don't press too
hard. Systematically
tackle every fraction of
an inch of the gold.

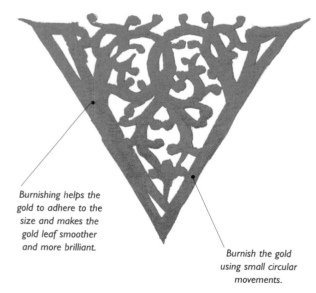

Burnishing helps the
gold to adhere to the
size and makes the
gold leaf smoother
and more brilliant.

Burnish the gold
using small circular
movements.

3 Brush away excess
gold with a large,
extra-soft brush.

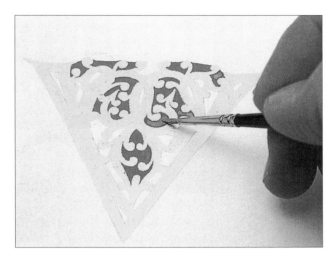

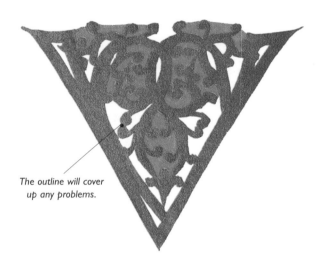

The outline will cover up any problems.

4 Using a sable 0 brush, mix purple gouache from ultramarine blue, light purple and zinc white. It should be the consistency of thin cream. Be careful not to go over the gold as you paint. If you do, carefully remove it with a clean brush and water. Remember, outlining can cover a multitude of such sins.

5 Continue the flat color with green (Winsor green, winsor blue, lemon yellow and zinc white). Don't let your hand dirty your work; rest it on a piece of paper. You can hold a tissue in your other hand to wipe the brush.

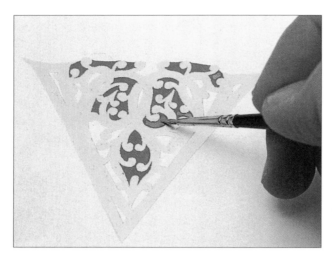

As the Ottonian style developed, geometric designs associated more with the Celtic, and other earlier styles were abandoned for motifs with a more classical origin. Where the geometry did live on, it started to grow and sprout—at first with almost bud-like protuberances, then styled leaves appeared which in time became more natural. The use of gold was important, giving a grander and richer appearance to the illumination, and therefore keeping the letter within the status of the patrons who commissioned the work. Try using the geometric styles in your own illustrations, combining patterns with either stylized or more natural plant forms.

6 *Add the final color, red (scarlet lake and a touch of lemon yellow) to the illumination and then use it to outline the gold. Use a size 00 brush with a good point for the outlining. The thicker paint adheres well to the gold, so this is not a problem.*

The Finished Letter

This piece is truly rich, smacking of imperial grandeur. You can imagine how it would have looked on the dyed purple vellum used by Ottonian illuminators. You can see the influence of metalwork design on such illumination, reinforced by the gilding. If you look carefully, you will see that the width of the outline varies, adding life to the illumination—this was considered to be part of the artistry of the professional.

Twelfth Century German S

This elegant 'S' comes from a twelfth-century German Bible, and is a test of your drawing skills as much as your coloring ability.

The creatures in this letter put one in mind of two puppies disputing over a leash. Whether they had any symbolic significance, we no longer know.

YOU WILL NEED

- **Tracing paper**
- **Project paper**
- **2H and 6B pencils**
- **Nos 1, 2, 0000, 00 brushes**
- **Gouache paints: yellow ochre, red ochre, permanent white, alizarin crimson, ultramarine, permanent green**

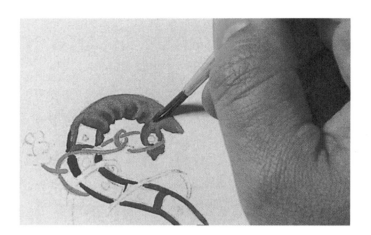

Design Tips

- **Lifting Off Color**

  If the creatures appear to be too dark after step 2, and also so that you can work some highlights into the folds of the necks, wet the painting with clean water. Squeeze out your brush between your fingers and then, with the squeezed-out brush, paint over the area where you wish the lightening of tone or highlight to be. Only use one stroke: if you use another you will simply replace the paint that you have just removed. If you still wish to remove more paint, clean the brush, squeeze it out again, and only then make a second pass. If you want to remove still more, wet the brush again and repeat the process. You need to be quick when doing this as the color soon soaks into the paper, and then cannot be removed.

  This lifting-off technique is very useful and has many applications, especially when painting around objects or where you wish to indicate light shining on an object. It can also come to your rescue when you find yourself with a wash that is about to swamp everything, or when two wet areas of different colors are bleeding into each other. In the latter instance you need to be very quick indeed in order to reverse a potential disaster.

- **Clean Water**

  Whenever you want to use a lighter color, always change your water, especially when you intend to use white. Even the slightest coloring in your water will dull your white, while a touch of blue will turn your yellows green.

1 Trace the design using a 2H pencil. Go over the back with a 6B pencil, and then trace it down onto your project paper.

2 Paint the two creatures' heads as follows. (Note that they are painted with yellow ochre on one side and red ochre on the other.) First paint both heads with water, using a No. 1 brush, to dampen them. Paint a little yellow ochre, diluted with water, on the top side and a little diluted red ochre on the bottom side. With a wet No. 1 brush, blend the two together, so that the dark hue—the red—is on the bottom and the light—the yellow—is on the top and they gradually blend into each other.

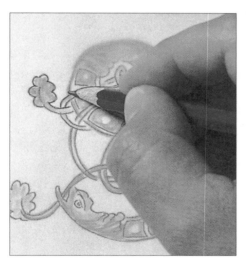

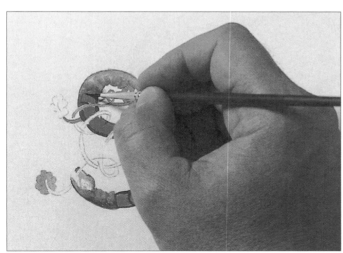

3 Join the two heads together with red ochre, carefully painting round the area to be occupied by the blue scales.

4 Mix some ultramarine and permanent white to make a bright pale blue and paint the scales.

5 Change your water and mix it with some permanent white to the consistency of thin cream. Use this to outline the blue scales and to paint the white dot in each.

7 Paint the two leaves, one with yellow ochre and the other with permanent green. If you wish to draw out some highlights where the veins go, do so with a squeezed-out brush, but make sure that you do it quickly.

6 Use alizarin crimson and yellow ochre to paint the leash.

8 Outline the image in red ochre.

13th Century Psalter

Between 1000 and 1400, the liturgical Psalter, more than any other type of book, was the bread and butter of the illuminator.

In general, the Psalter started with a calendar (which was the precedent for the book of hours), followed by eight sections of psalms, and ended with hymns and prayers. There was plenty of scope for the illuminator, with illustrations for the calendar, miniatures of Old and New Testament scenes, and after the twelfth century, historiated initials for the eight sections of psalms.

This High Gothic initial 'S' has been adapted from a Psalter made for the Duc de Berry in about 1380. The trailing ivy motif is more naturalistic than decoration used in earlier Gothic works, and shows the influence of the Italian Renaissance on the High Gothic style.

In this project, gesso is used as a binder for layers of transfer gold and loose gold leaf. Egg tempera is also used.

YOU WILL NEED

- **Pencil**
- **Tracing paper**
- **Vellum**
- **Mapping pen**
- **Waterproof black ink**
- **Gesso**
- **Fine, old brush**
- **Craft knife**
- **Dog-tooth burnisher**
- **Transfer gold**
- **Glassine**
- **Double thickness loose gold**
- **Large soft brush**
- **Pencil burnisher**
- **Egg**
- **Brushes—sable 0, 000, 00**
- **Ground pigments: cadmium red, ultramarine blue, permanent white**

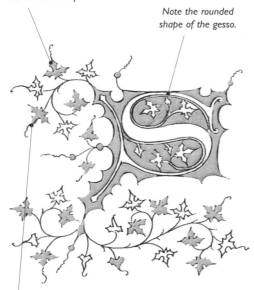

Push gesso into corners with brush tip.

Note the rounded shape of the gesso.

Untidy edges can be cleaned up with a knife.

1 Following light pencil tracing lines, outline the initial with a mapping pen, and black waterproof drawing ink on vellum. Apply the gesso with an old brush, spooning it on rather than painting it. Add more while it is well set to build up the shape. Add extra gesso wet-in-wet along the backbone of the shape with delicate jabs of the brush.

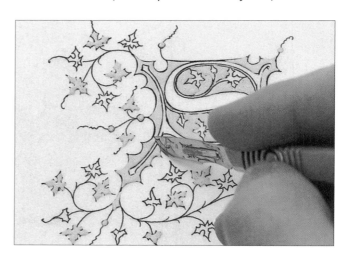

2 It is best to leave the gesso to dry overnight. Then any untidy edges or uneven shapes can be carefully scraped away with a sharp craft knife. Then use a dog-tooth burnisher straight onto the gesso to polish it slightly. This means that moisture from your breath can condense more easily on its surface for the next stage.

For economy, small pieces of gold leaf were used to fit individual patches of gesso.

The gold leaf will only adhere to the gesso.

Double-thickness loose gold leaf.

Before burnishing, allow gesso to reset.

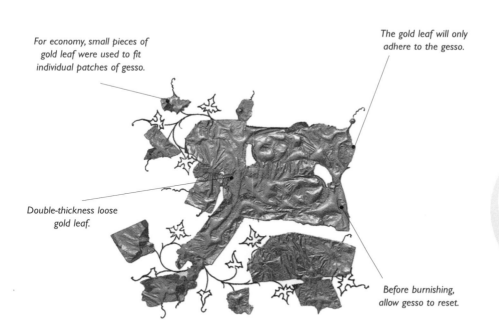

3 Add a layer of transfer gold, breathing hard on the gesso, and pressing on the transfer gold. Work gently at first to make sure the gesso has set firm.

4 Leave the transfer gold to set for about half an hour before burnishing through glassine paper. Pay particular attention to the edges to help the gold stick.

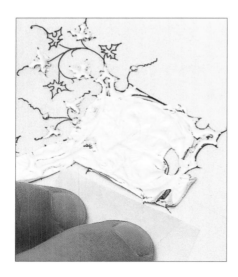

5   *Now add the double-thickness loose gold leaf. Breathe hard on the gesso and carefully transfer the gold to the gesso, pressing gently through the backing paper.*

6 *Allow the gesso to reset and then burnish directly on to the gold. Work the surface very gently. When the gold is well-adhered, brush off any excess with a solid brush.*

7   *Continue burnishing until full brilliance has been achieved. You might want to add another layer of gold and then re-burnish.*

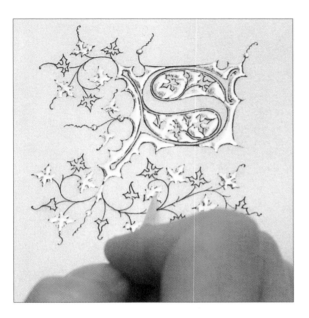

8 *Draw firmly around the edges of the gesso with a pencil burnisher. This will help you stick down any loose edges. Don't go over the gesso or you will leave an indented line. Brush excess gold away again, teasing it out of nooks and crannies.*

9 *Make up the red tempera, using cadmium red ground pigment. Apply the paint in small, thin interlocking strokes. Now make up and apply the ultramarine blue. Add color alongside the ink line of the tendrils.*

10 *For the highlighting, use your finest brush point, touched into the white. Dilute the white only a little, applying it with tiny hair-like strokes which join each other. If you over-paint the red, or blue, just cover with the appropriate color when dry. You can scrape off any excess paint, as the tempura lies on the surface of the vellum.*

The Finished Letter

The combination of the brilliant raised gold gilding and the jewel-like colors create a stunning piece of illumination. The shaped gesso allows the light to fall on the gold along one side, producing contrasts of brilliance. If applied correctly, it is very difficult to remove or break as the many examples surviving from medieval times testify.

Don't worry if it doesn't all work the first time. It takes practice to successfully combine all the elements needed for a perfect end result.

Fourteenth Century English I

This amazing capital 'I' comes from the Luttrell Psalter, which was written in the fourteenth-century for Sir Geoffrey Luttrell, a Lincolnshire knight. This letter has been copied because of its bizarre extravagance. You can certainly enjoy stretching your painting and drawing skills with this! The lesser initials have also been included to make the point that it is not only the great capital letters that interest us. The other capitals that appear on the page can be given a decorative treatment as well, in varying degrees according to their importance.

These capitals, drawn in a fat, Lombardic style, are plainly drawn and simply colored, but are made more significant by the pen-drawn decoration that surrounds them, forming white dots and a trifoliate decorative design. At first sight this looks rather complicated, but provided that you keep calm it is actually quite straightforward.

If you draw round the letters, leaving a white line and drawing round the trifoliate leaf shapes at the appropriate places as you progress, you will find that it is not as difficult as it first seemed.

Next draw the irregularly scalloped outer edge, and you subsequently only have to fill in the rest carefully, leaving out the little white dots as you do so.

YOU WILL NEED

- **Tracing or greaseproof paper**
- **Sharp pencil**
- **Ink or gouache paints: brilliant yellow, yellow ochre, burnt umber, light red, ultramarine, black**
- **Brushes**

1 Trace the large capitals and, if you want, also the lesser capitals.

2 Transfer the image to your project paper with a sharp pencil.

3 Ink in the lesser initials, leaving the coloring until last.

4 This project has been drawn in ink, but there is no need to ink the main design. Make a thin wash of brilliant yellow, and water and wash over the top half of the character. Leave the eye white. Squeeze out your brush and lift the highlights off the beak, forehead, cheek, and folds of material. Paint the tail.

5 While the yellow is still wet, mix yellow ochre and a little burnt umber, and paint the darker parts on the back of the head and the folds.

6 With a weak solution of light red and water, blend the dark tones with the lighter yellow, lifting off paint to provide the modeling on the face, and the folds of the cloth.

7 Paint over the tail with the same brown-reddish color.

8 Paint a light wash of ultramarine and water over the lower half of the creature, and quickly lift off the highlights on the face and the leading thigh. Leave the eye white.

9 Paint the dark parts with neat ultramarine and blend it with the light parts with a wet brush, lifting off paint if needed.

10 Paint the white lines, dots and circles on both halves of the creature and on the flowers.

11 Make a soft and creamy mix of black and burnt umber, and carefully paint the outlines. Place a dot of the mixture in each circle.

15th Century Whitevine

Painted in Rome in the fifteenth century, this initial 'P' has been extracted from a seething mass of whitevine on a page from a classical text with a decorated border and initial.

As you can see, the initial has been adapted, rather than directly copied, from the original, in which it was an integral part of the border. This adaptation meant that the artist needed to reconsider the color scheme. He tried out various color combinations on layout paper to see how they balanced with each other, before finding a formula which emphasised on curves.

The artist also chose to adapt the letter slightly using a Roman model. Although round hand was generally used for the text with this style of illumination, italic developed from the cursive way of writing round hand.

The spotting is typical of the period, too, some spots painted with shell gold and burnished so that they twinkle.

YOU WILL NEED

- **Pencil and tracing paper**
- **Technical pen**
- **Sepia waterproof ink**
- **Watercolor paper**
- **Gesso**
- **Transfer gold**
- **Glassine**
- **Dog-tooth burnisher**
- **Double-thickness loose gold**
- **Craft knife**
- **Pencil burnisher**
- **Large soft brush**
- **Shell gold**
- **Brushes—sable 0, 00**
- **Gouache Paints: scarlet lake, zinc white, alizarin crimson, Winsor blue lemon yellow, ultramarine blue, permanent white, Vandyke brown, lamp black**

Design Tips

- With loose gold leaf, you can fold the wasted edges around the gesso back on themselves with a piece of glassine paper or a brush. Press through the backing paper and then burnish. This improves the quality of the gold and saves on wastage.

- When spotting, make sure the paint is wet enough to form a circular point when touched on the page with the tip of the brush. Hold the brush almost vertically.

Edges will be cleaned up after application of second layer of loose gold.

Double-thickness loose gold leaf transfer.

Sepia waterproof ink.

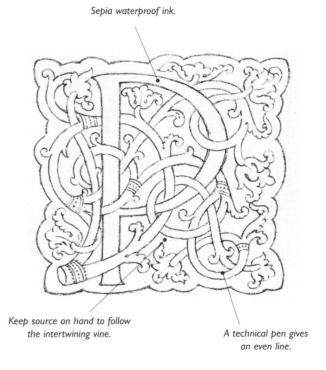

Keep source on hand to follow the intertwining vine.

A technical pen gives an even line.

Ink in the design with sepia waterproof ink using a technical pen. It works well for such a job as the flow is even. Apply the gesso and leave it to dry thoroughly overnight.

Clean edges with a pencil burnisher.

Contrasting patch of shell gold.

2 Press on a layer of transfer gold and leave gesso to re-set. Burnish through glassine first, then burnish directly.

3 Add a layer of double-thickness loose gold leaf, pressing through the backing paper. If the gold will not stick, scrape the gesso gently with a knife to remove any grease, breathe on the gesso and re-apply.

Refer to color rough for guidance.

Intense color with a little white added.

4 Burnish directly onto the gold. Add another layer and re-burnish. Once you have set the edges with a pencil burnisher, remove any excess gold with a soft brush.

5 Now paint in the small patches with shell gold. Allow them to dry thoroughly and then burnish.

6 Use the intense gouache paint quite diluted, with very little added white. Paint on the red (scarlet lake, zinc white and a touch of alizarin), then the green (Winsor blue, lemon yellow and white) then, finally, paint on the blue (Winsor and ultramarine blues and white).

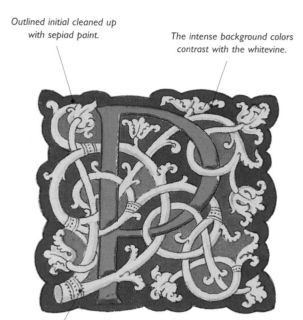

Outlined initial cleaned up with sepiad paint.

The intense background colors contrast with the whitevine.

Thin wash of Vandyke brown for shading.

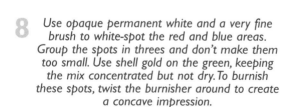

7 Paint a thin brown brush wash along one side of the vine and clean up the outline with a brownish mix of Vandyke brown, and lamp black to match the sepia ink.

8 Use opaque permanent white and a very fine brush to white-spot the red and blue areas. Group the spots in threes and don't make them too small. Use shell gold on the green, keeping the mix concentrated but not dry. To burnish these spots, twist the burnisher around to create a concave impression.

The Finished Letter

The graceful gilded 'P' stands out well from the busy background. The addition of the shading adds a three-dimensional quality which greatly enhances the final result. The spotting with gold creates reflective points like stars across the solid color.

Above: Initial 'P' from Eutropius' 'HISTORY OF ROME' 15th century.

GALLERY

Renaissance illumination initially centerd on fifteenth century Florence where an enlightened bookseller, Vespasiano di Bisticci, drummed up trade in the city by building libraries from aspiring humanist scholars.

Typical of fifteenth century Florentine decoration was a style known as Whitevine, where an initial is intertwined with a creeping vine—a contrasting white against a highly colored background.

Intertwining vines have always been recurring features of decoration, but this Renaissance Whitevine, often with a visible cut stem, has a solid, controlled appearance which is easily identifiable.

The sketch of an 'S' from Pliny's Historia Naturalis c. 1460, has a gold initial that is almost lost behind the rampaging Whitevine.

The original 'P' was intertwined with the border.

It was then redesigned as an integral letter which could stand on its own.

The artist did color try-outs for the project 'P' with concentric spirals of red and green. This was rejected in favor of a design using less red.

An 'I' can be difficult to decorate because of its simplicity. Copied from Pliny's Historia Naturalis this letter 'I' is interlaced with Whitevine like a flailing whip.

A late fifteenth century example from Milan, which could be framed with the twisted border design or used on its own.

A putto holds one side of a laurel wreath containing a monogram. Birds such as parrots often hide in the foliage.

A page decorated with Whitevine can appear like a seething mass of serpents, so use this style with some restraint. Borders from this period are more enclosed and narrower than contemporary Late Gothic equivalents and the colored background is usually given some relief with points of contrasting color and white.

Painting these dots is an art in itself: cluster them in threes, otherwise, you will have to judge the spacing by eye. Humanistic cursive minuscules combine well with Roman Capitals. Fit them together on the page, and decorate with all the accoutrements of the Whitevine style.

Right: A possible termination for a border.

Fifteenth Century French A

This initial was adapted from a fifteenth-century French manuscript and relies mostly on penwork for its effect. The drawing and painting of the initial are simple tasks, but the penwork around the initial and in the stem needs a little thought. It has been drawn with a technical drawing pen, but a mapping pen would do just as well. It is important both to make all the hoops the same size and to produce fine lines.

When first looking at this initial, you are attracted by its design possibilities. According to the demands of the text, the stem could be made any length, and the branches could be placed in any suitable position.

The design could be adapted to fit a left or right-hand margin or could go in the middle of the page, while a small miniature or heraldic device could be used in the place of the initial.

YOU WILL NEED

- **Tracing paper**
- **Project paper**
- **Pencil**
- **Ruler**
- **Right-angled set square**
- **Compasses**
- **Rubber**
- **Mapping pen**
- **Waterproof ink or gouache paint**

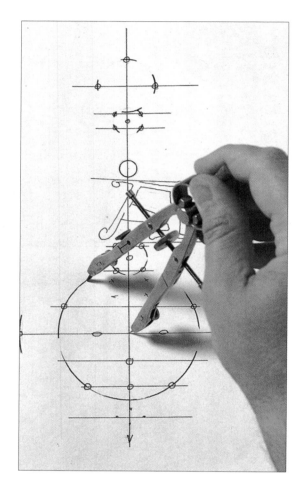

1 Draw a vertical line on a piece of tracing paper to act as the backbone of the design. Draw in a series of crossbars, making sure that they are at true right angles to the stem. Using your compasses, draw a series of circles centerd on the stem. Rub out the part of the stem where the capital letter will go.

2 Trace down the design onto our project paper.

3 To do the penwork, you will need waterproof ink of your chosen color or gouache paint. (If you are using gouache, mix it with water and transfer it to your pen with a brush.) Draw the initial and the surrounding penwork.

4 Draw in the design, trying to keep the work as fluid and neat as you can. The, to finish, color the initial.

Fifteenth Century Q

This project is copied from a fifteenth-century musical score. You are first attracted by the miniature—what is it all about?

In any event, the capital 'Q', which is simply drawn in gold strapwork and is decorated with acanthus leaves, and pen-drawn 'stamens', makes a very attractive project.

It does, however, need to act as the frame for a miniature illustration of some kind, but whether you copy this one or devise and execute one of your own is entirely up to you.

YOU WILL NEED

- **Tracing paper**
- **Greaseproof paper**
- **Tracing-down paper**
- **2H pencil**
- **Project paper**
- **Gouache paints: gold, red, ultramarine, permanent white, black, burnt umber**
- **Watercolor paints: burnt umber, Prussian blue, crimson lake**
- **Nos 1 and 0000 brushes**
- **PVA gilding medium**
- **Paper tube**
- **Gold leaf**
- **Burnisher**

1 Make a tracing of the image and trace it down onto your project paper, ensuring that it is upright.

2 Paint the PVA gilding medium onto the capital letter with the No 1 brush, and allow thirty-five minutes for it to dry.

3 To do the penwok, you will need waterproof ink of your chosen color or gouache paint. (If you are using gouache, mix it with water and transfer it to your pen with a brush.) Draw the initial and the surrounding penwork.

4 Paint the gold gouache (diluted to the right consistency) on the outer parts of the design.

5 Paint the red and blue areas, as well as the fat cardinal at the top of the group.

6 *Paint the miniature with watercolors. Start by painting the dark area at the top, behind the heads, with a mixture of burnt umber and Prussian blue. Then paint the floor with light brown, along with the barrel, darkening the paint with a little burnt umber. Darken the fat cardinal's color with some crimson lake, and then paint the rest of the figures, working from the largest parts to the smallest. Finally, paint the animals.*

7 *Outline the image with a mixture of black and burnt umber gouache, as well as some of the figures in he miniature.*

8 *Highlight the blue areas with some permanent white. Use a No 0000 brush and make sure that the paint is the consistency of thin cream.*

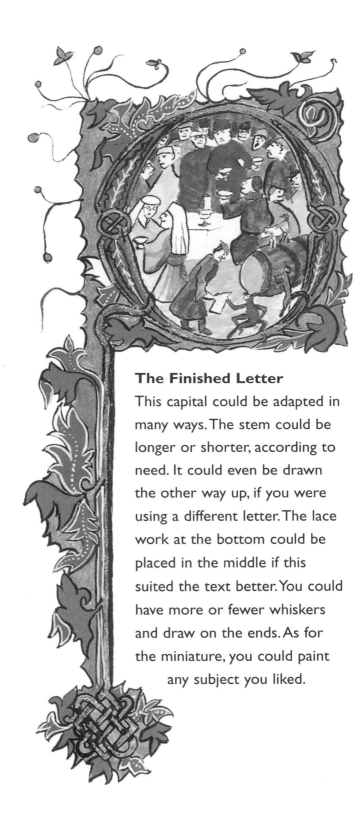

The Finished Letter

This capital could be adapted in many ways. The stem could be longer or shorter, according to need. It could even be drawn the other way up, if you were using a different letter. The lace work at the bottom could be placed in the middle if this suited the text better. You could have more or fewer whiskers and draw on the ends. As for the miniature, you could paint any subject you liked.

Fifteenth Century K

This exotic pink 'K' is taken from another
fifteenth century musical score, this time from a
French book of hours.
Although it looks quite large here, it would
originally have been drawn much smaller than this.
Books of music were placed on a
stand for a choir of monks to gather
around, books of hours, however, were
very small and could be slipped into a pocket.
This capital letter starts a prayer of
supplication – 'Lord have mercy' – that would have been sung in Greek at
the beginning of every Mass.

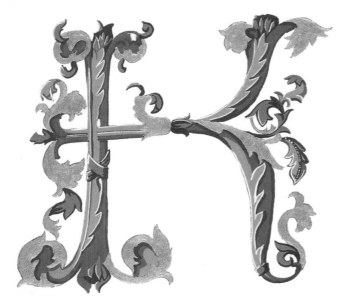

YOU WILL NEED

- **Tracing or
  greaseproof paper**
- **Tracing-down paper**
- **Project paper**
- **2H pencil**
- **Rubber**
- **Gouache paints:
  permanent white,
  ultramarine,
  alizarin crimson**
- **Gesso**
- **PVA gilding medium or
  spirit based gilding**
- **Nos 1 and 0000 brushes**
- **Gold leaf**
- **Paper tube**
- **Burnisher**

Design tips

- Gesso (which is made of plaster of Paris or a similar material mixed with a binder), is painted over the area to be gilded, leaving a raised area. When it is dry, gold leaf is applied to it. The gilded raised form glitters and catches the light, illuminating the page.

You can make gesso yourself, but if you will only be needing a small quantity use ready-made acrylic-based gesso that you can buy in small jars. If you are going to apply gesso, the secret is to lay a smooth, even base coat. When you open the jar, you will see that it contains a thick, white, cream-like substance which will need to be diluted with water if it is to be used for lettering.

If it is too thin and runny, it will not stand proud of the paper. If it is too thick, you cannot lay it smoothly. By constantly adding a little more water you can get the right consistency. Dip a brush into the gesso and lift it out, letting the water drip back onto the mix. If the water sits on the surface, the mixture is too thick, so add a couple more brushfuls of water.

Keep on testing and adding water, until the drip settles into the mix. When the mix has reached this stage, it is ready to use.

1 *Make a tracing of the image and trace it down onto your project paper. If your image is sharp enough, you will not need to draw over it.*

2 *With a no 1 brush, take up some prepared gesso, and paint round the form, taking care to paint into the points and corners. Now take a good brushful and start to fill in the form. Pushing, rather than painting it, gradually work over the form, filling in the area with gesso, so that any surface irregularities are removed. Work from the top downwards. When you have finished, put your work away in a warm spot to dry for at least a couple of hours.*

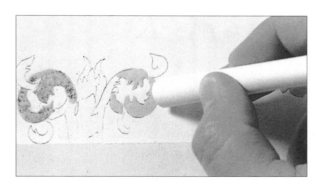

3 *When the gesso is smooth and hard, paint a coat of gilding medium over it. Leave it to dry. (If you use PVA gilding medium, you will find it difficult to paint a thin coat without leaving brush marks, which will show through the gold leaf and spoil the mirror-like surface for which you are aiming. You may prefer to buy a prepared, spirit-based gilding medium which dries quite smoothly, leaving no brush marks, but takes several hours to do so. If it is painted directly onto the paper, it makes it look transparent, so take dare round the edges of the form.)*

4 *Breathe through the paper tube onto the medium at the top of the page to moisten it. Lay the gold leaf on the area and burnish the backing paper. Rub down another layer of gold to make good any splits. When you have finished, burnish the gilded work through a piece of tracing paper, working over and round each piece. Then burnish the gold directly.*

5 *Paint the letter as follows. (Keep a piece of paper under hour hand to prevent damage to your gilding):*
The light-blue parts: with a permanent-white and ultramarine mixture. The pale-pink part: with an alizarin crimson and permanent white mixture.
The dark-blue parts: with neat ultramarine.
The dark-pink parts: with neat alizarin crimson.
Highlighting: highlight the pale-blue and pink parts with permanent white.
This letter is not outlined. If you want to do so, I suggest that you outline the pink areas with madder carmine, the blue areas with Prussian blue, and the gold areas with a black and burnt-umber mix.

Illuminated letters

Illuminated or decorated letters have been employed by calligraphers for nearly two thousand years to "light up" pages of text. In addition to this traditional application of decorative letterwork, designs based on a single letterform can also be used for greetings cards, letterheads and commemorative panels.

Illuminated letters can encompass a vast array of different types of design, from the fantastic illustrated compositions of medieval manuscripts, through intricate scrollwork, to the colorful modern graphic treatments of this century. What all the best illuminated letters have in common is a harmony between the letterform and the decorative treatment.

You do not have to be an expert illustrator to try your hand at decorative lettering. You can start by copying ideas from early manuscripts (try to find a book of reproductions from a library or museum), and adapting them to your own requirements—using your own color choices, for example. Later, try adding illustration ideas of your own. Simple plant forms are a great source of inspiration.

Using historical sources for guidance is an excellent way of learning about the tools and techniques of the craft, and about letterform design and illumination. However, the use of historical resources should not stop at analysing and copying, but rather this resource should be a springboard for developing your own contemporary ideas.

Versal letterforms were the traditional vehicle for medieval illumination; their built-up forms are ideal for the addition of color or gilding. However, almost any script can be used in a modern context.

In the project shown on the following pages, a single letter was decorated using gouache and gilding. The intention was to produce a design for a greeting card.

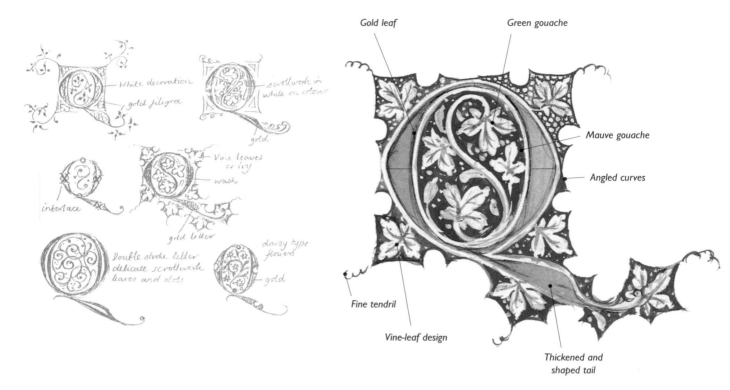

Gold leaf

Green gouache

Mauve gouache

Angled curves

White decoration

gold filigree

scrollwork in white on colour

gold

Vine leaves or ivy

wash

interlace

gold letter

daisy type flowers

gold

Double stroke letter delicate scrollwork leaves and dots

Fine tendril

Vine-leaf design

Thickened and shaped tail

Design Tips

• Planning the Illustration

The design is to be based around the letter 'Q' using a form of versal script known as Lombardic. The letterform, with it spacious counter and graceful tail, provides ample opportunities for decoration within, and around the letter. The scrolling form of the tail, in particular, provides a starting point for a design based on curling tendrils of vine leaves. A number of annotated sketches explore the possibilities for this type of design. A major decision to be made is how far to extend the decoration beyond the boundaries of the letterform.

• The Final Color Rough

The option eventually selected is a square design, broken by the tail, which includes vine motifs outside as well as inside the letter. The triangular silhouette of the four leaves placed around the 'O' form of the 'Q' makes up the corners of the square. The outside curves of the 'Q' are angled, and the tail is given extra weight. Preliminary color choices are made: gold for the letterform itself with mauve and green decoration.

1 With the tracing paper firmly taped in position, an accurate pencil tracing is made of the outlines of the final design. After untaping the paper, the outlines are drawn on the reverse side of the paper in a soft pencil.

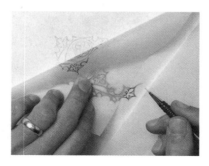

2 The design is transferred on to the chosen paper by placing the prepared tracing in position right side up. The outlines are drawn over again with a hard pencil so that the marks on the underside are transferred.

3 Gum ammoniac is applied to the letterform with a fine brush. The brush needs to be rinsed frequently in hot water to prevent the gum from clogging it. Breathing over the surface before the gold is applied restores tackiness.

4 Narrow strips of gold-transfer leaf are placed on the letterform, gold-side down. The backing sheet is removed after rubbing through it to adhere the gold to the gum ammoniac.

5 All parts of the letterform are covered in gold leaf, and the final piece of backing sheet is removed.

6 The gold is burnished with a burnishing tool through glassine paper. Tracing paper could be substituted. Afterward, any loose gold leaf is brushed away with a soft brush.

7 Sufficient quantities of the chosen colors of gouache are mixed to finish the job. The color is carefully applied with a fine sable brush.

8 For the final version, it is decided to use a muted green for the decoration inside the counter.

9 The last elements to be completed are the fine tendrils that extend from the corners of the design.

GALLERY

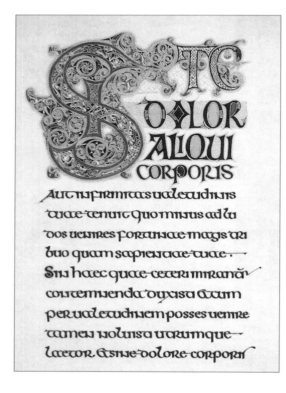

I LAY AMONG PTERIS AQUILINA—Mark van Stone
In this rendering of a 19th-century text medieval-style illumination has been used.

The design and execution of illuminated letters brings together a variety of skills that the calligraphy beginner needs to develop. Not only are you concerned with the letterform itself but also with the relationship of your illustration design to the letter, and the work as a whole. Select colors carefully to enhance the balance between letterform and decoration. The examples on this page show a variety of approaches.

VERSAL CONCERTINA BOOK—Donald Jackson
These elegant compressed versals show how a traditional letterform can be used in a contemporary context.

MEDIEVAL-STYLE ILLUMINATION—Mark Van Stone
Left: This Latin text is written and decorated in the style of the Lindisfarne Gospels. The watercolor decoration uses traditional Celtic knotwork motifs, and the following test is written in ink in insular half uncials.

Fifteenth Century Borders

These two borders are taken from a fifteenth-century manuscript, and show how two dissimilar designs can be combined on the same page. They are relatively simple in composition and can be adapted, lengthened or shortened according to the needs of the project in hand. The left-hand border, the inner one, is composed of acanthus-like elements that have been expanded to resemble heraldic mantling, with gold fruits and a ribbon winding round them. It has an uncomplicated dignity and could be used on either side of the page, or even between two columns of text. The ribbon could display a motto, piece of text or message. The little escutcheon at the top could carry an heraldic device, monogram or miniature.

YOU WILL NEED

- **Tracing paper**
- **Project paper**
- **2H pencil**
- **Ruler**
- **Gesso or PVA gilding medium**
- **Brushes**
- **Gold leaf**
- **Paper tube**
- **Burnisher**
- **Gouache paints: yellow ochre, permanent white, black, burnt umber, colors of your choice**
- **Pen**
- **Waterproof ink**

1 Either trace the design onto your project page or draw it yourself. If you do the latter, rule a center line and mark it at regular intervals to show where the top of the ribbon crosses it. Rule guidelines to the left and right to make sure that the acanthus leaves and gold fruits are the same width either side and all the way down.

2 Apply gesso or PVA gilding medium to the fruits. (If you use PVA, resist the temptation to apply a fat drop of it, which will shrink and wrinkle as it dries. Instead apply two or three coats.) Burnish on the gold leaf, starting at the top and working down.

3 Paint the ribbon to make it look as if it is made of a lustrous material, at least on the front side. Make a wash of yellow ochre and paint each section, lifting off the color in the center by squeezing out your brush and soaking up the color before it has soaked into the paper. You cold also apply some clean water to the center and lift it off. Treat each section in turn in this way. Mix a little of your wash with more yellow ochre to make it darker and paint two or three small vertical stripes at either end of each section. Finally, paint a thin strip of neat ochre at the downhill end of each section, to give the illusion of shadow.

4 When all is dry, write your text. Remember to write the letters at right angles to the direction of the ribbon, not vertical to the page.

5 Paint the acanthus leaves in the color of your choice. A useful tip is to mix your main colors with a little white, making them paler in tone. You can then use the neat color to apply the darker shadow tones.

6 Highlight the outward-rising curves of the acanthus leaves with permanent white.

7 Outline the image with a mixture of black and burnt umber. Remember to pain in the 'eyelashes' round the fruits.

Fifteenth Century P

This initial has been adapted from a fifteenth-century missal, and displays a flamboyant Lombardic capital 'P', as well as some delicate filigree pen decoration.

The coat of arms of the city of Paris has also been drawn within the 'P'. This is a very good way in which to display heraldic devices. The rest of the word is written in the Ronde style, a round letter form used in the French tradition, but you could use any other style that suited your particular project.

YOU WILL NEED

- **Tracing paper**
- **Project paper**
- **2H pencil**
- **Ruler**
- **Mapping or technical pen**
- **Black waterproof ink**
- **Gesso**
- **Brushes**
- **Gouache paint: yellow, ultramarine, permanent white, red, black, burnt umber**
- **Gold leaf**
- **Paper tube**
- **Burnisher**

1 Rule lines on your project paper to contain the word and capital. If you intend to include any other text, rule the lines for that too and write the text.

2 Make a photocopy of your design and use it to work out your color scheme.

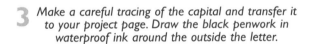

3 Make a careful tracing of the capital and transfer it to your project page. Draw the black penwork in waterproof ink around the outside the letter.

4 Paint the area to be gilded with gesso, pushing it into place with your brush, and filling all the little points and corners. (The little fleurs-de-lis on the coat of arms are particularly fiddly, so you may prefer to paint these in yellow paint.)

5 Apply the gold leaf with the burnisher.

6 Mix some ultramarine and permanent white gouache, and paint the blue areas.

7 Using neat ultramarine, paint round the inside of the center of the 'P', shading outward and then, with a wet brush, blending it into the pale blue area.

8 Paint the red areas.

9 Outline the image with a mixture of black and burnt umber. Highlight the blue areas with permanent white.

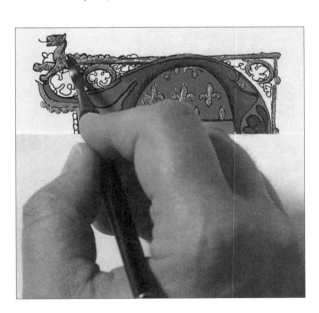

Sixteenth Century English S

This capital 'S' is striking in the imagination of its design and in the vigour of its style. The interwoven strapwork is typical of the penmanship of the sixteenth century. It appeared on an uncolored document, the capital being simply drawn with a pen.

You can produce some very striking effects with colored paper. There are some problems that you should be aware of, however. If you are tracing down a design you may find that the red tracing down paper does not show up. In this case, make yourself a sheet of contrasting color with some grease-proof paper, and a chalk pastel of an appropriate color. To do this, lay the pastel on its side on the greaseproof paper. Rub it all over the sheet to get as even a color as you can. Then wrap a piece of paper around your finger and rub it all over the greaseproof paper, spreading and working in the pastel until the surface of the greaseproof paper is completely covered.

YOU WILL NEED

- Sharp 2H pencil and a 6B pencil
- Tracing paper or tracing-down paper
- Brushes
- Gouache paint: pale green, ultramarine, cadmium pale yellow, permanent white, flame red, gold, black, burnt umber
- Pen and ink

1 Trace the design with a sharp 2H pencil and then go over the back with a fairly sharp 6B pencil.

2 Mix some pale green with ultramarine, cadmium pale yellow and water. Paint the head and lower body of the two dolphins.

3 Mix some light blue, permanent white and ultramarine and paint the top of the back, the bottom jaw and fin and tails.

4 Paint the tongues and small mid sections with a light red.

5 Paint the dark colors on the green, blue and red areas, and the fins and tails with dark blue.

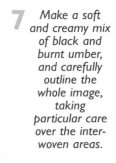

6 Paint the gold areas with gold gouache, carefully placing the dots on the interwoven section.

7 Make a soft and creamy mix of black and burnt umber, and carefully outline the whole image, taking particular care over the interwoven areas.

8 I have drawn the interwoven areas separately in pen and ink. It makes it easier to see the pattern and is also handy to keep for future reference.

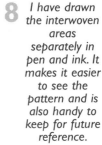

Design Tips

- Strap work is a very common and attractive element of designing letters, and borders and has been used in different styles over the centuries. At first sight it looks very complicated, but patiently follow each part through. It helps to remember that the design is often formed by two interlacing parts combining from different directions. Sometimes a third, unconnected, unending strap is interlaced with the two ends. If you like these designs, it is worth collecting tracings and keeping them in a scrap book for future reference and adaptation.

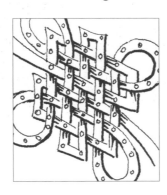

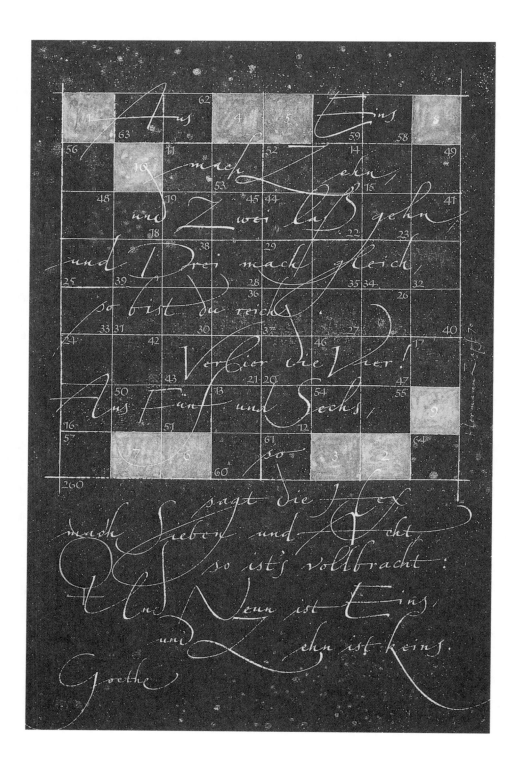

ADVANCED PROJECTS

Most calligraphers will, sooner or later, be required to design an invitation and even if you are new to calligraphy, you will be able to produce an attractive example with a well-written formal script.

With greater experience, a wide variety of more challenging and exciting design possibilities will emerge, such as asymmetrical layouts and contrasts of formal and free writing. Formal invitations can be greatly enhanced by calligraphy, used alone or combined with type. Handwritten letters and simple letter decoration—usually created by flourishing—can add the individual touch that type alone lacks.

Invitations

Formal scripts, such as italic, are suitable for occasions such as weddings, christenings, or banquets, but there are no hard-and-fast rules. The invitation could be written entirely in capitals, or in areas of upper and lowercase letters to suit the text and overall design. You might combine compatible scripts, use a suitably embellished capital, change to a larger nib for names or write them in a different script.

Designing an invitation for printing means preparing artwork in the form of a paste-up, with calligraphy written in black and with color instructions for the printer. If you are reproducing the invitations by photocopying, they can be copied in black and white, or color on to white, or colored paper thick enough to cut or fold into cards.

Your invitation will usually need to comply to a regular size and shape used by the printer, and if you work larger, you will have to prepare your artwork to scale.

The wedding invitation shown here had to give prominence to the names of the bride, and the groom, while conveying varying levels of information about the wedding and reception clearly and attractively.

Suzanne and Frank Brown
request the pleasure of your company
at the marriage of their daughter
Miranda
to
Mr. Steven Johnson

on Saturday, the twelfth of June
nineteen hundred and ninety-three
at eleven in the morning

St. Margaret's Church
Bennington, Vermont

and afterwards at the reception
The Laurels 517 Chestnut Drive

THE PRINTED INVITATION
The invitation is printed on a
white card with a silver
deckled edge. The result is
elegant and restrained.

Thumbnails

The first step in the planning process is to sketch out layout alternatives from the text supplied. At this stage, the format of the invitation, and the distribution of the words within that format are the main concerns. Four options, all with centerd text, are tried. The wide vertical format is selected for development.

Square format

Narrow vertical format

Horizontal format

Wide vertical format

Suzanne and Frank Brown

Compressed italic minuscules with capitals

Suzanne and Frank Brown

Compressed and sharpened italic minuscules with capitals

Suzanne and Frank Brown

Standard italic minuscules

SUZANNE & FRANK BROWN

Italic capitals with slight flourishes

Experimenting with Letterforms

Italic minuscules and capitals— being both formal and decorative—were the obvious choice for this kind of occasion. The precise details of width and spacing, however, need to be worked out. An all-capitals version and three versions of the minuscule from wide to narrow are tried.

Choosing the Paper

The choice of paper or card for calligraphic work that is to be printed is subject to considerations that are different from those taken into account when selecting a surface to write on. For printed work you are primarily concerned with color, weight, and texture. Obtain samples from the printer and judge them in relation to the color of ink you are using and the overall effect you are aiming to achieve.

1 The text is written in the chosen version of italic with a Mitchell No 4 nib to 5 nib widths x-height. Writing of this size is designed to be reduced in printing to the dimensions of the finished invitation.

2 A preliminary decision is made to render the names of the bridal couple in swash capitals, using a Mitchell No 3 nib.

3 An alternative version of the names in italic minuscules, also in the larger nib size, is tried for comparison.

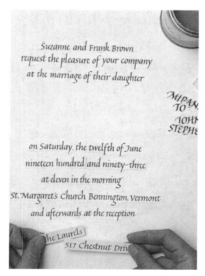

4 The text is cut into lines and a paste-up is started with spacing assessed by eye. When the arrangement is judged to be right, accurately measured lines can be ruled to guide the final paste-up.

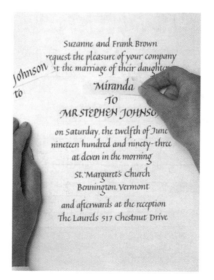

5 Once the capitalised version of the couple's names is pasted up, it is compared with the minuscule version. The decision is made to substitute the minuscule script.

6 With all the text satisfactorily pasted in position, margins are ruled in blue pencil to show the printer the final proportions required. The margins must be in proportion to the size of the final printed invitation.

GALLERY

Calligraphy in invitation design can be used on its own or in harmony with type. Flourishes are a natural choice for calligraphic enhancement of invitations, but other decorative elements may also be used to great effect. Sensitivity of design can extend to the choice of paper, the way in which the invitation is folded, and the addressing of the envelope. Creating invitations is an excellent way of putting calligraphy to practical use.

MATCHING INVITATIONS—Angela Hickey
This pair of wedding invitations—one to the wedding, the other to the reception—shows the elegant use of flourished italics.

WEDDING INVITATION—Bonnie Leah
This delicate design is printed on fine-quality white paper, with an original touch added by the use of Japanese lace-paper backing. Folded dimensions: 5¼in x 4in (13.5cm x 10cm).

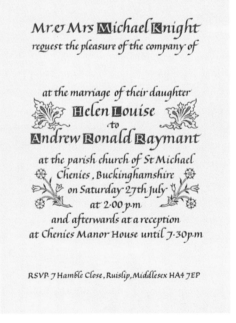

DECORATED INVITATION—Timothy Noad
In this original design for a wedding invitation, simple decorative motifs provide added interest. The text is written in formal italic, with emphasis provided by changes of scale.

Roman Capitals

The Roman letters 'AMDG' stand for the Latin words *ad majorem dei gloriam*: 'to the greater glory of God'. They have been put at the beginning of the projects to remind us that our study of illuminated letters is more than simply the pursuit of an artistic whim and that, if we can see it in a more spiritual light, we will find the patience to persevere when things get difficult. They also remind us that the basis of the script that we use today is founded upon the Roman capital letters that were carved in stone two millennia ago.

The transcription of these Roman letters makes a very useful first exercise. It will allow you to practice using some of your equipment on an easy project that has a good chance of success. Completing the project will boost your confidence.

YOU WILL NEED

- **Paper**
- **Masking tape**
- **T-square**
- **Right-angled set square**
- **Sharp 2H pencil**
- **6B pencil**
- **Rubber**
- **Masking fluid**
- **Nos 1, 6 and 0000 brushes**
- **Palette**
- **Gouache paint: yellow ochre, permanent white, red ochre**
- **4 drawing pins (optional)**

1   *Place your paper squarely on the drawing board using a T-square or parallel motion. Lightly tape it down.*

2   *Draw in the horizontal lines at the top and bottom of the rectangle that will contain the letters and mark the positions of the top and bottom of the letters. (If using a T-square make sure that the head remains in contact with the edge of the board or your lines will be neither parallel nor straight).*

3   *Keep a diagram of Roman capital letters to hand. Note the different proportions of the various letters, but use them as a guide rather than an exact measurement.*

4   *Slide the T-square down the paper so that your drawing area is a little above it. Take up the right-angled set square and rest it on the T-square. By sliding it back and forth you can draw all the vertical lines that you need to complete the rectangle and the position of the letters. (Note that it is easier to mark the middle of the letters).*

5   *Untape the paper. You should work on a flat surface from now on.*

6   *Lightly draw the rest of the letters, taking care to define thick and thin strokes. If you get it wrong, make your alterations with a rubber, but note that if you have drawn thick, bold lines by pressing down hard you will not be able to do so. Draw the curves of the 'D' and the 'G' freehand, remembering that they should fit into an 'O' shape.*

7   *Carefully trace the design from the original using a 2H pencil.*

8   *Turn over the tracing paper and go over the back of the design with a 6B pencil. Now turn it up the right way.*

9 Place tracing paper on your final working paper (shaded side down). Tape down, and copy over your drawing—making sure the tracing paper does not move.

10 With the No 1 brush, carefully paint masking fluid onto the letters. It is important that you cover the letters, but get no masking fluid on any other part of the paper.

11 Mix a little yellow ochre with enough water to make a milky consistency, and paint all over the rectangle with the No 6 brush to make a good, even wash.

12 When the wash is dry, carefully rub off the masking fluid with a rubber.

13 The letters should appear to be cut into stone; these 'cuts' have a dark and a light side. With a pencil, lightly draw the central line of the 'cuts' in the middle of each of the limbs of the letters. Mix a little permanent-white gouache with some of the previously prepared ochre wash, and paint the light side of the letters and the end of the slab, using the No 1 brush.

14 Mix a little red-ochre gouache with the wash and paint the dark side of the letters and the bottom of the slab.

15 Take a little clean water with a No 0000 brush and drop it into the mouth of a tube of permanent white to make the paint creamy enough to paint a highlight onto the exposed edges of your letters, and the part of the slab facing the light. You only need to make the lightest indication of a line.

16 When it is dry and you are satisfied with it, pin your work to the wall as a reminder in the future that your hard work can have successful results!

SIMPLE FLORAL TREATMENTS

These little examples have been drawn to show how effective simple flower decorations can be. They have been drawn in ink and painted with watercolor. Because this is transparent the pen line shows through and there is no need to outline. Were they painted with gouache, which masks the pen line, they would have to have outlines to neaten and tighten them up. They would however look brighter and more jewel-like. The letters would have looked better had they been outlined with paint, but they point out the folly of trying to outline in pen more eloquently than a written warning.

Sixteenth Century Border

This border is an adaptation of the ivy-leaf pattern. The miniature was copied from one by the Italian master Guilio Clovio, who worked in the first half of the sixteenth century. He is regarded as the Michaelangelo of miniature painting, one of the finest illustrators of manuscripts who has ever lived.

His borders typically contain classical figures, armour, architectural features, urns and diverse decoration, all delicately and excellently drawn and colored. The birds and creatures have both been added to signify creation, and to add some color and interest.

Design Tips

- Drafting Your Design

  When you embark on a project, it is important to consider the text and the decoration together, so that you do not spend hours on one part only to find that you have created an irreconcilable conflict with the other.

  The size of the miniature, the disposition of the frame, and the location of the little box for the capital letter will be determined by the length of the text. Experiment with drawing draft shapes and layouts on apiece of rough paper. Keep all your drafts: if they have not worked for this project, they may well help you with another.

  Do not be afraid to try something new. Learn from the past, but develop that knowledge.

Letterheads

Designing a letterhead is a rewarding and straightforward project for calligraphy beginners to tackle. This exercise can also provide interesting design challenges for slightly more advanced calligraphers who have a greater number of scripts, and decorative techniques at their disposal.

Calligraphy gives enormous scope as to the script, layout and design choices available, making it invaluable for creating a unique look for a letterhead. You will need to consider which type of lettering will be most appropriate to the person or business whose letterhead you are designing. Do you want the letterhead to look quiet and formal, or eye-catching and lively? If the former, either foundational hand or formal italic would be a good choice. It the latter, a vigorously written cursive italic might be suitable.

A further element that you may wish to incorporate is a motif or logo. This could be a simple graphic device or a sophisticated illustration, depending on your skill, and the requirements of your client.

The placement of each element in the design in relation to the whole needs to be carefully worked out. Do you want a close vertical texture for impact, or wide line spacing for elegance? Is the alignment to be to the right, left, centered or asymmetrical? And how is the letterhead to be placed on the page?

Beyond the design considerations, you also have to plan how the artwork is to be submitted to the printer. A preliminary discussion with the printer to establish the requirements can avoid expensive mistakes.

THE PRINTED VERSION
Calligraphic lettering provides an original
company identity that can be used on a
letterhead and a business card.

Design Tips

- **Selecting a script**

  The first task is to choose a script in keeping with the image that the person or business wants to project. Uncials or half uncials seem good first choices with their craft-based associations. Various scripts are tried.

- **Alternative Layouts**

  Having decided on a script, the next stage is to work out a layout. The main issues to be determined at this stage are the size of the lettering and its alignment. Rough pencil sketches are adequate for this purpose. It is decided that the name of the business should be rendered in the largest size. The relative size of the rest of the text needs to be worked out. Experiments with a logo are also tried at this stage.

- **The Final Design**

  Elements of the second and third layouts have been incorporated into the final design. The text arrangement of the second layout (with slight adjustments to text size) is combined with the logo suggestion of the third. The letterhead is to be centerd on the paper.

1 The writing of the large-size lettering is started between lines ruled to 4 nib widths. A Mitchell No 0 nib is used, producing lettering that is larger than it will appear in the final printed form. Reduction sharpens the letterforms.

2 As the letterhead is to be printed from a paste-up, small imperfections can be painted out in opaque white. This is a bleed-proof paint that covers any underlying ink effectively.

3 The artwork for the logo is drawn using a Mitchell No 0 nib. A textured watercolor paper is used, which gives a rough appearance to the work.

4 Final adjustments to the layout are made before pasting up the lettering and artwork. Guidelines for the paste-up are ruled.

5 Photocopies of each element—reduced in size where necessary—are pasted carefully in position to show the final effect.

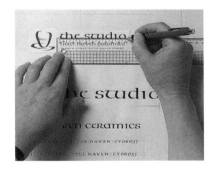

6 The intended size of each element is measured from the paste-up, and calculated as a percentage of the original so that instructions can be given for a PMT (photomechanical-transfer) reduction.

7 The exact positions of the artwork and lettering are also measured from the paste-up and noted.

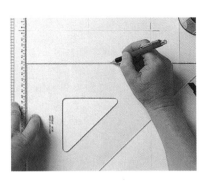

8 The margins and precise guidelines for the positioning of the letterhead on the paper are marked for a final 'camera-ready' paste-up for the printer. Non-reproducible blue pencil, which will not show in the printing, is used.

9 The final paste-up of the artwork is completed for printing. Instructions on color and paper type are given to the printer separately.

GALLERY

RIBBON-DECORATED LETTERHEAD—Bonnie Leah
This delicate stationery design shows the sensitive combination of
decorated calligraphic letterforms and type. The diamond shape and
ribbon decoration provide an original touch.
Dimensions: 11in x 8¹/₂in (28cm x 22cm).

VERTICAL LETTERHEAD
– Christopher Haanes
The combination of lively flourished italic with red
type makes for a sophisticated image. Further
interest is created by the vertical placement of
the calligraphy.

Letterheads provide a design challenge.
Whether you are commissioned to design a
formal and understated piece, or something
eye-catching, the creation of an appropriate
image is an excellent opportunity to practice
your design skills. The letterheads by
experienced calligraphers on this page
illustrate some of the interesting
possibilities available.

Poetry broadsheet

A broadsheet is a single sheet of paper containing text. This can be a single poem or section of a poem, several poems, or prose and can be linked by a theme. A broadsheet design should not be too complicated, or it may detract from the meaning of the text. A simple approach is usually the key to success.

The broadsheet is a useful project for the inexperienced calligrapher, and one to which you can return as you progress, because it offers plenty of opportunity for practicing newly acquired skills and using them creatively. Working on texts and themes will help you to release and develop your imagination, and find ways of interpreting your personal reactions to the passages you choose to write. This can be a stimulating experience and a source of fun. A finished broadsheet can be framed and displayed. The choice of quotations is crucial, and a personal interest in the theme will give the work excitement and a sense of discovery. If you enjoy the time that you spend working on the project, this will communicate itself to the viewer.

In the broadsheet shown here, texts were "hung" around a central piece of writing. The calligrapher was fascinated by the sense of wildness, and the closeness with nature reflected in some early Irish poems. The core text was powerful and deeply imaginative, and the additional quotations enhanced this feeling while also creating atmosphere. The theme linked the contrasts of beauty, and harshness in a landscape integrally bound up with the lives of its inhabitant birds and animals. The scripts were chosen to create an inter-play between the central and the surrounding texts, while harmonious colors, repeated shapes and images and gentle contrasts served to unify the design as a whole.

THE FINISHED WORK
The completed panel shows a delicate harmony of text and illustration. To display the work, a natural limed-wood frame is selected, whose muted color does not overwhelm the subtle lettering colors.

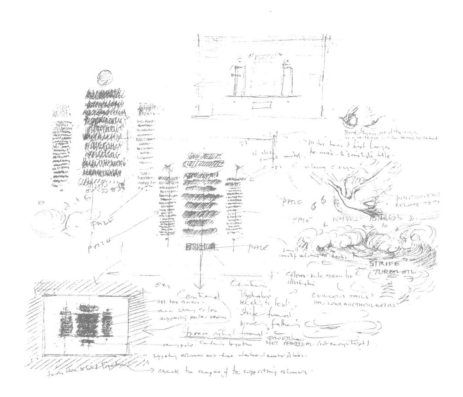

Design Tips

• The Evolving Idea

The initial design ideas for both the text and the illustration in this project are developed simultaneously. The calligrapher sketches broad areas to represent the component elements, so that the final design will form a unified whole.

The design is a triptych, with the main text placed centrally and the two subsidiary texts on either side. At this stage, the calligrapher's notes indicate that she intends the focus of the piece to be reinforced by rendering the main text in a darker tone than that of the subsidiary texts—a decision that is later partially reversed.

The thumbnail sketches with their accompanying notes show the development of the illustration ideas.

1 The initial writing of the text uses the selected colors in order to judge their effect. Different colors are tried on scraps of paper first.

2 Photocopies of the text are cut out and pasted in position. The central panel is placed first. Care is taken to ensure that the panels are evenly balanced with equal numbers of lines. Several attempts are needed.

3 With all the elements placed in position, measurements of the line spacing are taken from the paste-up to be transferred to the final version.

4 Further work is needed on the illustrations. The calligrapher experiments with different color treatments before making a final decision. Here, a muted yellow wash is painted over a pencil drawing.

5 The final writing is started. The central panel is completed first, because its position determines the placement of the other elements.

6 Using the paste-up as a guide, ruled lines to mark the position of the side panels are drawn in relation to the central panel.

7 The side panels are written along the ruled guidelines.

8 The illustrations are the last element to be added. They are carefully drawn in pencil before the colored washes are put in.

9 A final decision on margins is made once the work is completed. L-shaped cards are used to judge the margins and these are pencilled in. The broadsheet is later trimmed, and a mount is added for display.

GALLERY

Most of the panels of poetry shown in this gallery are examples of personal responses to the text, expressed in calligraphic terms. For calligraphers at all levels, poetry and literature in general can serve as a major stimulus for experimental creative work. Working from soundly understood letterforms, you can use poetry to explore variations in weight, slant and layout. Color, too, can be brought into play as a means of expressing the mood of the poem, from bright and energetic to quietly harmonious—the choice belongs to the calligrapher.

THE FISH—Janet Mehigan
Written in gouache in a light-weight italic script, this rendering of a poem by Rupert Brooke is an example of a simple layout. Dimensions: 98cm x 47cm (40in x 19in).

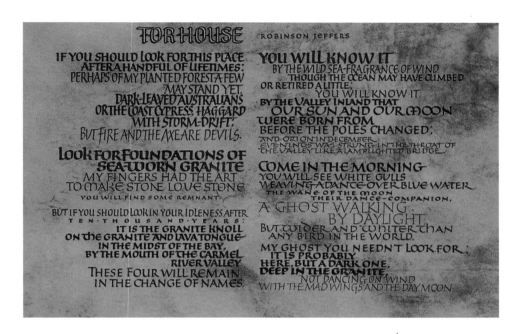

TOR HOUSE—Sheila Water
A wide range of capitals is used in this interpretation of a poem by Robinson Jeffers. Changes in weight, size and compression provide subtle variations in emphasis. The delicate color of the vellum gently unites the text areas. Dimensions: 23in x 15¹/₂in (58cm x 39cm).

IN THE HIGHLANDS
– Louise Donaldson
This calligraphic panel, based on a poem by Robert Louis Stevenson, uses different styles and sizes of lettering. Dimensions: 26in x 16¹/₂in (64cm x 40.5cm).

CROSSROAD—Nancy R. Leavitt
This imaginative interpretation of a text by Karl Young uses a close-knit vertical texture of different sized versals.
Color changes set off the lettering from the background, which links the various elements of the design.
Dimensions: 14in x 8³/₄in (37cm x 20cm).

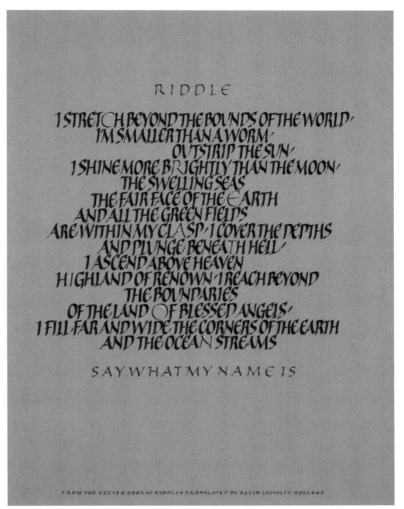

RIDDLE

I STRETCH BEYOND THE BOUNDS OF THE WORLD,
I'M SMALLER THAN A WORM,
OUTSTRIP THE SUN,
I SHINE MORE BRIGHTLY THAN THE MOON,
THE SWELLING SEAS
THE FAIR FACE OF THE EARTH
AND ALL THE GREEN FIELDS
ARE WITHIN MY CLASP, I COVER THE DEPTHS
AND PLUNGE BENEATH HELL,
I ASCEND ABOVE HEAVEN
HIGHLAND OF RENOWN, I REACH BEYOND
THE BOUNDARIES
OF THE LAND OF BLESSED ANGELS,
I FILL FAR AND WIDE THE CORNERS OF THE EARTH
AND THE OCEAN STREAMS

SAY WHAT MY NAME IS

FROM THE EXETER BOOK OF RIDDLES TRANSLATED BY KEVIN CROSSLEY-HOLLAND

CREATION—Gillian Hazeldine
This text from the Exeter Book of Riddles is rendered in heavy-weight capitals with a scattering
of light-weight Roman capitals, creating an interesting overall texture. The asymmetrical layout
adds to the sense of movement. Dimensions: 17³/₄in x 12in (45cm x 30cm).

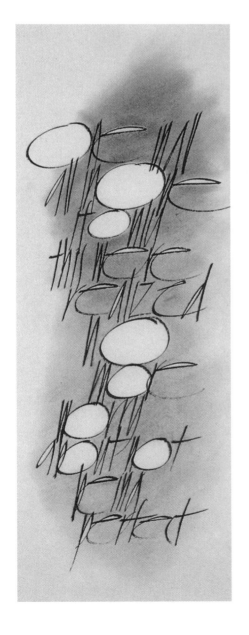

ONE IN ALL, ALL IN ONE—Paivi Vesanto
The compressed slanting letters of this italic-based
script give a strong diagonal emphasis to the design.
The exaggerated open letters left uncolored on a
Conté-crayon background produce an interesting
change of texture.
Dimensions: 9in x 27in (23cm x 69cm).

Posters

Calligraphy can be a striking alternative or complement to print in poster design. A calligraphic poster is a challenge, whatever your level of skill, giving you the chance to put your writing, and design abilities to practical use. Whatever its specific aim, the successful poster should catch the eye of the intended audience, and present the essential information clearly, so that it can be easily read at a quick glance. A poster can be reproduced at low cost and look attractive, even if it has to be in a single color.

Designing for one color can stimulate imaginative use both of contrasts created by the lettering itself, and of the space in and around the text. Color can be introduced, if required, by printing on colored paper or adding a splash of color by hand to each poster.

Some posters suffer from "over-load", with too much happening and no focus; others are simply dull. You can use lettering alone to create an eye-catching focus, or choose suitable imagery to fulfil this role. It is important to create an atmosphere in the poster that is suited to the subject by wise choice of styles and sizes of lettering, and by considered use or space and illustration (if needed). Whatever the subject—whether you are creating a notice for a classical concert, or an announcement for a contemporary dance performance—all the design elements in the poster must be carefully selected and balanced.

In posters, as in all design, there are no absolute rules, but experience provides helpful hints. The poster shown here is a low-budget design for a jazz concert, to be printed in black on a photocopier.

PRINTED POSTERS
The finished calligraphic artwork is seen here printed on to different colored papers. The green paper is selected for the final print run.

10 YEARS
TENTH ANNIVERSARY OF JAZZ AT THE WAREHOUSE

SPECIAL FREE CONCERT (WITH) ROY LEWIS BAND

(ON) THURSDAY 18th MAY (AT) 8pm (AT) THE WAREHOUSE

RIVERSIDE SELBY (NOTE:) FACILITIES FOR

WHEELCHAIR ACCESS
WHEELCHAIRS (AND) BAR

Assessing the Text

In most cases the client supplies the text for
the poster, as in this case, in the form of typed
copy. The first task is to organise the information
into 'bite-size' pieces, and sort them according
to their relative importance. Here, the
calligrapher also suggests ways of
making the wording punchier.

*Focus in lower half
of design with
diagonal
subsidiary elements*

*Focus in upper half,
aligned left*

*Focus in upper half,
aligned left to solid
band in margin*

*Focus in upper half,
main lettering
breaking into band
in left margin*

*Focus in upper half,
solid bands at top
and bottom,
aligned left*

Thumbnail Sketches

Various layout ideas are tried, incorporating
different sizes and styles of lettering. The word
'JAZZ' is picked out to provide the main focus
of the overall design.

1 The text if written out in preparation for a preliminary paste-up. At this point it is still possible to fine-tune the size and weight of the lettering. Here, the main word is written using a ¹/₂in (13 mm) Automatic pen. On consideration, this does not seem strong enough.

2 A paste-up is completed using photocopies of the lettering. 'JAZZ' has been re-written using a ³/₄in (20 mm) nib. At this stage, fine adjustments of text position are made.

3 Measurements of line spacing are taken from the paste-up and transferred to the final (camera-ready) paste-up.

4 The text is placed in its final position on the final paste-up.

5 The black bands and rules are carefully drawn in with indelible felt-tip pens. Any marks and imperfections—including the edges of the pasted-up text—are obliterated using correction fluid (or opaque white paint).

6 A fine marker pen is used to fill any unevenness in the rules and to ensure the black areas are 'solid'. The poster is now ready for reproduction. At this stage, the choice to print on white or colored paper is made.

GALLERY

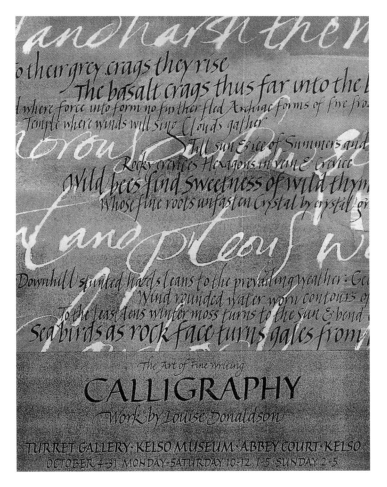

Calligraphic lettering used in poster design can create a visual impact quite different from that which can be achieved with type alone. Key words can be rendered in a style that is specifically designed to be in harmony with the overall message.

Extra-broad plain-stroke or multiline pens can be used to great effect in a design where one eye-catching word or image is required. This is also an area where you can adapt the letterforms or create new forms of your own, if this seems appropriate.

With posters, the freshness of the image if the key consideration.

EXHIBITION POSTER—Louise Donaldson
This attractive piece of work uses ruling-pen lettering in masking fluid under a graduated wash, alongside edged-pen calligraphy.
Dimensions: 26in x 16¹/₂in (66cm x 40.5cm).

TUSCANY—Jenny Kavarana
The diagonal lines of text, bold capitals, strong colors and a dark background all contribute to the strong image. The small white lettering makes a pleasing contrast and is united with the rest of the design by the ruled red lines. Dimensions: 24in x 17in (61cm x 43cm).

Eleventh Century English N

This eleventh-century initial is from a Bible illustrated in the Durham style.
The poor man is entangled in the snares of life, and seems beset by all the cares and worries of existence, which are epitomised by the strange creatures that surround him. Enjoy the challenge of working this delightful initial.

YOU WILL NEED

- **Tracing paper**
- **Tracing-down paper**
- **Project paper**
- **Sharp 2H pencil**
- **Nos 1, 0 and 0000 brushes**
- **PVA gilding medium**
- **Transfer gold**
- **Burnisher**
- **Gouache paints: cadmium primrose yellow, yellow ochre, ultramarine, dark green, burnt umber, red ochre, flame red, permanent white, black.**

Design Tips

• Tracing-down paper

Tracing down paper is essentially a sheet of tissue which is coated on one side with a powder (usually red) that comes off when under pressure. You place a sheet of tracing down paper under your tracing, and then go over it again with a sharp pencil. The pressure of the pencil causes the powder to stick to the paper, leaving a copy of the image on it. Take a piece of greaseproof paper and a set of soft chalk pastels. Select a pastel of a contrasting color to that of your project paper. Rub it all over the greaseproof paper, and then rub over it thoroughly with your finger (wrapped in a piece of paper).

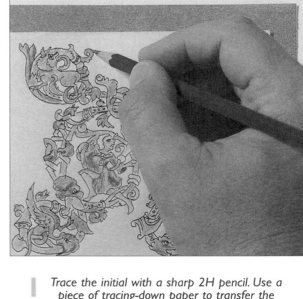

1 _Trace the initial with a sharp 2H pencil. Use a piece of tracing-down paper to transfer the image to your project paper. If you pencil over the back with a 6B pencil or scribble extensively over it you will find that it is difficult to see what you are doing when you trace it down._

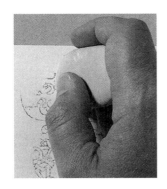

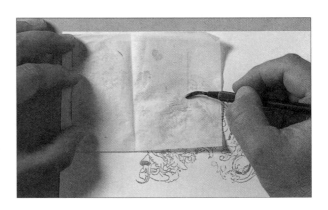

2 _Apply the PVA gilding medium to those areas that will be gilded. Allow the first coat to sink in and dry and then apply two or three coats, depending on how raised you want the gold to appear. Allow each to dry before applying the next. Then rub down three coats of transfer gold over the medium, working around the edges with the point of your burnisher. Burnish the gold thoroughly._

3 Paint the creatures in olive-green, mixed from cadmium primrose yellow, yellow ochre and ultramarine.

4 Outline the creatures in dark green with a No 0000 brush.

5 Paint the man in the following colors. Coat: a mixture of burnt umber, red ochre and yellow ochre; dark tones in burnt umber. Hair: a mixture of burnt umber and yellow ochre. Skin: a mixture of yellow ochre, flame red and permanent white.

6 Paint the blue areas with ultramarine.

7 Mix a little yellow ochre into your blue color and paint the green areas.

8 Outline the image in a burnt-umber and black mixture, using a No 0000 brush.

9 Highlight the green areas with yellow ochre and the blue with permanent white. Tidy up the edges with permanent white.

Eleventh Century Dutch R

This eleventh-century capital 'R', from the Chronicles of William of Jumieges, appears alive with writhing animation. It represents a slightly more ambitious project building on the drawing skills that you practiced in the last project. Study the image carefully before trying to draw it so that you have worked out exactly what is happening.

YOU WILL NEED

- **Tracing paper**
- **Project paper**
- **2H and 6B pencils**
- **Gouache paints: ultramarine, permanent white, brilliant yellow, flame red, red ochre, Prussian blue, black, permanent green, gold, burnt sienna**
- **Nos 1 and 0000 brushes**
- **A burnisher**

Design Tips

- ### Tracing from a Book

  If possible, do not trace directly from a book or other type of document. Photocopy the image and trace over the photocopy instead. If you are not permitted to photocopy the book or document, either because you would thereby be infringing copyright regulations, or because to do so would stress the book's binding or damage the document, draw the image freehand and then make a tracing from that

- ### Drawing your Own Copy

  When you first try to draw a copy of something, you may find it quite difficult. The following tip may help. Draw the image at one end of a piece of tracing paper. Fold the paper over and compare it with the original. Trace off the parts which are good, but alter the elements which were not so good. Fold the tracing paper over your second attempt, as before, and repeat the process. (You may have to do this four or five times.) You may end up with one or two sheets of tracing paper that are folded up like a concertina, but on the top copy you will have a drawing that is as close to the original as you can make it.

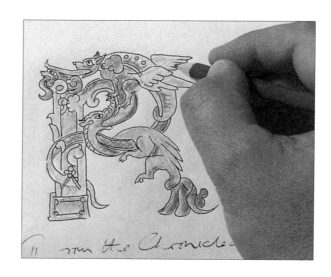

1 *Trace the image. (It may be quicker to scribble all over the back rather than draw over it with a 6B pencil.)*

2 *Mix some ultramarine and permanent white and paint the pale-blue areas.*

3 *Mix some brilliant yellow into your ultramarine, and permanent-white mixture to paint the green colors on the frog and the dragon.*

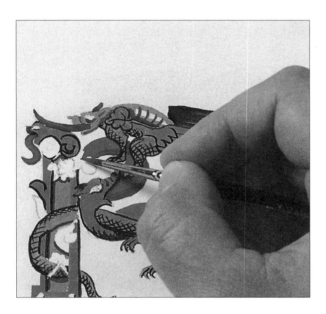

4 *Change your water and mix some flame red and permanent white to make the pink for the top dragon and the main stem.*

5 *Paint the shadows on the tongues and tail with red ochre.*

6 *Paint the shadows on the blue areas with Prussian blue (or ultramarine and black).*

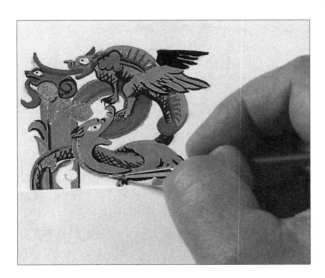

7 *Paint the shadows on the green areas with permanent green.*

8 *Paint the gold detailing with gold gouache. (If you want to give it a slightly smoother and more shiny appearance, you can burnish it with a burnisher. If you do not like the effect, apply another coat of gold paint, which you could reburnish if you wanted to. Experiment and see how you get on.)*

9 Mix some burnt sienna and black to make a very dark brown, and add a little water to give it a consistency like thin cream. With a No 0000 brush, outline the image.

10 Draw in the highlights with permanent white.

Manuscript book

Books in the form of the 'codex', or book form as we know it today were handwritten from Roman times until the Renaissance, and even after the invention of printing, rich patrons still commissioned manuscript volumes. The manuscript book continues to offer useful design experience to calligraphers at all levels, posing questions about the relationship between text area and margins, page size and shape, length of writing line, size, weight and styles of writing and, the choice of writing and binding materials.

Different paper surfaces can also be explored. Although hot-pressed paper is the easiest to write on, and most suitable for a formal manuscript book, a more textural surface can greatly enhance the atmosphere of a text whose words lend themselves to this approach.

Even the beginner can make an attractive manuscript book, because the book lends itself just as well to he straightforward treatment of a short text as to longer and more elaborate writing and designs. Books can be one or many sections, and illustration can range from a simple decorative element, such as a symbol, to ornate illumination. A single section is best for a first book. Traditionally, this consists of 16 pages—including a title page and several blank pages at the beginning and end of the book, so that there are about five to seven pages of writing—but there can be fewer if you prefer. You can include a discreet colophon at the back of the book, giving your name and the date of writing. You can then sew on a simple cover with or without decoration.

The text selected for this manuscript book is a short light-hearted essay by an Irish writer, John B. Keane, taken from his collection Strong Tea.

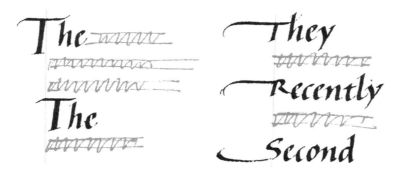

Design Tips

- ### Working Out the Letterforms
  Having decided on the format, it is possible to work out the treatment of the text in more detail. Although the text is humorous, it is decided not to over-emphasise this by using a zany script. A plain italic has the right feeling of simplicity. However, to give texture to the page and to provide variation in pace, larger colored capitals are chosen for the paragraph openings. Experiments for these are shown.

- ### Making a Cover
  A manuscript book needs a well-made cover to protect the inner pages. It should be made from heavy paper that will withstand handling. Once you have trimmed and folded the cover, sew it to the text pages.

- ### Folding the Cover
  The cover should be larger than the page dimensions; allow about $1/4$in - $1/2$in (6mm—13mm) extra at the top, bottom and outside edges. Give the cover generous flaps of about two-thirds the cover width. Once the cover is cut, score the outside folds of the spine, and flaps using a sharp tool such as a craft knife. Take care not to cut through the paper.

- ### Sewing the Cover
  Carefully position the folded folios inside the cover. Pierce the stitch holes from the inside fold of the center folio through the outside spine fold of the cover, as shown in the diagram. Using heavy-weight thread and a strong needle, pass the needle through the middle hole in the inside fold in the center folio, leaving a long loose end. Continue to sew following the sequence illustrated. Be careful not to divide the thread as you pass through a hole for the second time. To finish, tie the two loose ends together inside the book and trim.

1 Using a Mitchell No 4 nib and black watercolor, the calligrapher writes out the text for a rough paste-up.

2 Various styles—italic and versal—of introductory capitals are tried at different sizes.

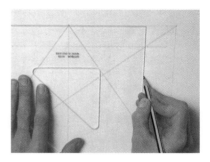

3 Margins are ruled on a sheet of paper for the paste-up.

4 Lines that will act as guides for the paste-up are ruled, based on preliminary decisions made when selecting the letterform.

5 The written-out text is cut out and pasted in position on the writing lines. Tweezers are useful for picking up and positioning small pieces of text.

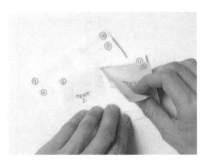

6 A manuscript book is made up of sheets folded in half—each comprising four pages of the book. It is a good idea to prepare a miniature book that allows you to check and number the pages.

7 After all decisions on layout and pagination have been made, the next stage is the final writing. With the versal capital pencilled in, the small black lettering is written first.

8 The versal capital is completed next in blue gouache, and, the introduction in small capitals is pencilled in.

9 The small capitals are written in pen in blue gouache.

10   *Once the writing is complete, the pages are trimmed (if necessary) and assembled in the correct order. The book is then placed on the chosen cover paper, and the dimensions of the cover are measured and marked.*

11   *The trimmed cover and book are sewn together with strong thread.*

12   *The finished book has a calligraphic cover that echoes the treatment of the inside pages.*

THE FINISHED BOOK

The cover, with its simple but decorative lettering harmonises with the straightforward calligraphy of the inside pages.

GALLERY

This selection of manuscript books illustrates a rich variety of approaches. It shows how a well-written classical format has great serenity and elegance, while a more experimental approach to the text has different strengths—most importantly, stimulating the inter-play of movement and stillness.

This selection also demonstrates that beautifully written lettering has its own decorative quality, but that illustration sensitively blended with the text can enhance the overall design. Whether you choose a simple or complex design, making a manuscript book is a feasible project for calligraphers at every stage of learning. It is an intimate design vehicle for a thoughtful and personal approach.

THE PROTHALAMION—Hazel Dolby
This spread combines grey gouache text and watercolor illustration. The generous margins enhance the delicacy of the whole. Dimensions 13¹/₂in x 10in (34cm x 25cm).

THE WORD—Kate Ridyard
In this book, the free italic-based script, written in red gouache with a ruling pen, contrasts strikingly with the black edged-pen italic.
Dimensions (spread): 12in x 4¹/₂in (30.5cm x 11.5cm).

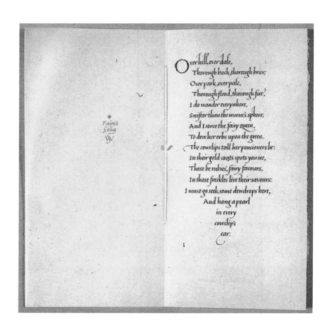

MONTAGNA-ACQUA—*Monica Dengo*
This title page from a book of the writings of Francois Cheng shows an interesting design, created by contrasting formal-italic edged-pen capitals with a lively italic written with a ruling pen. Both ink and gouache are used. Dimensions: 7⁷/₈in x 10⁵/₈in (20cm x 26cm).

FAIRY'S SONG—*Joan Pilsbury*
This elegant double-page spread of a Shakespearean text written on vellum in formal italic shows the timeless quality of a well-written italic. The initial 'O' is raised and burnished gold. The generous space around the text enhances the calm quality of the whole. Dimensions: 10in x 9³/₄in (25cm x 24.5cm).

Concertina Book

This type of simple folded book, which is also a display panel, is a popular application for calligraphy. It combines the opportunity of using a relatively long text at a convenient size with the challenge of having to design pages that work well when fully opened, as well as individually.

The need for the design to flow horizontally through the book provides some interesting possibilities for both the calligraphy and the illustration. Color can often provide a unifying element through the book.

Any page proportion is possible with a concertina book, making it an interesting design vehicle for unifying the mood of the text and the mode of presentation. Margin proportions can be varied to enhance interpretation—a text about open spaces might have a very wide top margin, for example.

The concertina book shown here makes use of an anonymous medieval poem about the seasons. The simplicity of the words seems to lend itself well to this intimate treatment, and the continuous nature of a concertina book works well with the idea of the seasonal cycle.

THE FINISHED BOOK
This horizontal-format book folds neatly into its cover. As the cover is fixed only at the front, the book can be opened and extended to show all its pages at a single view.

SPRING
FOR LAVENDER, BUSHY SWEET AND TALL
TEND UPON THE FEAST OF SAINT PAUL

SPRING
FOR LAVENDER BUSHY, SWEET AND TALL
TEND UPON THE FEAST OF SAINT PAUL

SPRING
FOR LAVENDER BUSHY SWEET AND TALL
TEND UPON THE FEAST OF SAINT PAUL

SPRING
FOR LAVENDER BUSHY SWEET AND TALL
TEND UPON THE FEAST OF SAINT PAUL

Design Tips

• Initial Layouts

The decision has already been made to use a horizontal format with illustrations based on the medieval symbols for the seasons. However, the size of the lettering, the relationship of the headings to the text and the position, and treatment of the motif need to be worked out in greater detail.

Various rough layouts are tried. The position of the motif at the left of the page remains constant, as does the rendering of the text in italic capitals. The major questions to be resolved are the size, weight and spacing of the text.

These rough layouts show the evolution of the idea, although none of these solutions is eventually selected for development. The idea of widely spaced lettering for the heading proves too weak, and a more conventional letter spacing is adopted.

1 The text is written and pasted up with the pen-drawn symbol. The verse is written with a Mitchell No 4 nib and the heading with a No 2¹/₂. At this stage, the final decision on the letter spacing of the heading is made.

2 The final paste-up shows the arrangement of the symbol, heading and verse on the page. A paste-up is needed for each page.

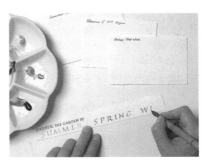

3 Final choices of paper and color are made. The project requires a paper that is suitable for both ink and watercolor. A pale cream textured paper is chosen after testing the selected colors on it.

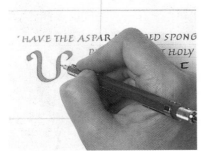

4 The motifs are to be stencilled. The first stage is to trace each pen-drawn motif in pencil.

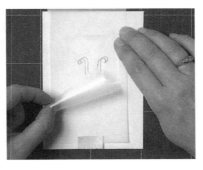

5 A piece of low-tack masking film is adhered over the tracing.

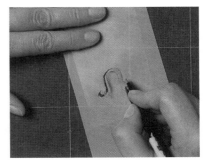

6 A craft knife is used to cut out the traced symbol, following the drawn outlines accurately.

7 The masking film is carefully peeled away from the tracing paper, and placed so that the symbol is in its final position on the paper. The surrounding paper is carefully masked. The chosen colors are mixed and spattered over the stencil using a stencil brush.

8 The text is written on the pages in black ink, in the positions specified by the final paste-up.

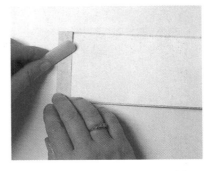

9 The cover is cut to allow ¹/₈in (3mm) extra at the top and bottom, plus ¹/₂in (13mm) at the front and a 1in (25mm) flap with 2in (50mm) tab at the back. The folds of the cover are scored. The front flap is glued to the first page only.

GALLERY

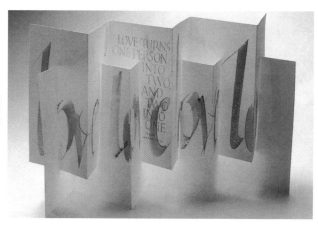

LOVE—Mary Noble
This unusual book consists of two concertina sheets with slits that are slotted together vertically. Dimensions: 10in x 25in (25.5cm x 64cm).

The different concertina books illustrated on this page indicate the wide scope open to you in designing a concertina book. As the examples show, this type of book is an attractive and manageable project for a calligraphy beginner.

ANGLO-SAXON RIDDLE—Anne Irwin
The well-planned simplicity of this concertina book is the key to its success. Rubber-stamp motifs are used alongside text written in a basic Roman book-hand. Dimensions (opened): 3in x 108in (7.5cm x 275cm).

ZODIAC—Patricia Lovett
This attractive concertina book based on the signs of the zodiac, incorporates subtle illustrations over painted background squares. Dimensions: 5in x 8in (2.5cm x 20.5cm).

Fifteenth Century Whitevine

This style of design, known as the 'white vine' first appeared in
the tenth century. It became very popular on its reappearance in
Italy in the fifteenth century. The pen-drawn vine-and-leaf design is picked out
in different colors and is enhanced by the colors that surround it.
The vines were usually left white, but some were colored cream
and some green, some were even multi-colored, especially when the vine
design was drawn as a geometric spiral. The design was often drawn
both within the letter, and spreading round it and down the page.

YOU WILL NEED

- **2H pencil**
- **Tracing or greaseproof paper**
- **Project paper**
- **Tracing-down paper**
- **Rubber**
- **Ruler**
- **Masking tape**
- **Nos 1 and 0000 brushes**
- **PVA gilding medium**
- **Paper tube**
- **Gold leaf**
- **Burnisher**
- **Gouache paints: ultramarine, blue, red, brilliant yellow, yellow ochre, gold, black, burnt umber**
- **Waterproof ink**
- **Lettering pen**

1 Take a piece of tracing or greaseproof paper and
draw two horizontal lines (between which the
inscription will be written), and two vertical lines
(which will contain the vine design). Draw in the
lettering, the outlines of the capital letter and the
design. Retrace and alter as often as you feel
necessary to achieve the size, and shape that best
occupies the space.

2 Draw the vine design in detail, making sure
the tracing paper does not move.

3 Rule two guidelines (for the lettering and design) on
your project paper. Using waterproof ink and a
lettering pen, write the word, leaving out the capital.
Trace down the capital letter and design.

4 Paint two coats of PVA gilding medium onto the
capital letter, flower centers and little buds. Allow
to dry.

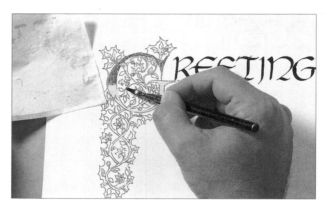

5 Breathe on the area to be gilded through the paper
tube to make the medium sticky, and lay the gold leaf
onto the form, rubbing it down with a burnisher.

6 Paint the blue and the red areas.

7 Paint the green areas with a mixture of brilliant yellow,
yellow ochre and ultramarine.

8   *Paint the gold areas on the outside of the initial and the vine area, making sure that the gold gouache is thick enough.*

9   *Outline everything with a mixture of black and burnt umber. Apply spots of gold leaf to any bare patches in the gilding and reburnish if necessary.*

Using the same design, a different word has been written, taking some liberties with the text to make it fit in the space. Also, the color pattern has been experimented with, to give a stained-glass effect. Instead of gold leaf on the initial, gold paint has been used. Outlining in gold paint has also been experimented with .

1 0 *'Greetings', written in French. The same tracing has been used, adapting it to a capital 'S'. I have painted the whole design in the one color. The effect is so strong that I did not outline it—even adding gold to the buds and flower centers would diminish the impact.*

1 1 *'Greeting', written in German. Again, a single color has been used for this (the green was mixed from ultramarine and yellow ochre).*

Fifteenth Century English Border

This project involves a capital letter taken from a fifteenth-century poem about St. Edmund, which is thought to have been written in the scriptorium of the abbey at Bury St. Edmunds in England. The decorative elements are fairly simple, but their effectiveness depends on a crispness of execution. The work needs to be done with flair and panache.

YOU WILL NEED

- **Tracing paper**
- **Project paper**
- **2H pencil**
- **Gesso**
- **PVA gilding medium**
- **No 1 brush**
- **Gold leaf**
- **Paper tube**
- **Burnisher**
- **Gouache paints: gold, red, ultramarine, green, brown, black, burnt umber, permanent white.**

1 Trace the image and transfer it to your project paper. (Remember that this should serve only as a guide.) The position of the box for the second capital depends on the text.

2 Mix a little PVA gilding medium with gesso and apply a drop of the mixture to each berry using an old No 1 brush.

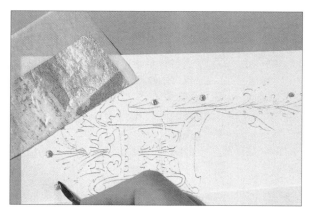

3 Breathe through the paper tube onto each berry in turn, starting at the top of the page. Take a sheet of gold leaf and, using the burnisher, rub it down over each berry.

4 Apply gold paint round the capital and down the stem.

5 Paint the blue, red and green areas, having first mixed a little white with each color.

6 Paint the blue of the capital. Mix a lighter shade of the blue and paint the lighter part of the capital and the other light-blue areas. Paint the blue tips of the stamens.

7 Outlines all the areas of color with the appropriate, undiluted color.

8 Paint the brown shadows on the red acanthus stems and trumpet shapes.

9 Outline the gold areas with a mixture of black and burnt umber.

10 Highlight the blue areas with permanent white.

Decorative borders

Although good calligraphy should be able to stand alone, there are situations in formal or creative work where decoration can enhance the written text. Decorative borders from Eastern and Western historical manuscripts are an infinitely varied source of reference for contemporary calligraphy.

These borders may influence your own designs but, try to use them in new and creative ways. The wealth of designs in Western manuscripts includes simple colored linear borders, which sometimes consist of different-colored bands of varying widths.

These may be plain, divided into decorated rectangles or, feature repeating patterns of geometric or inter-twined plant elements. Sometimes the border is an extension of a decorated initial letter. A myriad of plant designs, including complex floral designs, are found in Flemish, French and Italian manuscripts from the late medieval period onwards.

Possibilities for contemporary borders abound. Apart from plants and geometric shapes, patterns and symbols from different cultures or religions can be a source of ideas. Whatever the design, small illustrations can be introduced at intervals, perhaps enclosed in circles or other shapes. As with any other form of decoration, the border must be appropriate to the subject and script and form an integral part of the work as a whole. Plant borders may be contained by colored or gilded lines of suitable width or, left with the plants themselves forming the outer edges of the design.

THE FINISHED WORK
The delicate floral border, together with the elegant italic text, would be overwhelmed by a heavy frame and mount. A fine gold frame discreetly complements both the calligraphy and the decoration.

In these vernal seasons of the year when the air is calm and pleasant it were an injury and sullenness against Nature not to go out and see her riches and partake in her rejoicing

Border on all sides   *Border at top*   *Border at left*

Design Tips

- ### First Thoughts

  For this project, the first step is to decide on the page format, and on the placement of the floral borders on the page.

  Various options shown below are sketched as thumbnails. The final design is vertical with a single border along the left margin.

- ### Designing the Border

  The decision on the final design arises from trial illustrations. The choice is between designs of varying complexity, and whether to include repeating elements.

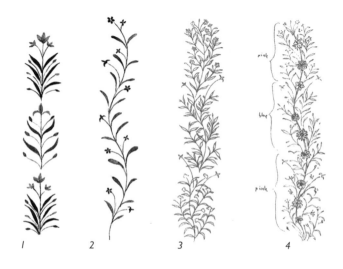

1 Simple alternating flower-and-foliage motif with a strong central linear element.

2 Undulating central stem with non-repeating design.

3 Three-part design of non-repeating complex flower-and-stem pattern.

4 Complex flower-and-stem pattern with strong central emphasis. Repeating color combinations.

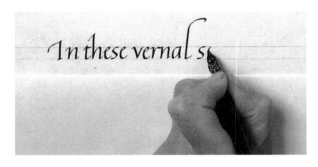

1 The text is written for a final paste-up using a Mitchell No 3 nib.

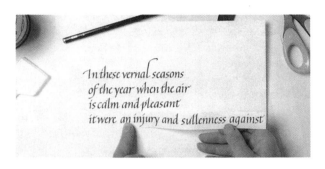

2 The text is pasted up line by line. Each line is cut to length only when the line length is established.

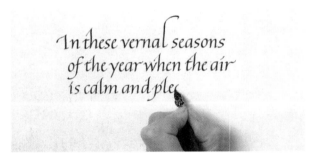

3 The final writing out of the text follows the paste-up. A heavy, hot-pressed paper is used.

4 A tracing is made of the chosen design for the floral border. Placing a pad of paper under the drawing will help you to obtain a good-quality line.

5 The traced design is transferred to its final position on the writing sheet by placing carbon paper between the tracing paper and the paper. Simply draw over the tracing, pressing firmly. Any unwanted marks can be removed from the paper with an eraser.

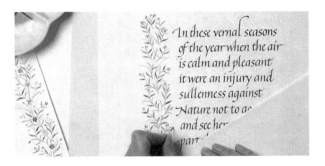

6 The final illustration is colored by applying water-color with a fine brush.

GALLERY

Decorative borders have been a particularly attractive enhancement of calligraphic work for many centuries in both East and West. Whether realistic, stylised or invented, floral borders are particularly suited to flowing calligraphic forms. In Western manuscripts, such as Renaissance Books of Hours, the fine details of the painting and gilding are superb. In a simpler form, this kind of illustration is readily accessible to the calligraphy beginner. Whether you are creating a manuscript book or a panel of calligraphy, you will find it rewarding to combine border design with calligraphy.

CALLIGRAPHIC PANEL
– Carina Westling
This panel of flowing cursive italic is enhanced by finely painted, and gilded borders using an inter-laced design. The unusual decision to use two contrasting L-shapes creates an effective balance in conjunction with the circular focal decoration.

DRAPERS' COMPANY 500th-ANNIVERSARY CHARTER
– Joan Pilsbury and Wendy Westover
This charter, written on vellum in italic with raised and burnished gold versal capitals, is a superb example of a formal document. The beautifully detailed watercolor and gouache borders use plant designs and heraldic elements with gold details.
Dimensions: 66in x 54in (168cm x 137cm).

REMEMBRANCE BOOK—Gaynor Goffe
This simple repeating border painted in gouache is one of a series in a book of remembrance. The border elements of this page are designed to reflect the life of the deceased. Dimensions: 10in x 7in (25cm x 18cm).

Eleventh Century English Q

This capital 'Q' is taken from an eleventh-century manuscript of the Winchester school in England. The skilful juxtaposition of primary colors, together with the small touches of gold, give this capital letter a stunning, jewel-like brilliance.

YOU WILL NEED

- **Tracing paper**
- **Project paper**
- **2H and 6B pencils**
- **Gouache paints:**
  ultramarine, flame red,
  brilliant yellow,
  permanent white, burnt
  sienna, black, cadmium
  primrose yellow
- **Nos 0, 1 and**
  0000 brushes
- **PVA gilding medium**
- **Transfer gold**
- **Paper tube**
- **Burnisher**

Design Tips

- **Mixing paint**

  Make sure that you mix enough paint for the project, if you subsequently find that you have not got enough it is very difficult to mix more that matches your original shade exactly. If you find that you have to use a shade which you will have to mix yourself, it is often worth buying a tube of the equivalent color. This will both save you time and ensure that you have the right shade to hand.

- **Tracing**

  Take care that you do not move your tracing paper while you are working. It is worth sticking the tracing paper down with low-tack masking tape so that it cannot move.

- **Preparing PVA Gilding medium**

  PVA gilding medium is a pink color. It consists of a glutinous liquid that contains a thickening agent held in suspension. This tends to settle in the bottle and needs to be stirred up. Do not shake the bottle and thereby make it full of bubbles, however. (If you get bubbles on your paper you should pop them with a pin or brush.) Instead, turn your bottle upside down, end to end, until the medium has been well mixed, or else stir the medium with a brush—but ensure that you do not make any bubbles.

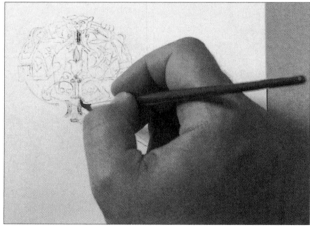

1   Trace the design. (Take care, because the original is not symmetrical.) Trace the image down onto your project page.

2   Apply the PVA gilding medium to the parts that will receive the gold. Use a No 0 brush to apply the sizing. Resist the temptation to apply a thick drop because when it dries it will shrink and wrinkle. First apply one thin coat and then allow it to dry and sink into the paper. When it is dry, build up the letter form with as many additional thin coats as you need to create the right thickness.

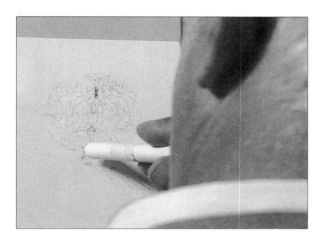

4 Burnish the gold through the backing paper or a piece of tracing paper and then burnish directly onto the gold.

3 Apply the transfer gold. Before it will stick to the PVA gilding medium the glue in the medium needs to be re-softened. To do this, roll up a little tube of paper to about the size of a cigarette and breathe onto the medium gently. Lay your transfer gold onto the medium, backing paper upwards, and rub it gently with the pointed end of the burnisher. The gold will stick to the letter form and come off the backing paper. Apply another coat directly on top of the first, and then a third. (Note that gold will stick to gouache paint if it has been moistened by a warm breath, so do the writing first, then the gilding and finally the painting.)

5 Mix a weak mixture of cadmium primrose yellow and ultramarine and paint the background using a No 1 brush. (Alternatively, you could use gold gouache paint for this, which would contrast quite well with the burnished gold.) Note that it is important to do the background first, so that you do not leave any little corners of unpainted white paper showing through.

6 Paint the red areas with flame red and the pink with permanent white added to the red.

7 Change your water and paint the blue areas with ultramarine. Add a little cadmium primrose yellow to the ultramarine and paint the green areas.

8 Outline with a mixture of burnt sienna and black and paint the seeds in the pods using a No 0000 brush. Then add the highlights by making a thread-like line on the light side.

9 Apply the white dots to the blue areas using a No 0000 brush. (Your paint needs to be fairly thick and stiff for this, if it is too wet it will run into the blue.)

GLOSSARY

Arch—The part of a LOWER-CASE letter formed by a curve springing from the STEM, as in 'h', 'm', 'n'.

Ascender—The rising stroke of a LOWER-CASE letter.

Base line—Also called the writing line, this is the level on which a line of writing rests, giving a fixed reference for the relative heights of letters and the drop of the DESCENDERS.

Black letter—Term for the dense, angular writing of the GOTHIC period.

Body height—The height of the basic form of a LOWER-CASE letter, not including the extra length of ASCENDERS or DESCENDERS.

Book hand—Any style of alphabet commonly used in book production before the age of printing.

Boustrophedon—An arrangement of lines of writing, used by the Greeks, in which alternate lines run in opposite directions.

Bowl—The part of a letter formed by curved strokes attaching to the main STEM and enclosing a COUNTER, as in 'R', 'P', 'a', 'b'.

Broadsheet—A design in calligraphy contained on a single sheet of paper, vellum or parchment.

Built-up letters—Letters formed by drawing rather than writing, or having modifications to the basic form of the structural pen strokes.

Calligram—Words or lines of writing, or massed areas of text, arranged to construct a design.

Carolingian script—The first standard MINUSCULE script, devised by Alcuin of York under the direction of the Emperor Charlemagne at the end of the eighth century.

Chancery cursive—A form of ITALIC script used by the scribes of the papal Chancery in Renaissance Italy, also known as *cancellaresca*.

Character—Typographic term to describe any letter, punctuation mark or symbol commonly used in typesetting.

Codex—A book made up of folded and/or bound leaves forming successive pages.

Colophon—An inscription at the end of a handwritten book giving details of the date, place, scribe's name or other such relevant information.

Counter—The space within a letter wholly or partially enclosed by the lines of the letterform, within the BOWL of 'P', for example.

Cross-stroke—A horizontal stroke essential to the SKELETON form of a letter, as in 'E', 'F', 'T'.

Cuneiform—The earliest systematic form of writing, taking its name from the wedge-shaped strokes made when inscribing on soft clay. Cuneus is a Latin word meaning 'wedge'.

Cursive—The description of a handwriting form that is rapid and informal, where letters are fluidly formed and joined, without pen lifts.

Demotic script—The informal SCRIPT of the Egyptians, following on from HIEROGLYPHS and HIERATIC SCRIPT.

Descender—Tail of a LOWER-CASE letter that drops below the BASE LINE.

Diacritical sign—An accent or mark that indicates particular pronunciation of a letter or syllable.

Ductus—The order of strokes followed in constructing a pen letter.

Face abb Typeface—The general term for an alphabet designed for typographic use.

Flourish—An extended pen stroke or linear decoration used to embellish a basic letterform.

Gesso—A smooth mixture of plaster and white lead bound in gum, which can be reduced to a liquid medium for writing or painting. It dries hard for use in creating a raised letter for GILDING.

Gilding—Applying gold leaf to an adhesive base to decorate a letter or ornament.

Gothic script—A broad term embracing a number of different styles of writing, characteristically angular and heavy, of the late medieval period.

Hand—An alternative term for handwriting or SCRIPT, meaning lettering written by hand.

Hairline—The finest stroke of a pen, often used to create SERIFS and other finishing strokes, or decoration of a basic letterform.

Hefratic script—The formal SCRIPT of the ancient Egyptians.

Hieroglyphs—The earliest form of writing used by the ancient Egyptians, in which words were represented by pictorial symbols.

Ideogram—A written symbol representing a concept or abstract idea rather than an actual object.

Illumination—The decoration of a MANUSCRIPT with gold leaf burnished to a high shine; the term is also used more broadly to describe decoration in gold and colors.

Indent—To leave space additional to the usual margin when beginning a line of writing, as in the opening of a paragraph.

Ionic script—The standard form of writing developed by the Greeks.

Italic—Slanted forms of writing with curving letters based on an elliptical rather than circular model.

Layout—The basic plan of a two-dimensional design, showing spacing, organisation of text, illustration and so on.

Logo—A word or combination of letters designed as a single unit, sometimes combined with a decorative or illustrative element; it may be used as a trademark, emblem or symbol.

Lower-case—Typographic term for 'small' letters as distinct from capitals, which are known in typography as upper-case.

Majuscule—A capital letter.

Manuscript—A term used specifically for a book or document written by hand rather then printed.

Massed text—Text written in a heavy or compressed SCRIPT and with narrow spacing between words and lines.

Minuscule—A 'small' or LOWER-CASE letter.

Ornament—A device or pattern used to decorate a handwritten or printed text.

Paleography—Study of written forms, including the general development of alphabets and particulars of handwritten manuscripts, such as date, provenance and so on.

Palimpsest—A MANUSCRIPT from which a text has been erased and the writing surface used again.

Papyrus—The earliest form of paper, a coarse material made by hammering together strips of fiber from the stem of the papyrus plant.

Parchment—Writing material prepared from the inner layer of a split sheepskin.

Phonogram—A written symbol representing a sound in speech.

Pictogram—A pictorial symbol representing a particular object or image.

Ragged text—A page or column of writing with lines of different lengths, which are aligned at neither side.

River—The appearance of a vertical rift in a page of text, caused by an accidental, but consistent, alignment of word spaces on following lines.

Roman capitals—The formal alphabet of capital letters, devised by the Romans, which was the basis of most modern, western alphabet systems.

Rubricate—To contrast or emphasize part or parts of a text by writing in red; for example, headings, a prologue, a quotation.

Rustic capitals—An informal alphabet of capital letters used by the Romans, with letters elongated and rounded compared to the standard square ROMAN CAPITALS.

Sans-serif—A term denoting letters without SERIFS or finishing strokes.

Script—Another term for writing by hand, often used to imply a CURSIVE style of writing.

Scriptorium—A writing room, particularly that of a medieval monastery in which formal manuscripts were produced.

Serif—An abbreviated pen stroke or device used to finish the main stroke of a letterform, a hairline or hook, for example.

Skeleton letter—The most basic form of a letter demonstrating its essential distinguishing characteristics.

Stem—The main vertical stroke in a letterform.

Textura—A term for particular forms of GOTHIC SCRIPT that were so dense and regular as to appear to have a woven texture. Textura is a Latin word, meaning woven.

Transitional script—A letterform marking a change in style between one standard SCRIPT and the development of a new form.

Uncial—A BOOK HAND used by the Romans and early Christians, typified by the heavy, squat form of the rounded '0'.

Vellum—Writing material prepared from the skin of a calf, having a particularly smooth, velvety texture.

Versal—A large, decorative letter used to mark the opening of a line, paragraph or verse in a MANUSCRIPT.

Weight—A measurement of the relative size and thickness of a pen letter, expressed by the relationship of nib width to height.

Word break—The device of hyphenating a word between syllables so it can be split into two sections to regulate line length in a text.

x-height—Typographic term for BODY HEIGHT.

INDEX

A

AMDC (Roman Capitals), 386

Ampersands, 265

Aries, 305

Ash, 256, 258

B

Birthday Party Invite, 231

Book Cover, 419

Bookbinding, 297

Border, Decorative, 429

Brushed Pens and Pencils, 42

Brushes, 31

C

Calendar, 250

Calligraphy in Modern World, 20

Calligraphy, History of, 12

Centerd Layout, 242

Color, Applying, 56

Color, Using, 55

Concertina Book, 420

Copperplates, 204

Copperplates, Alphabet, 206

Copperplates, Fine Gothic, 209

Copperplates, Humanistic, 213

Copperplates, Pointed Pen, 208

Copperplates, Round Hand, 212

Copperplates, Round Text, 210

Copperplates, Script, 207

Copperplates, Square Text, 211

Cursive Script, 135

Cutting and Pasting, 52

Cutting Tools, 39

D

Design of Letterforms, 22

Double Pencils, 84

Drawing Board, 37

E

Edged Pen, 81

Egg Tempura, 46

Eleventh Century A, 333

Eleventh Century N, 410

Eleventh Century Q, 435

Eleventh Century R, 412

Eraser, 38

F

Fifteenth Century A, 361

Fifteenth Century Borders, 373, 430

Fifteenth Century K, 366

Fifteenth Century P, 221

Fifteenth Century P, 376

Fifteenth Century Q, 363

Fifteenth Century W, 218

Fifteenth Century Whitevine, 352, 414

Floral Treatments, 390

Flourishes for Italics, 263

Flourishing, 59, 260, 264

Flowers, Heraldic, 241

Flowers, Meaning, 238

Foundational Hand, 82

Foundational Pen Strokes, 84

Fourteenth Century I, 349

G

Glossary, 442

Gold Leaf, 369

Gothic, 164

Gothic, Blackletter, 166

Gothic, Cursive, 168

Gothic, Majuscule, 176

Gothic, Rotunda, 170

Gothic, Textura, 172

Graded Wash, 70

H

Halley's Comet, 282

Headings, 76

Hedgerows, 252

Henry II Periscopes, 335

Heraldic Design, 312

Heraldry, 310

I

Illumination, History
of, 318

Illumination, Styles, 320

Illustrations, 292

In The Bleak Midwinter,
280

Inks and Paints, 33

Interpreting Text, 274

Introduction to Italics, 18

Invitations, 382

Italic, Alphabet, 188, 202

Italic, Capitals, 122

Italic, Cursive, 132

Italic, Fine, 198

Italic, Flourished, 199

Italic, Humanistic, 200

Italic, Skeleton, 112

Italic, Weighted, 113

Italic, Formal, 203

Italics, Formal, 110

J

Jolly Miller, 294

L

Large Pens, 120

Late Nineteenth Century
Revival, 18

Layout Basics, 49

Layout, Types, 51

Letter Construction, 93

Letterheads, 393

Letterheads, Ribbon-
Decorated, 396

Lettering, 302

Lettering, Brush, 308

Lower-case
(development), 102

M

Manuscript Book, 416

Margins, 62

Masking Fluid, 43

Modern, Broken
Letter, 193

Modern, Cursive, 182

Modern, Fine Capitals, 178

Modern, Fine Pen, 186

Modern, Flourished, 185

Modern, Gothic, 179

Modern, Modulated, 196

Modern, Script, 184

Modern, Squared
Capitals, 194

Modern, Triple-stroke, 180

Modified Tenth Century,
161

N

Ninth Century M, 351

Numerals, 108

O

Oak, 256

P

Paper, Types, 35
Pater Noster, 136
Pen, Handmade, 30
Pen, Loading, 30
Pencils, 38
Poetry Broadsheet, 397
Poster, 406
Power of Language, 10

Q

Quills, 44
Quotations, Writing, 88

R

Reed Pen, 306
Roman Alphabets, 137

Roman Capitals, 95, 141
Roman Lettering
(Modern), 144
Roman, Lower-case, 142
Rough Sketches, 230
Ruler, 38
Ruling Pen, 78

S

Scaling Down, 89
Script Alphabet, 184
Set Square, 38
Seventh Century Fish, 329
Sixteenth Century Border, 391
Sixteenth Century R, 230
Sixteenth Century S, 378
Sizing, 50
Sub-heading, 76
Swash Capitals, 262
Swashes, 260

T

Template, 438, 439, 440, 441
Text Area, 227
Textura, Alphabet, 174
Texture and Staining, 71
Texture, Creating, 118
Textured Wash, 71
Thirteenth Century
Border, 214
Thirteenth Century
Psalter, 342
Triple-stroke Alphabet, 180
Twelth Century S, 339

U

Uncials, 146
Uncials, English, 151
Uncials, Half, 151

V

Vellum, 40, 266
Versal, Alphabet, 154
Versals, 152
Versals, Elaborated, 158
Versals, Lombardic, 156
Versals, Ornamental, 160
Versals, Roman, 155

W

Watchpoints, 86
Watercolor Washes, 66
Words and Images, 286
Writing on a Wash, 73
Writing Surfaces, 284, 404
Writing Tools, 28